A Southern Vanguard

A Southern Vanguard

THE JOHN PEALE BISHOP
MEMORIAL VOLUME

Edited by ALLEN TATE

Essay Index Reprint Series

 BOOKS FOR LIBRARIES PRESS
FREEPORT, NEW YORK

STANDARD BOOK NUMBER:
8369-1726-X

LIBRARY OF CONGRESS CATALOG CARD NUMBER:
76-107740

PRINTED IN THE UNITED STATES OF AMERICA

This Volume is
Offered to the Memory of

JOHN PEALE BISHOP
(1892-1944)

Contents

Stories

Preface

THIS ANTHOLOGY IS COMPOSED OF STORIES, poems, and critical essays offered for the John Peale Bishop Memorial Literary Prize Contest conducted between April 1 and September 15, 1945, by *The Sewanee Review* and Prentice-Hall, Inc. The prizes were awarded as follows: $200
to Andrew Lytle for his story, THE GUIDE; $200 to Malcolm Cow-
ley for his essay, WILLIAM FAULKNER'S LEGEND OF THE
SOUTH; and $100 to Randall Jarrell for his poem, THE MARCHEN.
The judges were Gorham Munson, Editor of the Trade Book Department of Prentice-Hall, Inc., and myself, who at the time of the contest
was Editor of *The Sewanee Review*. The winning titles and a few
others which are acknowledged elsewhere in this volume, were published in *The Sewanee Review*. Under the conditions of the contest
non-Southern writers were invited to compete for the essay prize, provided their subjects were Southern; the entrants for the fiction and
poetry prizes had to be of Southern birth or identified with the Southern States by residence or by interest.

Mr. Munson and I deemed it highly appropriate that the contest be
held in memory of John Peale Bishop, a Southern writer of great distinction whose literary life spanned almost exactly the period between
the two great wars. Bishop was born on April 21, 1892, in Charles Town,
Jefferson County, West Virginia, one of the "lost counties" of Virginia;
he died on April 4, 1944 at Hyannis, Massachusetts. Elsewhere I have
written a personal memoir and I will not repeat it here. Bishop's value
for the Southern writer of the coming generation must first of all lie
in his value for the imaginative life wherever he is read; without a
certain universal interest we should not expect for his work even a
sectional attention. More than any Southerner of his time he was aware
of the South in relation to Europe and the North, and the tension of

this conflict expressed itself in a kind of sensibility which America had not produced before. Southern writers of the post-war period will have to find out what Bishop did or run the risk of catching up with what he did only after rediscovering it for themselves a generation later.

The winners of the prizes are all writers whose careers began well before 1939, and it was perhaps to be expected that their maturity of experience and craft would put them, from any reasonable point of view, ahead of their younger competitors: performance, not promise, had to guide the judges in their decisions. But the promise here is not negligible; and although I should scarcely hold that this anthology "represents" the new Southern talent, it contains a large portion of it. There are five or six writers here, not yet published in books, of whom much is to be expected; and I think it is fair to predict from the contents of this anthology that the best Southern writers in the next few years will be writers of fiction.

ALLEN TATE

Acknowledgments

"Poetry and Painting" and "A Dream," by the late John Peale Bishop, are included in this anthology with the kind permission of the poet's widow, Mrs. Margaret H. Bishop, and of the Editor of *The Sewanee Review*. I wish also to thank the Editor of *The Sewanee Review* for permission to reprint here certain titles which appeared in that journal: "The Märchen," by Randall Jarrell; "William Faulkner's Legend of the South," by Malcolm Cowley; "Myth-Makers and the South's Dilemma," by Louis B. Wright; "The Guide," by Andrew Lytle; and "A Long Fourth," by Peter Taylor.

Thanks are due the following publishers for their courtesy in giving permission to quote in the Essay section from works in copyright: Charles Scribner's Sons for quotations from *Aleck Maury, Sportsman,* by Caroline Gordon, *Look Homeward, Angel,* by Thomas Wolfe, and *The Fathers,* by Allen Tate; Alfred A. Knopf for quotations from *Blue Girls,* by John Crowe Ransom, and *The Sacred Wood,* by T. S. Eliot; Harcourt, Brace Co., Inc. for quotations from *Selected Essays* and *The Use of Poetry,* by T. S. Eliot, *Cass Mastern's Wedding Ring,* by Robert Penn Warren, and *The Wide Net, A Curtain of Green,* and *The Robber Bridegroom,* by Eudora Welty; Random House, Inc. for quotations from *Ulysses,* by James Joyce, and *Light in August* and *Absalom! Absalom!* by William Faulkner; Harper & Brothers for quotations from *You Can't Go Home Again,* by Thomas Wolfe; The Macmillan Company for quotations from *Autobiographies,* by William Butler Yeats; Robert M. McBride and Co. for quotations from *Jurgen,* by James Branch Cabell; and G. P. Putnam's Sons for quotations from *Reason in Madness,* by Allen Tate.

A. T.

ESSAYS

Poetry and Painting
John Peale Bishop

I SHALL BEGIN THIS ESSAY BY QUOTING a passage from one of the *Reactionary Essays on Poetry and Ideas* by Allen Tate. He is speaking of the confusion which results when the common center of experience, out of which the separate arts achieve their special formal solutions, disappears. Then the arts, deprived of their proper sustenance, begin to live one on another. "Painting," he says, "tries to be music; poetry leans upon painting; all the arts 'strive toward the condition of music'; till at last seeing the mathematical structure of music, the arts become geometrical and abstract, and destroy themselves."

The passage occurs in an essay on my own poetry. And it is because Mr. Tate feels, quite rightly, that in some of my poems I lean very far toward the painters, finding in an art not theirs solutions which are possibly proper only to them that he has asked me here this evening.[1] There may have been malice in his invitation. He may have asked me here only to witness my confusion. But the confusion is not mine alone. It has perhaps always existed. It was present we know in the mid-eighteenth century when Gotthold Lessing wrote his famous essay on The Limits of Painting and Poetry, which he called *The Laocoön*. The distinction that Lessing made still seems to hold good. It would still seem to be sound to say that succession in time is the sphere of the poet, as space is that of the painter. And yet, paradoxically enough, it is with that movement in the arts which Lessing did something to initiate that the confusion becomes serious. I do not want to make too much of Lessing. There is a tendency among critics to play up their predecessors; in order to increase the prestige of criticism, they ascribe to the critics of the past a power for creation which in all probability they

[1] This essay was read as a lecture under the auspices of the Creative Arts Program at Princeton University, January 29, 1940.

3

never had. However, Lessing was in at the beginning of a movement of which we have not yet seen the end. And it is worth considering his position for a moment, if we are to understand why the clarity of his distinction between poetry and painting should have been followed by a century in which these arts are confused as they had not been before in the history of the West.

Now one of the reasons why Lessing, whose distinctions are so clear, gave rise through his influence to such confusion is that he was, as any of his contemporaries would have been, interested in the means which each art employed in what he called its imitations, only in so far as they limited the artist in his choice of subject. It was possible for him, in the eighteenth century, consumed as he was by admiration for the Greeks and Romans, to take the means for granted. We cannot. And more, we know that for the artist the assumption of limitations is the beginning of liberation and that, in the complete work of art, while we always know what the means are, we never know what the end is. I can say how Shakespeare wrote full Fathom Five. I cannot possibly tell you what he wrote. All I can say is that it is poetry. I can make out from the canvas, stroke by stroke, how Cézanne painted, but if I were to tell you that what he had painted was some apples and a tablecloth, you would know that I had said nothing.

The art of poetry is, like that of music, made manifest in a control of time. The poet has words to work with and words are his only sounds; it is by controlling their sequence in time that he seems to control time; it is upon their sensuous disposition that he must depend to convey a sense of duration. A painter is known by his spatial power. What he does when he applies paint to canvas is to create from what was without depth an illusion of enduring space. Only a moment in any action can be shown within that space. What goes before and after that moment in time, which must be seen in space, can at most be imagined.

Let us go back before the great modern confusion to see what happens in that space. I am going to take the painting of a battle, which is all action, one of the several paintings which Paolo Uccello made of the Rout of San Romano, that one which is now in the National Gallery in London—or was before it was buried against air raids—and which is reproduced in Thomas Craven's *Treasury of Art Masterpieces*. The horsemen press in from the left with their lances lifted, under white banners tormented by the wind. The white charger of the turbaned swordsman in the foreground rears, snorting in the delight of battle. The lance of the fantastically helmeted Florentine is already lowered to meet the oncoming Siennese. At the right, the fighters on each side are hacking at one another, with swords, across their horses heads. On a far hillside can be seen, beyond the fray, foot soldiers, and above them on the hill, made small by distance, two more horsemen. The moment the painter has chosen to depict is that of first contact between the Florentines and the Siennese, a moment all action, a moment composed in space of many actions, and yet, in point of time, but a moment. The motion of the warriors is motionless, the plunging of the horses arrested. What has been is, and, in what is actually seen, what is about to be is foreseen. The spatial imitation of a moment (and that is all the Rout of San Romano is) is still an imagination of time.

We cannot ignore time in a painting, and particularly we cannot ignore it in Paolo Uccello. For Uccello it was who introduced perspective into European painting, and perspective is the means which allows the painter to include in his composition the consciousness of time; for it is by means of perspective that we see the distance one from another of objects in space, and all distance, like astronomical distance, may be expressed as time. But however great the temporal element, it has been converted in Uccello's composition into terms of space. That is why the Rout of San Romano is one of the truly great paintings of the European tradition. The opposing bodies of men and horses are not pitted against each other merely in battle; they are here opponents in space. The lifting and lowering of lances, the raising and breaking of swords, all those movements which in life could not have achieved their meaning unless in time, are here brought into spatial relations, and create their meaning by simply being. And all are under complete control. Since their aim is to kill, all these movements were they living would be violent. The impression they convey is one of absolute calm. Man has been added to nature. The order of art has been imposed on human disorder.

In Paolo Uccello's battle we have the actions of time set before us as a complex of space. The poet who wishes to present a battle should have no trouble in rendering the succession of actions. But a battle must take place somewhere.

And one might suppose that Shakespeare could show us how it is done. The difficulty is really to find a battle in Shakespeare's plays. It would seem that nothing would be easier, for we carry away from his plays the impression that they resound from beginning to end with the conflict of arms, so long a reverberation do words like Philippi, Agincourt and Bosworth leave in our ears. But when you go through the plays looking for the poet's equivalent to the painter's Rout of San Romano, you discover that the poet was almost as wary of fighting as his Falstaff. He is at times forced on the very field, but when he gets there, he, as likely as not, pretends like Falstaff that he has slaughtered his bravest enemy, while actually he has merely gone through the motions of fighting. His failure is not one of valor; for he does not fail. He is simply discreet enough to know that real battles are always fought in real space and that an imaginary battle must take place in imaginary space. He can imagine space, but his danger, since he was a dramatic poet, was that the space he had imagined could be confounded, at what ridiculous risk he knew, with the real stage on which his actors stood, hacking at one another with the theatre's harmless swords.

> O for a Muse of fire, that would ascend
> The brightest heaven of invention,—
> A kingdom for a stage, princes to act,
> And monarchs to behold the swelling scene!
> Then should the warlike Harry, like himself,
> Assume the port of Mars; and at his heels,
> Leasht-in like hounds, should famine, sword and fire
> Crouch for employment. But pardon, gentles all,
> The flat unraised spirits that have dared
> On this unworthy scaffold to bring forth
> So great an object: can this cockpit hold
> The vasty fields of France? or may we cram
> Within this wooden O the very casques
> That did affright the air at Agincourt?

Obviously not. All that the cockpit ever held was a company of actors and all that ever did affright the air in that wooden O were the words of the poet. What then does Shakespeare do? Since he can't put the battle of Agincourt on the stage, he diverts the interest to something he can show. Agincourt was one of the most interesting battles ever fought. But while it is being prepared for, while it is being forced into conclusion, the attention is centered on the relation between the sovereign and subject. Not only was this profoundly interesting to Shakespeare—and presumably to his audience—but it was a relation which could perfectly be shown in a succession of scenes, which present now one aspect, now another, but which never, even in the sum, exceed the possibilities of the stage.

The poet, though his art is one of time, cannot get away from space. For our minds are so made that space is a necessary concept. The greatest expanse of space which Shakespeare ever attempted to put on the stage is in *Antony and Cleopatra*, where, if we but listen to the words, we shall hear the tramplings of armies over three continents. But it is a space that we hear; it comes to us in names, and if we see a plain before Actium, it is only in the mind's eye. Of the battle itself we have only the noise of a sea-fight and then a short report in which we are told how Cleopatra fled:

> She once being looft,
> The noble ruin of her magic, Antony,
> Claps on his sea-wing, and like a doting mallard,
> Leaving the fight in height, flies after her;
> I never saw an action of such shame:
> Experience, manhood, honour, ne'er before
> Did violate so itself.

The action at Actium becomes the act of Antony; the issue of the battle has already been decided where for the poet decision is possible: in Antony's violation of his own manhood. And that being the work of time, it is perfectly possible for the poet to handle it, his medium being words and his art being so to control them that they create by their sensuous succession an illusion of time.

What conclusions are we to draw from this? The poet of *Antony and Cleopatra* has not been limited in staging that ancient tragedy to a sequence of actions in time. Shakespeare's subject demanded that his actions range over the whole of the known and subjugated world, and we may suspect that what attracted Shakespeare to that particular tragedy at a time when, as a poet, he must have been conscious as never before of his powers, was its spaciousness. Certainly beyond any other of his plays *Antony and Cleopatra* is conceived in space and charged with the emotions which arise from its contemplation. He is limited by his means, for verses are only articulate sounds, which must so follow one another that they create time in a sensuous flow, which, unlike time itself, is under the control of the poet. He is not limited in his subject. The battle, which we should expect, had Lessing been as sound as he seemed on the limits of poetry and painting (since a battle is composed of nothing but actions successive in time), to have been a most appropriate subject for the poet, has actually been presented much more successfully by the painter, as a conflict of bodies immobilized in space. What we are concerned with in Shakespeare's play is what is happening to Antony, and Actium is only a point in the long process, whose significance, since Antony is a living man, only time can let out. And Shakespeare was not at a loss when it came to making the life of Antony, which, in so far as it is history, belongs to the past, into the continuous present which is poetry. His means is verse. Shakespeare, I think it is safe to say, was not much interested in action for its own sake, but no poetry was ever written in which more happens, for in no other does so much more happen within the words in a given movement of time. A great deal also happens in the Rout of San Romano, but what counts is not the conflict of armies which prompted the painter, but the use of their lineaments and colors to control space. The exhilaration and the calm which is produced by art is due to the sense it gives of release from the conditions of living, not by its denying those concepts without which life is to us inconceivable, but by controlling them. Only through the means of art can the conviction be created that man controls time and space. It is in the means of art, then, that we must look for its end.

Lessing's contention that each art is at its best where its power is least to be disputed is doubtless still sound. Each artist is limited by his means, but in those limitations is the source of his power. Why not then, asked Picasso, make the means the end? The power of the painter is only shown in his ordering of space. Why should he not then limit himself to paintings in which the spatial relations should be apparent, in which indeed nothing else should appear. When all is said and done, the subject signifies nothing, the subject is merely a pretext; why not then discard the subject, or if the subject refuses to disappear, let its own life dissolve so that nothing is left but living form?

An Impressionist like Monet had devoted his long life to preserving in pigment the changing appearance of an hour. And Impressionism, conscious of the moment of mutability, had at last, as Lhote said, committed plastic suicide and been drowned like Ophelia among the water lilies which are the last great work of Monet's age. Picasso for a time at least sought nothing else but form, for nothing in art is permanent but form.

If we look at such a painting of Picasso's as The Three Musicians we cannot but be aware that in this canvas space has been superbly created. The whole composition seems to have been made up of surfaces which like those of geometry are without a third dimension, and yet the illusion of depth is there. If we look closely we can see how it has been produced, by color and by lines, though no one line leads us more than a little way. There is in the painting nothing that we should ordinarily call perspective; there is at most only a primitive approach to it. To find anything that is so nearly a pure creation of space, we should have to go back to Paolo Uccello. In the Rout of San Romano the perspective is still primitive, though for not the same reason as in the work of Picasso. Picasso greatly admires Uccello and would probably admit that his art has been influenced by the Italian. And it is almost certain that we would not now find so much satisfaction in the Rout of San Romano, if we had never seen a Picasso. For the art of the present can contribute to the art of the past. History is not a one way road. But it will not do to allow this contrary traffic to confuse us. The artist of one century can never repeat the art of another.

Paolo Uccello replaced a visible world, where all was disorder, with a world of sensuous form and color, where all is disposed according to some invisible source of order. Pablo Picasso projects an invisible world, in which all is disorder, with a world of abstract form and color, where all is arranged according to some purely material order. Man is so made that he cannot conceive the world except as time and space. But there is a great difference in the world of Italy in the fifteenth century, when time seemed to have been conquered by a dream of eternity, and our own world, in which we suppose a conquest of space through material, not to say mechanical means. Picasso is a great admirer of Uccello.

That abstract painting was incomplete was soon clear, but what it lacked, what Picasso had so lately and with absolute logic eliminated, was not clear. At least it was not clear to anybody that counted until Chirico brought back perspective. But he did not bring back the elaborate perspective that had been lost. The aim was no longer *trompe l'oeil,* but in Cocteau's perfect phrase *trompe l'esprit.* It was not the eye, but the spirit that was to be taken in. And it was to be tricked in exactly the way we are tricked in dreams into believing that what is

past is present. Picasso had also painted much from memory, his harle-
quins, his guitars, his three musicians all are memories of Spain when
he was a young man. But Chirico's recollections have something of the
quality of hallucination; his paintings are excursions into a childhood
spent, for all his Italian parentage, in Greece. There is, of course, a
difference between painting an object or a person remembered and
attempting to paint memory itself. Picasso is sound and sane; Chirico
is a man under compulsion and perhaps a little mad; Salvador Dali
simulates paranoia. But the point is not there; the point is that the
contemporary mind cannot pretend that it is without the consciousness
of time. But when time reappeared in the early paintings of Dali it
was most self-consciously. It came back marked on those marvellous
limp watches in a painting called The Persistence of Memory. And not
only has Dali restored perspective. He uses it with a skill that is nothing short of ostentation.

The presumption is that perspective was brought back into painting
to satisfy an emotional need. Certainly those empty squares with their
arcades in shadow, those streets deserted of all but statues of Chirico,
or the immense plains of Dali, where the small muscled shapes of men
cast disproportionate shadows, are sources of disquietude. I cannot altogether say why they trouble us. But it is not at all necessary for the
purpose that I should. I merely want to suggest that the moment a
painter insists upon his third dimension of perspective he has already
introduced a fourth, which is time. And when time appears in a painting, it comes somewhat as the messenger in a Greek play comes, not
by chance, but as an instrument of necessity.

I have stayed long over the painters, because it is more difficult to
discern the temporal element in painting than it is to discover why the
poets have never been able to get along without the concept of space.

> Here is no water but only rock
> Rock and no water and the sandy road
> The road winding above among the mountains
> Which are mountains of rock without water
> If there were water we should stop and drink
> Amongst the rock one cannot stop or think . . .

This is the Dali desert before Dali. In this passage from *The Waste
Land* images of space do occur but successively and not as they would

in one of Dali's paintings, simultaneously. And the dry rocks and the sandy road winding toward the mountain where there is still no water are but symbols of a spiritual drought, due to the disappearance of faith in the truth of Christianity, which is itself a disaster of time.

The early poems of Eliot are often situated with great care in space. In "Sweeny Among the Nightingales" Apeneck Sweeny, that extraordinary sensual man, is found in a Parisian dive; but for a moment we are also allowed to see him standing on the great earth itself:

> The circles of the stormy moon
> Slide westward toward the River Plate.

It is an earth still dark with the tragic blood of Agamemnon:

> The nightingales are singing in
> The Convent of the Sacred Heart

> And sang within the bloody wood
> When Agamemnon cried aloud
> And let their liquid siftings fall
> To stain the stiff dishonoured shroud.

On Sweeny's sordid surroundings the poet suddenly intrudes with the terror of time.

The pure poet is one for whom a poetic solution is possible for any problem which his life imposes upon him. A pure painter is likewise one for whom the solution of any problem is in painting. Shakespeare is such a poet; Uccello such a painter. Once the problem is solved, it no longer exists as a problem; it is present in the solution but solely as a force, as a tension. The public is interested in problems; it is seldom interested in the solution; it is seldom interested in art.

The ultimate question concerning any work of art is out of how deep a life does it come. But the question that must first be asked is whether it has a life of its own. And the life of art is in its form. There have been poets among the painters. Chirico is one. There have been poets who not only leaned on the painters, but picked their pockets and stole their palettes as well. Baudelaire was one. But Chirico does not write verse, while in Baudelaire all his colors have their correspondences in sound.

When all the arts strive toward the condition of music, painting becomes abstract and poetry attempts to live on its own technical resources. This is behaving like the child who copies the answers from the back pages of his arithmetic book without having consulted the problem. But that behavior is at the moment unlikely. Today the artist is more like the child who from his schoolroom desk looks first at the window beyond which lies life with all its turmoil and play, and then at the enclosing walls and the door that is slow in opening. In the meanwhile the problem waits, unsolved, but not insoluble. But the problem is one which demands to be solved on its own terms, not those of the playground or the street.

It is the mind that imposes these conceptions of time and space. It is his art that confines the poet to the conventions of time, as it is the art of the painter that holds him to a conventional space. The mind is free; but it is the mind of a condemned man.

William Faulkner's Legend of the South

Malcolm Cowley

WILLIAM FAULKNER IS ONE OF THE WRITERS who reward and even in a sense demand a second reading. When you return to one of his books years after its publication, the passages that had puzzled you are easier to understand and each of them takes its proper place in the picture. Moreover, you lose very little by knowing the plot in advance. Faulkner's stories are not the sort that unwind in celluloid ribbons until the last inch of them has been reflected on a flat screen, with nothing to imagine and nothing more to see except the newsreel, the animated cartoon and the Coming Repulsions; instead his books are sculptural, as if you could walk round them for different views of the same solid object. But it is not merely a statue that he presents: rather it is a whole monument or, let us say, a city buried in the jungle, to which the author wishes to guide us, but not at once or by following a single path. We start out along one road, winding between walls of jungle growth in the humid afternoon, and it is not long until we catch a glimpse of our destination. Just beyond us, however, is a swamp filled with snakes, and the guide makes us turn back. We take another road; we gain a clearer picture of the city; but this time there are other dangers in front of us, quicksands or precipices, and again the guide makes us return. By whatever road we travel, we always catch sight of our goal, always learn more about it and are always forced back; till at last we find the proper path and reach the heart of the city just as it is about to be overwhelmed by fire or earthquake. . . . Reading the same book a second time is like soaring over the jungle in a plane, with every section of the landscape falling into its proper perspective.

And there is another respect in which our judgment of the author changes when we return to not one but several of his novels in succession. On a first reading what had chiefly impressed us may have been their violence, which sometimes seemed to have no justification in art or nature. We had remembered incidents and figures like the violating of Temple Drake, in *Sanctuary;* like the pursuit and castration of Joe Christmas, in *Light in August;* like the idiot boy who fell in love and eloped with a cow, in *The Hamlet;* and like the nameless woman, in *The Wild Palms,* who bore her child unaided in the midst of a Mississippi River flood, on an Indian mound where all the snakes in the Delta had taken refuge. After a second reading, most of these nightmares retain their power to shock, but at the same time they merge a little into the background, as if they were the almost natural product of the long unbearable Mississippi summers; as if they were thunder showers brewed in the windless heat. We pay less attention to the horrors as such, and more to the old situation out of which they developed and the new disasters it seems to foreshadow.

The situation itself, and not the violence to which it leads, is Faulkner's real subject. It is, moreover, the same situation in all his books— or, let us say, in all the novels and stories belonging to his Yocknapatawpha County series. Briefly it is the destruction of the old Southern order, by war and military occupation and still more by finance capitalism that tempts and destroys it from within. "Tell about the South," says Quentin Compson's roommate at Harvard, who comes from Edmonton, Alberta, and is curious about the unknown region beyond the Ohio. "What's it like there?" Shreve McCannon goes on to ask. "What do they do there? Why do they live there? Why do they live at all?" And Quentin, whose background is a little like that of the author and who often seems to speak for him—Quentin answers, "You can't understand it. You would have to be born there." Nevertheless, he tells a long and violent story that he regards as the essence of the Deep South, which is not so much a region as it is, in Quentin's mind, an incomplete and frustrated nation trying to recover its own identity, trying to relive its legendary past.

There was a boy, Quentin says—I am giving the plot of *Absalom, Absalom!*—a mountain boy named Thomas Sutpen whose family drifted into the Virginia tidewater. There his father found odd jobs on a plantation. One day the father sent him with a message to the big house, but he was turned away at the door by a black man in livery. The mountain boy, puzzled and humiliated, was seized upon by the ambition to which he would afterwards refer as "the design." He would own a plantation, with slaves and a liveried butler; he would build a mansion as big as any in the tidewater; and he would have a son to inherit his wealth.

A dozen years later, Sutpen appeared in the frontier town of Jefferson, Mississippi and, by some transaction the nature of which was never explained—though it certainly wasn't by honest purchase—he obtained a hundred square miles of land from the Chickasaws. He disappeared again, and this time he returned with twenty wild Negroes from the jungle and a French architect. On the day of his reappearance, he set about building the largest house in northern Mississippi, with timbers from the forest and bricks that his Negroes molded and baked on the spot; it was as if his mansion, Sutpen's Hundred, had been literally torn from the soil. Only one man in Jefferson—he was Quentin's grandfather, General Compson—ever learned how and where Sutpen had acquired his slaves. He had shipped to Haiti from Virginia, worked as an overseer on a sugar plantation and married the rich planter's daughter, who had borne him a son. Then, finding that his wife had Negro blood, he had simply put her away, with her child and her fortune, while keeping the twenty slaves as a sort of indemnity. He explained to General Compson in the stilted speech he had taught himself that she could not be "adjunctive to the forwarding of the design."

"Jesus, the South is fine, isn't it?" says Shreve McCannon. "It's better than the theatre, isn't it? It's better than Ben Hur, isn't it? No wonder you have to come away now and then, isn't it?"

Sutpen married again, Quentin continues. This time his wife belonged to a pious family of the neighborhood, and she bore him two children, Henry and Judith. He became the biggest landowner and cotton planter in the county, and it seemed that his "design" had already been fulfilled. At this moment, however—it was Christmas in 1859—Henry came home from the University of Mississippi with an older and worldlier new friend, Charles Bon, who was in reality Sutpen's son by his first marriage. Charles became engaged to Judith. Sutpen learned his identity and, without making a sign of recognition, ordered him to leave the house. Henry, who refused to believe that Charles was his half-brother, renounced his birthright and followed him to New Orleans. In 1861 all the male Sutpens went off to war, and all of them survived four years of fighting. Then, in the spring of 1865, Charles suddenly decided to marry Judith, even though he was certain by now that she was his half-sister. Henry rode beside him all the way back to Sutpen's Hundred, but tried to stop him at the gate, killed him when he insisted on going ahead with his plan, told Judith what he had done, and disappeared.

"The South," Shreve McCannon says as he listens to the story. "The South. Jesus. No wonder you folks all outlive yourselves by years and years." And Quentin says, remembering his own sister with whom he was in love—just as Charles Bon, and Henry too, were in love with Judith—"I am older at twenty than a lot of people who have died."

But Quentin's story of the Deep South does not end with the war. Colonel Sutpen came home, he says, to find his wife dead, his son a fugitive, his slaves dispersed (they had run away even before they were freed by the Union army) and most of his land about to be seized for debt. But still determined to carry out "the design," he did not even pause for breath before undertaking to restore his house and plantation as nearly as possible to what they had been. The effort failed; he lost most of his land and was reduced to keeping a crossroads store. Now in his sixties, he tried again to beget a son; but his wife's younger sister, Miss Rosa Coldfield, was outraged by his proposal ("Let's try it," he had said, "and if it's a boy we'll get married"); and later poor Milly Jones, with whom he had an affair, gave birth to a baby girl. At that Sutpen abandoned hope and provoked Milly's grandfather into killing him. Judith survived her father for a time, as did the half-caste son of Charles Bon by a New Orleans octoroon. After the death of these two by yellow fever, the great house was haunted rather than inhabited by an ancient mulatto woman, Sutpen's daughter by one of his slaves. The fugitive Henry Sutpen came home to die; the townspeople heard of his illness and sent an ambulance after him; but old Clytie thought they were arresting him for murder and set fire to Sutpen's Hundred. The only survivor of the conflagration was Jim Bond, a half-witted, saddle-colored creature who was Charles Bon's grandson.

"Do you know what I think?" says Shreve McCannon after the story has ended. "I think that in time the Jim Bonds are going to conquer the western hemisphere. Of course it won't be quite in our time and of course as they spread toward the poles they will bleach out again like the rabbits and the birds do, so they won't show up so sharp against the snow. But it will still be Jim Bond; and so in a few thousand years, I who regard you will also have sprung from the loins of African kings. Now I want you to tell me just one thing more. Why do you hate the South?"

"I don't hate it," Quentin says quickly, at once. "I don't hate it," he repeats, speaking for the author as well as himself. *I don't hate it,* he thinks, panting in the cold air, the iron New England dark; *I don't. I don't! I don't hate it! I don't hate it!*

The reader cannot help wondering why this somber and, at moments, plainly incredible story had so seized upon Quentin's mind that he trembled with excitement when telling it and felt that it revealed the essence of the Deep South. It seems to belong in the realm of Gothic romances, with Sutpen's Hundred taking the place of the haunted castle on the Rhine, with Colonel Sutpen as Faust and Charles Bon as Manfred. Then slowly it dawns on you that most of the characters and incidents have a double meaning; that besides their place in the story, they also serve as symbols or metaphors with a general application. Sutpen's great design, the land he stole from the Indians, the French architect who built his house with the help of wild Negroes from the jungle, the woman of mixed blood whom he married and disowned, the unacknowledged son who ruined him, the poor white whom he wronged and who killed him in anger, the final destruction of his mansion like the downfall of a social order: all these might belong to a tragic fable of Southern history. With a little cleverness, the whole novel might be explained as a connected and logical allegory, but this, I think, would be going beyond the author's intention. First of all he was writing a story, and one that affected him deeply, but he was also brooding over a social situation. More or less unconsciously, the incidents in the story came to represent the forces and elements in the social situation, since the mind naturally works in terms of symbols and parallels. In Faulkner's case, this form of parallelism is not confined to *Absalom, Absalom!* It can be found in the whole fictional framework that he has been elaborating in novel after novel, until his work has become a myth or legend of the South.

I call it a legend because it is obviously no more intended as a historical account of the country south of the Ohio than *The Scarlet Letter* is intended as a history of Massachusetts Bay or *Paradise Lost* as a factual description of the Fall. Briefly stated, the legend might run something like this: The Deep South was settled partly by aristocrats like the Sartoris clan and partly by new men like Colonel Sutpen. Both types of planters were determined to establish a lasting social order on the land they had seized from the Indians (that is, to leave sons behind them). They had the virtue of living single-mindedly by a fixed code;

but there was also an inherent guilt in their "design," their way of life, that put a curse on the land and brought about the Civil War. After the War was lost, partly as a result of their own mad heroism (for who else but men as brave as Jackson and Stuart could have frightened the Yankees into standing together and fighting back?) they tried to restore "the design" by other methods. But they no longer had the strength to achieve more than a partial success, even after they had freed their land from the carpetbaggers who followed the Northern armies. As time passed, moreover, the men of the old order found that they had Southern enemies too: they had to fight against a new exploiting class descended from the landless whites of slavery days. In this struggle between the clan of Sartoris and the unscrupulous tribe of Snopes, the Sartorises were defeated in advance by a traditional code that prevented them from using the weapons of the enemy. But the Snopeses as price of their victory had to serve the mechanized civilization of the North, which was morally impotent in itself, but which, with the aid of its Southern retainers, ended by corrupting the Southern nation. In our own day, the problems of the South are still unsolved, the racial conflict is becoming more acute; and Faulkner's characters in their despairing moments foresee or forebode some catastrophe of which Jim Bond and his like will be the only survivors.

This legend of Faulkner's, if I have stated it correctly, is clearly not a scientific interpretation of Southern history (if such a thing exists); but neither is it the familiar plantation legend that has been embodied in hundreds of romantic novels. Faulkner presents the virtues of the old order as being moral rather than material. There is no baronial pomp in his novels; no profusion of silk and silver, mahogany and moonlight and champagne. The big house on Mr. Hubert Beauchamp's plantation (in *Go Down, Moses*) had a rotted floorboard in the back gallery that Mr. Hubert never got round to having fixed. Visitors used to find him sitting in the spring-house with his boots off and his feet in the water while he drank a morning toddy, which he invited them to share. Visitors to Sutpen's Hundred were offered champagne: it was the best, doubtless, and yet it was "crudely dispensed out of the burlesqued pantomime elegance of Negro butlers who (and likewise the drinkers who gulped it down like neat whiskey between flowery and unsubtle toasts) would have treated lemonade the same way." All the planters lived comfortably, with plenty of servants, but Faulkner never lets us forget that they were living on what had recently been the frontier. What he admires about them is not their wealth or their manners or their fine houses, but rather their unquestioning acceptance of a moral code that taught them "courage and honor and pride, and pity and love of justice and of liberty." Living with single hearts, they were, says Quentin Compson's father:

> . . . people too as we are, and victims too as we are, but victims of a different circumstance, simpler and therefore, integer for integer, larger, more heroic and the figures therefore more heroic too, not dwarfed and involved but distinct, uncomplex, who had the gift of living once or dying once instead of being diffused and scattered creatures drawn blindly limb from limb from a grab bag and assembled, author and victim too of a thousand homicides and a thousand copulations and divorcements.

The old order was a moral order: that was its strength and the secret lost by its heirs. But also—and here is another respect in which Faulkner's legend differs from the plantation legend as presented in a novel like *Gone with the Wind*—it bore the moral burden of a guilt so great that the War and even Reconstruction were in some sense a merited punishment. There is madness, but there is a metaphorical meaning too, in Miss Rosa Coldfield's belief that Sutpen was a demon and that his sins were the real reason ". . . why God let us lose the War: that only through the blood of our men and the tears of our women could He stay this demon and efface his name and lineage from the earth." Quentin's father is quite sane, in his sober moments, and yet he expresses almost the same idea about Sutpen's guilt and its consequences. He is telling the story of the Sutpens when he remarks that the Civil War was ". . . a stupid and bloody aberration in the high (and impossible) destiny of the United States, maybe instigated by that family fatality which possessed, along with all circumstance, that curious lack of economy between cause and effect which is always a characteristic of fate when reduced to using human materials."

Colonel Sutpen himself has a feeling, not exactly of guilt, since he has never questioned the rightness of his design, but rather of amazement that so many misfortunes have fallen on him. Sitting in General Compson's office, he goes back over his career, trying to see where he had made his "mistake," for that is what he calls it. Sometimes the author seems to be implying that the sin for which Sutpen and his class are being punished is simply the act of cohabiting with Negroes. But before the end of *Absalom, Absalom!* we learn that miscegenation is only part of it. When Charles Bon's curious actions are explained, we find that he was taking revenge on his father for having refused to recognize him by so much as a single glance. Thus, heartlessness was the "mistake" that had ruined Sutpen, not the taking of a partly Negro wife and Negro concubines. And the point becomes clearer in a long story called *The Bear* (in *Go Down, Moses*), probably the best single piece that Faulkner has written. When Isaac McCaslin is twenty-one, he insists on relinquishing the big plantation that is his by inheritance; he thinks that the land is cursed. It is cursed in his eyes by the deeds of his grandfather: "that evil and unregenerate old man who could summon, because she was his property, a human being because she was old enough and female, to his widower's house and get a child on her and then dismiss her because she was of an inferior race, and then bequeath a thousand dollars to the infant because he would be dead then and wouldn't have to pay it." It follows that the land was cursed—and the War was part of the curse—because its owners had treated human beings as instruments; in a word, it was cursed by slavery.

All through his boyhood, Faulkner must have dreamed of fighting in the Civil War. It was a Sartoris war and not a Snopes war, like the one in which he afterwards risked his life in a foreign army. And yet his sympathies did not wholly lie with the slaveholding clan of Sartoris, even though it was his own clan. The men he most admired and must have pictured himself as resembling were the Southern soldiers—after all, they were the vast majority—who owned no slaves themselves and suffered from the institution of slavery. The men he would praise in his novels were those "who had fought for four years and lost . . . not because they were opposed to freedom as freedom, but for the old reasons for which man (not the generals and politicians but man) has always fought and died in wars: to preserve a status quo or to establish a better future one to endure for his children." You might define his position as that of an anti-slavery Southern nationalist.

His attitude toward Negroes will seem surprising only to Northerners. It seems to have developed from the attitude of the slaveholders, which was often inhuman but never impersonal—that is, the slave might be treated as a domestic animal, but not as a machine or the servant of a machine. Apparently the slaveholding class had little or no feeling of racial animosity. Frederick Law Olmsted, a sharp and by no means a friendly observer, was struck by what he called "the close cohabitation and association of black and white." In his *Journey in the Seaboard Slave States,* the record of his travels in 1853-54, he said: "Negro women are carrying black and white babies together in their arms; black and white children are playing together (not going to school together); black and white faces are constantly thrust together out of the doors, to see the train go by." He described the relation between masters and servants as having "a familiarity and closeness of intimacy that would have been noticed with astonishment, if not with manifest displeasure, in almost any chance company at the North." In Faulkner's historical novels, we find this closeness of intimacy compounded with closeness of blood, for the servants are very often the illegitimate half-brothers or sisters of their white companions—not only more often than in life, a mild way of putting it, but also more often than in any Abolitionist tract. He describes the old South as inhabited by two races that lived essentially the same life, if on different levels. Thus, he says in *Absalom, Absalom!* that the young planters were

. . . only in the surface matter of food and clothing and daily occupation any different from the Negro slaves who supported them—the same sweat, the only difference being that on the one hand it went for labor in fields where on the other it went as the price of the spartan and meagre pleasures which were available to them because they did not have to sweat in the fields: the hard violent hunting and riding; the same pleasures: the one, gambling for worn knives and brass jewelry and twists of tobacco and buttons and garments because they happened to be easiest and quickest to hand; on the other for the money and horses, the guns and watches, and for the same reason; the same parties: the identical music from identical instruments, crude fiddles and guitars, now in the big house with candles and silk dresses and champagne, now in dirt-floored cabins with smoking pine knots and calico and water sweetened with molasses.

"They will endure. They are better than we are," Ike McCaslin says of the Negroes, although he finds it more painful to utter this heresy than it is to surrender his plantation. "Stronger than we are," he continues. "Their vices are vices aped from white men or that white men and bondage have taught them: improvidence and intemperance and evasion—not laziness . . . and their virtues are their own: endurance and pity and tolerance and forbearance and fidelity and love of children, whether their own or not or black or not." In Faulkner's novels, the Negroes are an element of stability and endurance, just as the octoroons (like Charles Bon and Joe Christmas) are an element of tragic instability. His favorite characters are the Negro cooks and matriarchs who hold a white family together: Elnora and Dilsey and Clytie and Aunt Mollie Beauchamp. After the Compson family has gone to pieces (in *The Sound and the Fury*), it is Dilsey the cook who endures and is left behind to mourn. Looking up at the square, unpainted house with its rotting portico, she thinks, "Ise seed de first and de last"; and later in the kitchen, looking at the cold stove, "I seed de first en de last."

The increasing hatred between two races is explained in Faulkner's novels partly by the heritage of slavery and Reconstruction; partly by the coming into power of a new class which, so far as it consists of families with landless and slaveless ancestors, has a tradition of hostility to the Negroes. But Faulkner also likes to think that the lynch mobs were often led by the descendants of his old enemies, the carpet-baggers—

> . . . that race threefold in one and alien even among themselves save for a single fierce will for rapine and pillage, composed of the sons of middle-aged Quartermaster lieutenants and Army sutlers and contractors in military blankets and shoes and transport mules, who followed the battles they themselves had not fought and inherited the conquest they themselves had not helped to gain . . . and left their bones and in another generation would be engaged in a fierce economic competition of small sloven farms with the black men they were supposed to have freed and the white descendants of fathers who had owned no slaves anyway whom they were supposed to have disinherited, and in the third generation would be back once more in the little lost county seats as barbers and garage mechanics and deputy sheriffs and mill and gin hands and power-plant firemen, leading, first in mufti then later in an actual formalized regalia of hooded sheets and passwords and fiery Christian symbols, lynching mobs against the race their ancestors had come to save.

Faulkner's novels of contemporary Southern life continue the legend into a period that he regards as one of moral confusion and social decay. He is continually seeking in them for violent images to convey his sense of despair. *Sanctuary* is the most violent of all his novels; it is also the most popular and by no means the least important (in spite of Faulkner's comment that it was "a cheap idea . . . deliberately conceived to make money"). The story of Popeye and Temple Drake has more meaning than appears on a first hasty reading—the only reading that most of the critics have been willing to grant it. George Marion O'Donnell went over the novel more carefully and decided that it formed a coherent allegory. Writing in the *Kenyon Review,* he said that the pattern of the allegory was something like this:

> Southern Womanhood Corrupted but Undefiled (Temple Drake), in the company of the Corrupted Tradition (Gowan Stevens, a professional Virginian), falls into the clutches of amoral Modernism (Popeye), which is itself impotent, but which with the aid of its strong ally Natural Lust ("Red") rapes Southern Womanhood unnaturally and then seduces her so satisfactorily that her corruption is total, and she becomes the tacit ally of Modernism. Meanwhile Pore White Trash (Goodwin) has been accused of the crime which he, with the aid of the Naif Faithful (Tawmmy), actually tried to prevent. The Formalized Tradition (Horace Benbow), perceiving the true state of affairs, tries vainly to defend Pore White Trash. However, Southern Womanhood is so hopelessly corrupted that she willfully sees Pore White Trash convicted and lynched; she is then carried off by Wealth (Judge Drake) to meaningless escape in European luxury. Modernism, carrying in it from birth its own impotence and doom, submits with masochistic pleasure to its own destruction for the one crime that it has not yet committed—Revolutionary Destruction of Order (the murder of the Alabama policeman, for which the innocent Popeye is executed).

Mr. O'Donnell deserves very great credit as the first critic to discuss Faulkner as a moralist, the first to compare him in passing with Hawthorne, and almost the first to see that he is engaged in creating Southern myths. In his comments on *Sanctuary,* however, he has been entirely too ingenious. There is no doubt that his allegorical scheme can be read into the novel, but it hardly seems possible that the author intended to put it there. Faulkner tells us that *Sanctuary* was written "in about three weeks." It was completely rewritten two years later, in the effort "to make out of it something which would not shame *The Sound and the Fury* and *As I Lay Dying* too much"; but I doubt that Faulkner had or took the time to give every character a double meaning. Lee Goodwin, for example, is not Pore White Trash, capitalized, but a tough, frightened moonshiner dishonorably discharged from the Army. Tawmmy is not the Naif Faithful, capitalized; he is simply faithful and stupid. If Temple Drake has any symbolic value, she represents the South as a whole, or the younger generation in the South, rather than Southern Womanhood (a phrase that makes Faulkner wince); but it is also quite possible that she represents nothing but a rather silly co-ed. Popeye, however, is another question; and at this point Mr. O'Donnell's reading is not only ingenious but comes very close to Faulkner's conscious or unconscious intention.

Popeye is one of several characters in Faulkner's novels who stand for something that might be called "amoral Modernism," considering that they are creatures of the time and have no social morality whatever; but it might also be called—more accurately, I think—the mechanical civilization that has invaded and partly conquered the South. Popeye is always described in mechanical terms: his eyes "looked like rubber knobs"; his face "just went awry, like the face of a wax doll set too near a hot fire and forgotten"; his tight suit and stiff hat were "all angles, like a modernistic lampshade"; and in general he had "that vicious depthless quality of stamped tin." He was the son of a professional strikebreaker, from whom he inherited syphilis, and the grandson of a pyromaniac. Like two other villains in Faulkner's novels, Joe Christmas and Januarius Jones, he had spent most of his childhood in an institution. He was the man "who made money and had nothing he could do with it, spend it for, since he knew that alcohol would kill him like poison, who had no friends and had never known a woman" —in other words, he was the compendium of all the hateful qualities that Faulkner assigns to finance capitalism. *Sanctuary* is not the connected allegory that Mr. O'Donnell presents in outline (he doesn't approve of allegorical writing by novelists), but neither is it the accumulation of pointless horrors as which it has been dismissed by other critics. It is an example of the Freudian method turned backwards, being full of sexual nightmares that are in reality social symbols. In the author's mind, the novel is somehow connected with what he regards as the rape and corruption of the South.

And the descendants of the old ruling caste, in Faulkner's novels, have the wish but not the courage or the strength of will to prevent this new disaster. They are defeated by Popeye (like Horace Benbow), or they run away from him (like Gowan Stevens, who had gone to school at Virginia and learned to drink like a gentleman, but not to fight for his principles), or they are robbed and replaced in their positions of influence by the Snopeses (like old Bayard Sartoris, the president of the bank), or they drug themselves with eloquence and alcohol (like Mr. Compson), or they retire into the illusion of being inviolable Southern ladies (like Mrs. Compson, who says, "It can't be simply to flout and hurt me. Whoever God is, He would not permit that. I'm a lady"), or they dwell so much on the past that they are incapable of facing the present (like Reverend Hightower, of *Light in August,* who loses his wife and his church through living in a dream world), or they run from danger to danger (like young Bayard Sartoris) frantically seeking their own destruction. Faulkner's novels are full of well-meaning and even admirable people, not only the grandsons of the cotton aristocracy, but also pine-hill farmers and storekeepers and sewing-machine agents and Negro cooks and sharecroppers; but they are almost all of them defeated by circumstances and they carry with them a sense of their own doom.

They also carry, whether heroes or villains, a curious sense of submission to their fate. "There is not one of Faulkner's characters," says André Gide in his dialogue on *The New American Novelists,* "who, properly speaking, has a soul"; and I think he means that not one of them exercises the faculty of conscious choice between good and evil. They are haunted, obsessed, driven forward by some inner necessity. Like Miss Rosa Coldfield (in *Absalom, Absalom!*), they exist in "that dream state in which you run without moving from a terror in which you cannot believe, toward a safety in which you have no faith." Or, like the slaves freed by General Sherman's army (in *The Unvanquished*), they follow the roads toward any river, believing that it will be their Jordan:

> They were singing, walking along the road singing, not even looking to either side. The dust didn't even settle for two days, because all that night they still passed; we sat up listening to them, and the next morning every few yards along the road would be the old ones who couldn't keep up any more, sitting or lying down and even crawling along, calling to the others to help them; and the others—the young strong ones—not stopping, not even looking at them. "Going to Jordan," they told me. "Going to cross Jordan."

All Faulkner's characters, black and white, are a little like that. They dig for gold frenziedly after they have lost their hope of finding it (like Henry Armstid in *The Hamlet* and Lucas Beauchamp in *Go Down, Moses*); or they battle against and survive a Mississippi flood for the one privilege of returning to the state prison farm (like the tall convict in *The Wild Palms*); or, a whole family together, they carry a body through flood and fire and corruption to bury it in the cemetery at Jefferson (like the Bundrens in *As I Lay Dying*); or they tramp the roads week after week in search of men who had promised to marry them (like Lena Grove, the pregnant woman of *Light in August*); or, pursued by a mob, they turn at the end to meet and accept death (like Joe Christmas in the same novel). Even when they seem to be guided by a conscious design, like Colonel Sutpen, it is not something they have chosen by an act of will, but something that has taken possession of them: ". . . not what he wanted to do but what he just had to do, had to do it whether he wanted to or not, because if he did not do it he knew that he could never live with himself for the rest of his life." In the same way, Faulkner himself writes, not what he wants to, but what he just has to write whether he wants to or not. And the effect produced on us by all these haunted characters, described in hypnagogic prose, is that of myths or fairy tales or dreams, where again the people act under compulsion, toward fatally predetermined ends.

In addition to being a fatalist, Faulkner is also an idealist, more strongly so than any other American writer of our time. The idealism disguises itself as its own opposite, but that is because he is deeply impressed by and tends to exaggerate the contrast between the life around him and the ideal picture in his mind. No other American writer makes such a use of negative turns of speech: his stories abound in words like "paintless," "lightless," "windowless," "not-feeling," "unvisioned." He speaks of "that *roadless* and even *pathless* waste of *unfenced* fallow and wilderness jungle—*no* barn, *no* stable, *not so much as* a hen-coop; just a log cabin built by hand and *no* clever hand either, a meagre pile of clumsily cut firewood sufficient for about one day and *not even* a gaunt hound to come bellowing out from under the house when he rode up." In the same story (*The Bear*), he speaks of ". . . the empty fields without plow or seed to work them, fenceless against the stock which did not exist within or without the walled stable which likewise was not there." He speaks of faces watching "without alarm, without recognition, without hope," and he speaks of the South under Reconstruction as "a lightless and gutted and empty land." Always in his mind he has an ideal picture of how the land and the people should be—a picture of painted, many-windowed houses, fenced fields, overflowing barns, eyes lighting up with recognition; and always, being honest, he measures that picture against the land and people he has seen. And both pictures are not only physical but moral; for always in the background of his novels is a sense of moral standards and a feeling of outrage at their being violated or simply pushed aside. Seeing little hope in the future, he turns to the past, where he hopes to discover a legendary and recurrent pattern that will illuminate and lend dignity to the world about him. So it is that Reverend Hightower, dying in the dingy ruin of his plans, sees a vision of Bedford Forrest's troopers, who lived without question by a single and universally accepted code:

He hears above his heart the thunder increase, myriad and drumming. Like a long sighing of wind in trees it begins, then they sweep into sight, borne now upon a cloud of phantom dust. They rush past, forwardleaning in the saddles, with brandished arms, beneath whipping ribbons from slanted and eager lances; with tumult and soundless yelling they sweep past like a tide whose crest is jagged with the wild heads of horses and the brandished arms of men like the crater of the world in explosion. They rush past, are gone; the dust swirls skyward sucking, fades away into the night which has fully come. Yet, leaning forward in the window . . . it seems to him that he still hears them: the wild bugles and the clashing sabres and the dying thunder of hooves.

The New Criticism and the
Southern Critics
Robert Wooster Stallman

I

THERE IS ONE BASIC THEME IN BOTH the criticism and poetry of the
Southern poet-critics: Allen Tate, John Crowe Ransom, Cleanth
Brooks, Robert Penn Warren, and John Peale Bishop. It is the dis-
location of modern sensibility—the issue of our glorification of the
scientific vision at the expense of the aesthetic vision. This theme of
spiritual disorder, which the late Paul Valéry exploited, shows through
the current of the critical ideas of I. A. Richards, Yvor Winters, and
R. P. Blackmur. It is T. S. Eliot's major premise: the loss of order and
integrity in the modern consciousness and its unifying relation to an
ordered society and a tradition or culture. It is the obsessive burden of
contemporary criticism. The theme operates at the critical level as a
standard for measuring the poetic achievement of our age and of other
ages. It operates thus through these thematic variations: *the loss of a
tradition, the loss of a culture, the loss of a fixed convention, the loss of
a world-order.* The location of this theme at the critical level forms the
introduction to this examination of the Southern poet-critics. My analysis of their canon of criticism and poetry centers upon the most representative spokesman for the school: Allen Tate. My purpose is to order
into a synthesis the critical ideas of Tate, Ransom, and the New Critics.[1]

[1] This essay intends to clarify the position of Tate and the Southern critics, rather
than to pass judgment upon it. Adverse criticism of their position is made by Francis X.
Roellinger, Jr., in "Two Theories of Poetry as Knowledge" (*Southern Review:* Spring,
1942), and by Hoyt Trowbridge in "Aristotle and the 'New Criticism'" (*Sewanee Review:* Autumn, 1944). My study draws upon the complete critical writings of the Southern critics, together with all significant review-essays on their criticism. The only Southern poet-critics as yet bibliographed are Tate, Bishop, and R. P. Warren. Tate's checklist,
catalogued by Willard Thorp, and Bishop's, by J. Max Patrick and R. W. Stallman, appear in the *Princeton University Library Chronicle* (Apr., 1942, and Feb., 1946, respec-
tively). My checklist of Warren appears in the *University of Kansas City Review* (Spring,
1947). Except for this, my annotated *Bibliography of Modern Criticism* is still in manuscript form.

The loss of a tradition: The loss for the poetic discipline of an antecedent discipline in a religious or social tradition extending moral and intellectual authority to the poet. As the subject of Yvor Winters' *Primitivism and Decadence* is the effect upon what he calls the "Experimental Generation" of the loss of an antecedent discipline such as tradition, culture, or convention provide (the resultant loss is a poetry of structural confusion), so the theme of Eliot's *After Strange Gods* is the limiting and crippling effect upon our literature of a separation from a living and central tradition. The effect, Eliot states, is twofold: confusion as to the boundaries of criticism, and extreme individualism in views—the expression of a personal view of life that "is merely part of the whole movement of several centuries towards the aggrandisement and exploitation of *personality*." Tradition, as Tate (following Eliot) defines it, "is a quality of judgment and of conduct, rooted in a concrete way of life," that we inherit from our immediate past, or if we are makers of tradition (and it demands our constant rediscovery), the quality of life that we create and pass on to the next generation. Tradition (the term includes more than "traditional religious beliefs"), no less than religion, is formed of a structure of absolutes, imperatives or points of moral and intellectual reference which man requires to realize his nature, absolutes "implicit and emergent in experience at all times, and under certain conditions, explicit and realized." Our age lacks a scheme of experience such as Christianity afforded medieval Europe. It lacks the unity of life: a living center, a coherent way of thinking about experience, a unified conception of man in relation to God and nature. From Tate's traditionalist perspective history is seen, as by Eliot and Hilaire Belloc, as the decline of moral standards from the 12th Century to our day. In the decay of Protestantism is to be found the chief clue to our understanding of English literature. Eliot and Hulme and Tate are at one in this perspective. Tradition is the foundation for the critical viewpoint of both Eliot and Tate. (The source of Eliot's more recent standards of judgment is the Christian tradition, as Tate points out.) Eliot's conception of an immutable order is ultimately religious, whereas Tate's, like Valéry's, is ultimately aesthetic.

The loss of a fixed convention or fundamental agreement between the poet and his society, the loss of which, in Pound and Eliot for instance, has cost our age "The Expense of Greatness." This burden echoes throughout contemporary criticism from Blackmur and Tate to Spender and Auden. Never were poets, John Middleton Murry complains, more profoundly divided from the life of society than in our time. Dante and the great ages of poetry, as Blackmur (following Eliot) states, had at hand a convention or culture: "a group of ideas, and a faith, with the discipline that flows from them . . ." There is no such agreement today. MacLeish, Tate records, lacks what Milton had: "an objective convention that absorbed every implication of his personal feeling." Our modern poet, deprived of that rational structure from which he derives value and authority, is under the constant necessity of either resurrecting a dead convention (Millay is the example Tate cites) or erecting a new convention of his own (Yeats is the occasion for Blackmur's point). For Tate, as for Blackmur, the work of a great poet is a body of new convention—a new order of language. The pattern of a culture manifests itself in language, in the medium of the poet's words, and it is only in terms of language ("the embodiment of our experience in words") that a convention exists or survives. A convention, as defined by Tate (Blackmur's definition is identical), is simply the way in which language has been used by the poets of a preceding generation, used so powerfully that we can but carry on its major significance. The criticism of Tate and Blackmur is built upon this commonplace—in Blackmur it is the governing criterion, the conditioning fact of his judgment on Housman, Sandburg, Cummings, Emily Dickinson, Wallace Stevens:—does the poet make "a genuine attempt to use in his poems the maximum resource of poetic language consonant with his particular talent"? The operation of this principle in Tate's criticism is illustrated by his judgment on Millay. By using the language of the preceding generation "to convey an emotion peculiar to her own," and by making that language—a language not rooted in contemporary sensibility—personal, Millay restored to life a dead convention. This is at once her distinction and her limitation. She preserved in the easiest traditional style, the style of the preceding decadent age, the personality of her own age—without altering either. (*Reactionary Essays*)

The loss of a culture: a pattern of ideas and conduct imbedded in a homogeneous society; the loss of belief in the supernatural—in religion and myth; the loss of an objective system of truth. What Blake's genius required and lacked, Eliot observes, "was a framework of accepted and traditional ideas which would have prevented him from indulging in a philosophy of his own, and concentrated his attention on the problems of the poet. . . . The concentration resulting from a framework of mythology and theology and philosophy is one of the reasons why Dante is a classic, and Blake only a poet of genius. The fault is perhaps not with Blake himself, but with the environment which failed to provide what such a poet needed. . . ." (Observe here Eliot's criterion of "historical fatality.") Eliot's theme informs Tate's standard of judgment on E. A. Robinson, MacLeish, and Cummings: the loss of a systematic philosophy and the consequent substitution, for an external framework of ideas or an impersonal code, of a personal philosophy of experience—personality as the core of meaning, personal sensation as the center of experience. "It is the present fate of poetry," Tate sums up in his critique of MacLeish, "to be always beginning over again. The kind of 'culture' in *Conquistador* is purely literary; the kind of experience in it is the sentimentality of moral isolation. The refinement of the craftsmanship hovers over a void." Lacking an epos, myth, or code, E. A. Robinson had to repeat his ground again and again, writing a poem that would not be written. On Cummings the judgment of Tate and of John Peale Bishop come to the same point: the aggregate of Cummings's poems is an image of his unique personality. What *The Waste Land* means (Part II, as explicated by Tate in his essay on "What is a Traditional Society?") is that in ages which suffer the decay of religion we get the expression of chaos and violence; "it means that men who have lost both the higher myth of religion and the lower myth of historical dramatization have lost the forms of human action; it means that they are no longer capable . . . of forming a dramatic conception of human nature . . ." In place of the dramatization of the human soul, as located by Tate and Bishop in Emily Dickinson's poetry, we get from a contemporary poet like MacLeish the peculiarly modern situation: the dramatization (in *Conquistador*) of personality against an historical setting. The difference between Emily Dickinson, for whom the New England Idea (puritan theocracy) made possible modes for tragic action, and a contemporary New England poet like Mark Van Doren is measured by Bishop, in his review of Van Doren's *Collected Poems,* in terms of the loss of this sustaining tradition. What his poetry lacks is "the soul sufficient to itself," that authentic New England note of spiritual integrity whose loss Emily Dickinson set down with incomparable intensity. (*Nation:* Dec. 23, 1939) This criterion of "historical fatality," the prejudice of Bishop and Tate, is Eliot's standard of judging the poet as a fatal event in cultural history. It is a criterion historical rather than critical, as Blackmur observes in his examination—the finest piece of criticism yet written—of Emily Dickinson. It leads a critic less discriminating than Tate to explore the conditions producing poetry rather than the poetry itself.

The loss of a world order which can be assimilated to the poetic vision (a world order such as Shakespeare had in his medieval pattern of life, or a world order such as Emily Dickinson had in her New England Puritan Christianity). The loss of a code of moral and intellectual "terminal points" by which the poet can test his experience; the loss of what Shelley called a "fixed point of reference" for the poet's sensibility. The loss of a common center of meaning, from which the separate arts achieve their special formal solutions, has resulted, Tate points out in criticizing the poems of Bishop that are conceived as paintings, in that *mélange des genres* which the late 19th Century French poets developed to an advanced stage, that confusion and self-imitation of the arts whereby the arts tend to destroy themselves (the medium of one art being extended into the medium of another). Tate's objection to the poem as painting rests upon the contention that "There is no satisfactory substitute in poetry for the form-symbol." A poem for these critics—Tate, Ransom, Winters, Warren, Blackmur—requires a rational structure, a scheme of objective reference to give order and meaning to the poet's emotional experience. The assumption—a fallacy common to poets of our time (pointed out by Winters in MacLeish's poetry, and by Blackmur in Sandburg's)—that order or adequate form can be created simply by the poet's act of self-expression, by his imitation of disorder in what Winters labels as Expressive or Imitative Form, fails the poet as a solution for his problem: to achieve a rational order of value. Nor can the poet solve that problem by substituting for a structure of meaning, personal emotion undisciplined by a structure of ideas or events (emotion functioning as itself the theme of the poem). It is for want of formal structure that the poems of MacLeish and Cummings and Hart Crane are criticized by Tate: A mechanism of personal sensation takes the place of theme in MacLeish's *Conquistador;* the personality attached to *Viva* is the only meaning in Cummings's poems; the coherence of *The Bridge* is not structural, it has merely the coherence of the personal feeling or tone of the poet. Crane's poetic career Tate sets down as "a vindication of Eliot's major premise—that the integrity of the individual consciousness has broken

down." Crane's world had no center. Lacking an individual consciousness, he fell back "upon the intensity of consciousness rather than the
clarity, for his center of vision. And that is romanticism." The failure
of *The Bridge* ("The poem is the effort of a solipsistic sensibility to locate itself in the external world, to establish points of reference") is
symptomatic of the failure of modern poetry generally. What Tate
isolates in Crane is "the special quality of his mind that belongs peculiarly to our own time." Namely, the disorder. That disorder, far from
being the deliberately cultivated "disorder" of Rimbaud, was with
Crane original and fundamental. Keeping to Tate's critical approach,
Bishop in his essay on Thomas Wolfe isolates the affinity of Wolfe and
Crane to their world: they voice its breakdown in the consciousness of
continuity, and that is their significance for it. As here in his examination of Hart Crane, Tate's analysis of *The Bridge* extends beyond the
poem to the relation of its inner confusion with the outer disorder and
cross-purposes of the contemporary *milieu,* so too in his examination of
other poets (Eliot, Pound, Bishop, Dickinson) his criticism scrutinizes
both the conscious intention of the poet, as it is framed by the poem,
and his unconscious intention—the cultural mind of his world-order as
it relates to the poet and his poetry.

The problem of the modern poet, as summed up by Samuel Hoare
in *Standards of Criticism* (1933), is the problem of transferring to the
poetic process a unified point of view synthesized out of the complexity
of relations (social, physical, intellectual) which in the modern world
are not readily solvable into a unity. "The modern can never avoid the
suspicion that whatever attitude he takes up is only a partial expression
of himself and a partial activity. And he has no scale of values which
would justify him in concluding that this part is the most important,
that this activity is the fundamental activity. Without this great poetry
is impossible." The dilemma of the poet is forced no less upon the critic.
The critic whom Blackmur singles out as belonging somewhat more
conspicuously than other critics to this common category is Yvor
Winters:

Men everywhere are unwilling to trust, to confide, either in the work
their own minds do or in that which they see actually performed by the
minds of others, though that is all they have in either case finally to
depend on. They are driven rather to accept or dismiss, to foster or

destroy, the little work actually done in terms of work not done at all, but merely imputed. At least, this is so of every imaginative field; of religion, of politics, of philosophy, and of literary criticism.

("A Note on Yvor Winters")

Intellectual chaos—our "conscious awareness of the apparent unrelatedness of things" (the central affinity, according to Eliot, between our age and Donne's)—has been the background of American poetry, Tate complains, and "the sore distress of American criticism." (Marxian criticism is for Tate "the latest disguise of this heresy.") We lack a tradition of criticism, a body of ideas, points of critical reference. As Tate remarks, "the split mind of the poet meets its counterpart in the disfranchised intellect of the critic."

II

The final object of criticism for Tate, and likewise for Herbert Read, is the positing and criticizing of dogmas in pursuit of standards of judgment and value. Tate's criticism, though he disclaims the act of "the systematic literary critic," achieves nevertheless a synthesis of dogmas; they do not conflict with each other, as they do in Read's criticism, but form a coherent system of principles unified by a single point of view. Tate's point of view, which is influenced no less than Read's by T. E. Hulme, is that there is a radical division between the realm of faith, the religious, the contemplative, the qualitative, the spiritual or supernatural; and the realm of reason, the practical, the quantitative, the physical (the universe of matter).

It was Hulme's thesis that our spiritual disunity is the result of our failure to recognize the gap between the orders of *the divine*—the "Religious Attitude" which postulates absolute values in the light of which man is judged as essentially limited and imperfect ("endowed with Original Sin")—and *the human*—the "Humanist Attitude" that "life is the source and measure of all values, and that man is fundamentally good." The confusion of these two orders, the location in the plane of *humanity* of the concept of Perfection that properly belongs to the divine, Hulme designated as the essence of Romanticism. "The view which regards man as a well, a reservoir, full of possibilities, I call the romantic; the one which regards him as a very finite and fixed creature, I call the classical." His identifying formulation of romanticism with humanism and of classicism with the religious attitude is followed by Eliot and likewise by Tate.

Classicism, in Eliot's terms, means the discrimination between *reason* and *faith;* and romanticism—the confusion of reason and faith, which historically occurred after the collapse of the Scholastic School. This confusion, Eliot complains, has been the background of the modern consciousness since the Renaissance. The most urgent business of criticism today, Middleton Murry declares, is the task of creating a new synthesis analogous, but not correspondent, to the medieval synthesis of faith and reason, which was projected into the Thomist system. Not until a new synthesis is achieved, Murry maintains, will any work of art of the first magnitude be possible again. But "the Classicism of the Middle Ages can serve us only as a symbol, not as a pattern, of a new synthesis." For the terms of the modern antinomy do not correspond with the terms of the medieval antinomy between faith and reason, because faith his disappeared. "The post-Renaissance discarded the act of faith from its psychology and the object of faith from its reality; but only, as Whitehead shows in *Science and the Modern World,* by introducing an unconscious act of faith into the structure of its scientific knowledge." The dictum of St. Thomas, the fundamental proposition of the Thomist system that there cannot be faith and knowledge concerning the same object, is no longer valid in our experience. The objects and faculties of faith and reason are for the modern mind no longer distinct or distinguishable. The old antinomy between faith and reason, which was replaced by the post-Renaissance dichotomy between art and science, has its modern representation in the opposition between *qualitative knowledge* (or "intuition"), the faculty, as Whitehead defines it, by which concrete reality is prehended) and *quantitative knowledge* (or "intelligence"). The modern problem, Murry states in the essay from which I draw this summary ("Towards a Synthesis," *New Criterion:* May, 1927), is to reach a synthesis between these two orders of knowledge. Tate's description of our modern dilemma is summed up in similar terms. His opposition to the positivist procedure, which reduces all knowledge to the quantitative kind, has the same foundation as Murry's opposition to the scientific materialism of our time.

Hulme defined the mood, the perspective, of our age; and this is his importance, almost exclusively so, as an influence rather than as an

original thinker. Both Eliot and Tate have thoroughly orientated themselves in Hulme's *Speculations;* his dicta, in the same or in different
settings, appear throughout their writings. In Hulme is grounded
Tate's opposition to Emerson's conception of man, a conception which
dissipated, as Robert Penn Warren points out, all tragic possibilities in
that culture for dramatizing the human soul. Hulme, instead of Blackmur, might have phrased this passage to account for the great wastes in
Emily Dickinson and Whitman:

> The great bulk of the verse of each appears to have been written on the
> sustaining pretense that everything was always possible. To see bound-
> less good on the horizon, to see it without the limiting discipline of the
> conviction of evil, is in poetry as in politics the great stultifier of action.
> . . . With no criterion of achievement without there could be no crite-
> rion of completion within.

Tate is a disciple of Hulme in his campaign against the modern age
of science, the age of romanticism, the post-Renaissance self-sufficient
spirit of humanism, humanitarianism, protestantism, capitalism, progress, the economic and perfectible man. Both Tate and Read are followers of Hulme in holding a non-supernatural doctrine of original
sin; in sharing Hulme's belief that human nature contains certain radical imperfections; that the individual, far from being "an infinite reservoir of possibilities" (the romantic view of man), is a finite and limited
creature (the classical view); and that "it is only by tradition and or-
ganisation that anything decent can be got out of him." Hence neither
Tate nor Read can fully assent to Humanism, as Read, again following
Hulme, defines it:—"the belief that the only values that matter are human values." But Tate, unlike Read, (who falls back upon what F. C.
Flint calls "a Henry James' combination of social standards,") accepts
a system of supernatural religion as necessary for those standards by
which man, the imperfect being, can measure his own imperfections.
The necessary background for the realization of human and social
values, Tate insists, is a universal scheme of reference, a living center of
action and judgment such as we find in an objective religion. "The religious unity of intellect and emotion, of reason and instinct, is the sole
technique for the realization of values."

The disunity of the modern mind is the single theme of Tate's *Reason in Madness.* Our intellectual disunity, Tate and Ransom claim, has

been created by the disruption and confusion of these two categories: the aesthetic vision concerned with quality and the scientific vision concerned with quantity. It has its origin and expression in the modern intellectual movement variously known as positivism, pragmatism, instrumentalism; in the scientism of our age that has forced out the religious attitude and reduced to irrelevant emotion the spiritual realm under the illusion that all experience can be ordered scientifically. The decline of organized religion, Tate suggests, accounts for the recent revival of utilitarian aestheticism. Dewey's theory of the integrating power of art, a theory which attributes to art all the psychological virtues of a religion, makes of art a makeshift religion. Under the formula that "all art is action," he identifies art and religion and science as "satisfying the same fundamental needs." Tate, in "The Aesthetic Emotion as Useful" (*This Quarter:* Dec., 1932), rejects this equation and exposes the fallacy of the pragmatic aesthetic upon which this equation is based. Both Tate, in *Reason in Madness,* and Ransom, in *The New Criticism,* attack victoriously the "demi-religion of positivism" and perform for contemporary criticism, as one of their critics acknowledges, an invaluable service by exposing the pretensions of the positivists' scientific position. Following a modern aesthetician like Eliseo Vivas, they regard the aesthetic and the practical as opposites. Art, contrary to Dewey's pragmatic aesthetic, is neither another kind of religion nor another kind of science. Poetry is poetry and not science or religion.

The canon of the Southern critics is based upon the division of art and religion and science into equally valid, objective, and independent categories of experience. Art and religion are the vehicles of qualitative experience, but the two positions are not identical. Likewise science and religion, as Arnold stated, are two different things. It was Arnold's faith, as Tate interprets it in "Literature as Knowledge," that poetry, now that religion had yielded to the "fact" of science, could take over the work of religion. Though the "fact" of science had undermined religion, it could still support poetry. Arnold's view has its modern version in I. A. Richards's *Science and Poetry.* Richards here endorsed Arnold's dictum that what is valuable in religion, as in science, is art. But Richards misunderstands the nature of the aesthetic emotion; underlying the claims his early criticism makes for poetry, Montgomery Belgion points out in his critique of Richards ("What is Criticism?" *Criterion:* Oct., 1930), is a notion that poetry and life are equivalent. Both Belgion and Tate do away with the whole of Richards's utilitarian theory of art. Richards, however, has repudiated his early scientism; with his present position, as laid down in *Coleridge on the Imagination* (1934), Tate acknowledges an essential agreement. Tate's analysis of Arnold's position shows it up as giving the case for poetry away to the scientist. His poetics turns poetry into a "descriptive science or experience at that level, touched with emotion." For Tate and Ransom, science and poetry are the opposite poles of truth.

Tate and Ransom attempt to solve anew Arnold's problem: to place poetry on an equal footing with science. Against such modern theories of poetry as the early theory of Richards, that poetry is a device for "ordering" experience, performing thus the emotional therapeutic offices of religion, or the theory of Kenneth Burke that a work of art is a psychological machine deliberately designed to arouse emotions, Tate and Ransom urge the claim that poetry is primarily of the intellect and that poetry "is an independent form of knowledge, a kind of cognition, equal to the knowledge of the sciences at least, perhaps superior." As Tate says in his Preface to *The Language of Poetry*, poetry, "although it is not a science, is not nonsense." It is this view that Richards has recently taken: *"Poetry is the completest mode of utterance."* A similar insight has been expressed by Paul Valéry and T. Sturge Moore. As Tate frames it, "the high forms of literature offer us the only complete, and thus the most responsible, versions of our experience." Tate and Ransom claim for art the cognitive ingredient which Richards, in his former positivist position, discredits. The knowledge poetry gives us is a special kind of knowledge and not, as Richards once persuaded us to think, merely an inferior kind of science which is more useful than science itself. The arts, Tate contends, "give us a sort of cognition at least equally valid with that of the scientific method." Though Tate's theory of poetry as knowledge is fundamentally the same as Ransom's, the knowledge Tate postulates is "independent" and "complete." The order of completeness achieved in a work of the imagination is not of the "experimental" order achieved by the positivist sciences, but of an "experienced" or (in Richards's terms) a "mythical" order. The world of poetry "is neither the world of verifiable science nor a projection of ourselves; yet it is *complete*. And because it is complete knowledge we may, I think, claim for it a unique kind of responsibility, and see in it at times an irresponsibility equally distinct." (*Reason in Madness*)

Science and poetry, as Ransom defines their relation in his treatment of religion in *God Without Thunder*, present two different descriptions of the world. Whereas science presents an abstract description, poetry attempts a total description of the object, including both the quantitative elements (the knowledge which is "useful") and the qualitative elements (the knowledge which is "useless"). The difference between art and science is marked out in similar terms by Ramon Fernandez: art qualifies, individualizes, where science schematizes and collects relations. The reality of art differs from the reality of science, not in its subject matter, but in its mode of feeling that subject. Tate defines the religious experience as "experience, immediate and traditional, fused— Quality and Quantity—which is the means of validating values." Mere quality is as vacuous as mere quantity; both are compounded in actual reality. Poetry is a vision of the whole. The abstract structures of science, Ransom asserts, sacrifice "the body and substance of the world." Poetry's representation of the world is an alternative to the world pictured by science. "The World's Body," which is missed by the abstract structures of scientific knowledge, is restored by the concrete particulars of poetry. In an Editorial Note in *Poetry* (May, 1932), Tate writes: "As poetry grows increasingly abstract, it competes with science, or as Aristotle might have put it, competes with some form of history, and is hence less an imitation of perceived forms than practicable versions of what happens. The local, the immediate, and the concrete are the take-off of poetry, and the terms of some long-settled familiarity with the concrete features of experience are doubtless the origin of its form." The problem of the poet—it is the oldest problem of aesthetics—is fundamentally the problem of what the poet shall "imitate" and to what end. In "Poetry and Politics" (*New Republic:* Aug. 2, 1933), Tate rejects the hope of Edmund Wilson that poetry will become an adjunct of politics. The mixed modes of art and politics result in neither art nor politics; art as propaganda is an escape from reality. "Art arises in particulars, and it arrives at order at the point of impact between the new particulars and whatever organized experience the poet has been able to acquire." In the indeterminate particulars of the poem reside the "realistic cognitions" that Ransom and Tate claim for poetry. The universal is represented through the particular. Ransom, practising his imitation theory of knowledge upon a philosophical poem by Hardy, observes of Hardy's language: "It is not content with the concepts, but is constantly stopping to insert or to attach the particularity which is involved in images; a procedure which might be called the imaginative realization of the concepts. A genuine poetic energy will work with both these dimensions at once." (*Southern Review:* Summer, 1940) The critic focuses his inquiry upon the poem. Rational inquiry, Tate holds, is the only mode of criticism. "We must return to, we must never leave, the poem itself. Its 'interest' value is a cognitive one; it is sufficient that here, in the poem, we get knowledge of a whole object."

Poetry is one way of knowing the world: "if the poem is a real creation, it is a kind of knowledge that we did not possess before." The knowledge of poetry is the unique and formed intelligence of the world's phenomena. In the poem, the imaginatively realized content of the world is subject to no change and is therefore known with equal truth for all time. For Tate, as for Schopenhauer, art aims at nothing outside itself. This formalist creed of Tate and Ransom has been accused of aestheticism or art for art's sake, but their principle of art for art's sake must be interpreted very differently from the aestheticism of the 'Nineties. Rightly understood, the principle of art for art's sake has tremendous implications. Middleton Murry's defense, in *Aspects of Literature,* bears out Tate's position: "Art is autonomous, and to be pursued for its own sake, precisely because it comprehends the whole of human life; because it has reference to a more perfect human morality than any other activity of man." Tate's principle of art for art's sake opposes critical programs that inflict upon art the values of science, of metaphysics, or of a social philosophy. He repudiates the program of Edmund Wilson for an art-science: the view that art and science, as they come to apply themselves more directly to life, may yet arrive "at a way of thinking, a technique of dealing with our perceptions, which will make *art and science one."* (My italics) Wilson's position, which is almost irreconcilable with Tate's, follows the optimistic dictum of Whitehead that the poetic and the scientific impulses, being radically different, must unite harmoniously, if at all, that they can meet only in compromise. This compromise, Tate observes in his review of *Axel's Castle (Hound & Horn:* Summer, 1931), is at the heart of Wilson's rejection of the Symbolists. His optimism has kinship with Edwin Muir's faith in Wordsworth's dictum that "as soon as the world of science becomes somehow as 'familiar' as the primitive world of religious myth, our cultural integrity and our literature will be restored. This belief ignores the hopeless breach between the abstractionism of science and the object itself, for which the abstraction stands and to which it is the business of the poet to return." (*Nation:* Nov. 17, 1926)

Tate's criticism campaigns against modern schools of critics who judge art scientifically, practically, industrially, according to what it contains as "useful" knowledge; who first view art as being of necessity like science, a quantitative or pragmatic instrument, and then criticize it for its pragmatic values. As Tate remarks, "the kind of criticism that dominates our intellectual life is that of the French mathematician who, after reading a tragedy by Racine, asked: *'Qu' est ce que cela prouve?'* It proves nothing; it *creates the totality of experience in its quality* [my italics]; and it has no useful relation to the ordinary forms of action." (*Reactionary Essays*)

The necessity of art, Tate explains in the essay containing the core of his poetics, "Poetry and the Absolute" (*Sewanee Review;* Jan., 1926), springs from the irresistible need of the mind for absolute experience, a need which cannot be adequately satisfied in ordinary experience nor in an absolute metaphysics which classifies this ordinary experience into moral states and defines it intellectually. It is satisfied in the absolute which poetry constructs in its "portrait of reality" rather than in the absolute which philosophy constructs. Here, in the created absolute of poetry, Tate finds that satisfaction which Hulme looked for, and failed to find, in philosophy. As a Platonist in aesthetics Hulme discredited the subject-matter of art and consequently misunderstood the aim of poetry. "He did not understand that it is the absolute intensification of perception beyond its moral situation which is the unique quality of poetry: the intensification of perception into 'something rich and strange' wholly superior to subject-matter in the ordinary state." The ultimate value of experience is in its ordered intensification. The only coherent reality that we can experience is through art, for it is there that the unformed reality is formed, coherent, absolute. The disparate and conflicting elements of our experience have their only final coherence in the formal re-creation of art. Art does not explain our experience, rather it apprehends and concentrates our experience within the limitations of form. Poetry is the fusion of "an intensely felt ordinary experience, an intense moral situation, into an intensely realized art." The poet as maker strives toward the signification of experience that becomes, within the dimensions of the poem, absolute. The example Tate cites is Donne's *Funeral;* the poem "has form—completeness, finality, absolutism." Valéry describes this quality of perfect poetry by simile, comparing it "to a distant sailing-vessel—inanimate but articulate seemingly with an absolute life of its own." Absolute form, the ordered intensification of experience, results from a perfectly realized interaction between the poet's personality, which is the variant, and the poet's subject-matter, which is the constant in Tate's formula for the poet-poem relationship. "The absolutism adheres between the poet and his poem, between the reader and the poetry, not between them and the world. And this immediately explains the necessity of art."

The chief end of criticism is to understand this relation of the poet, or reader, to the poem. But how shall the critic, disciplined in the aesthetic attitude, apply it as a criterion by which to measure the absolute quality of different poems and to reject the poem from which this quality is missing? Tate offers no formula for the aesthetic critic:

> The test of an absolute creation must be applied *a posteriori*: it must be variously derived and as variously phrased. One may say that Mr. Yeats's poems, 'Upon a Dying Lady,' survive the test, in any formulation. . . . He has presented a newly-created emotion never before felt by anyone and never to be felt creatively by anyone else; he has contributed an absolute signification to an old and relative fact. It is absolute because it is unique and contains no point of relation to any other signification of that fact.

The great poems are absolute; there is nothing beyond the poem. In the perfectly realized poem there is no overflow of unrealized emotion or action. There is no ulterior motive. "If it contains an originally ulterior motive, such as Dante's moral contempt for his enemies in Hell, it is absorbed and becomes implicit in form, rather than explicit and didactic." Poets must be selected by some absolute, even a provisional one. This principle Tate repeats in his criticism of Spender's poems (*New Verse:* May, 1933), a review which is, incidentally, an important note on the problem of Poetry and Belief. "All his [Spender's] best poems convey single emotions. And these *single emotions* are created, in the sense that a table or chair are created; they are not believed."

The poem as related to the poet's, or reader's, beliefs—the question whether it is necessary to share the poet's beliefs in order to enjoy fully his poetry—raises a major problem in contemporary criticism. The problem has been discussed in relation to Dante and Shelley by Eliot (*Selected Essays* and *The Use of Poetry*), in relation to Hopkins by Herbert Read (*Collected Essays*), in relation to Yeats by Blackmur (*The Expense of Greatness*) and by Cleanth Brooks (*Modern Poetry and the Tradition*), and more generally by Richards (*Science and Po-*

etry and *Practical Criticism*). Here Richards expressed the opinion that poetry, since it is compacted of "pseudo-statements" or assertions of attitudes which, being scientifically false, cannot compete with the "certified scientific statements" of the objective world, has a future only insofar as it can get along without its pseudo-statements—with its assertion of attitudes fortified by a minimum of beliefs, or preferably without beliefs at all. In *Reactionary Essays,* Tate dismisses this part of Richards's theory as palpably absurd: poetry—a tissue of lies—orders our minds with falsehoods! His theory here comes at last to the same end as the positivists' assumption that poetry has no meaning at all. The knowledge or truth that poetry gives us is inadequate, immature, untrue. "But the statements in a genuine work of art," Tate counters, "are neither 'certified' nor 'pseudo-'; the creative intention removes them from the domain of practicality." Both in creation and enjoyment, Eliot notes, "much always enters which is, from the point of view of 'art,' irrelevant." One irrelevance, Brooks states, as is the truth or falsity of the belief that poetry expresses. Belgion, in the essay cited, shows up Richards's mistake in thinking that what, in the way of acceptance, is demanded of a poem is the poet's own belief. And Tate, in his note on Spender, sums up Belgion's point: "It is not what a poet 'believes' (Mr. Richards's theory) but rather what total attitude he takes towards all aspects of his conduct, that constitutes the 'content' side of the aesthetic problem." Belief, as applied to the arts, is a statistical and sociological category.

Eliot resolves the Problem of Belief thus: "When the doctrine, theory, belief, or 'view of life' presented in a poem is one which the mind of the reader can accept as coherent, mature, and founded on the facts of experience, it interposes no obstacle to the reader's enjoyment. . . ." With this final interpretation, which Eliot makes in *The Use of Poetry* (1933), all later critics concur. Tate interprets the problem in terms of the structural integrity of the poetic work. The question of the specific merit of a poetic statement as truth or falsehood does not arise when the beliefs of the poem are ordered into an intrinsic whole. It is on this ground that he rejects Shelley's poetry, not because Shelley's ideas are immature but because his statements as explanations of experience are not an integral part of a genuine poem.

The genuine poem is the "result" of an organic, an objective, relation between the poem and the events which produced it; the poem gives us both the thought or emotion *and* the situation from which they spring. In "Hardy's Philosophic Metaphors," Tate remarks that Hardy's abstractions are beyond the range of his feelings, "since he rarely shows us the experience that ought to justify them, that would give them substance, visibility, meaning." In *Reactionary Essays* Tate judges Crane and Cummings by the same criterion: the criterion of the Objective Correlative. In Cummings the idea is in excess of an occasion that remains "unknowable," and we are brought back to the poet's personality as the only reference of an emotion in excess of what is stated. Where the emotion is undisciplined by a structure of ideas or events of which it is a part, we get, as from Crane, "poetic sentimentality." In Donne and in Emily Dickinson, to the contrary, "There is no thought as such at all; nor is there feeling; there is that unique focus of experience which is at once neither and both." Emily Dickinson's abstractions are not separately visible from her sensuous illuminations of them; "like Donne, she *perceives abstraction* and *thinks sensation*." As in all great poetry, there is a clash of opposites which issues in a tension between abstraction and sensation. Permanent poetry, Eliot holds, is a fusion of these two poles of the mind: emotion and thought. Tate reframes Eliot's view: poetry does not give us "an emotional experience" nor "an intellectual experience"; it gives us a poetic experience. Blackmur defines this poetic experience in his commentary on Wallace Stevens's *Ideas of Order*. Ideas are principles, notions, abstractions; but they are also things seen. "It is the function of poetry . . . to experience ideas of the first kind with the eyes of the second kind, and to make of the experience of both a harmony and an order: a harmonium." (*The Expense of Greatness*)

Blackmur here echoes Tate in his conception of the poetic imagination. It is the power of creating the inner meaning of experience; it restores the speculative or abstract imagination to the condition of the concrete and the actual. The abstract imagination is the opposite of the poetic imagination, as Tate distinguishes these faculties in "Three Types of Poetry." The didactic imagination constructs a poetry of the scientific will (allegoric or propaganda art). A poetry of the will, as distinct from a poetry of the imagination, ignores the whole vision of experience for some special moral, or social, or political interest; the meaning is *forced,* the total context of the human predicament over-simplified, unexplored. Such poetry is "one-sided" and is inferior both as poetry and as science. "Platonic" poetry is Tate and Ransom's descriptive term for this didactic poetry which brings poetry into competition with science, as Brooks says, falsifying their relationship. Unlike the Metaphysical poet, the Platonic poet, Ransom asserts, discourses in *terms* of things, "but on the understanding that they are translatable at every point into ideas," or he elaborates "ideas as such, but in proceeding introduces for ornament some physical properties." Ransom holds an Aristotelian or objective "realist" world-view as the foundation of poetry as opposed to a Platonic or subjective "idealistic" one. He differentiates the subject-matter of poems according to its "ontology," or the reality of its being. The poem's status is objective. The knowledge of poetry is unique, radically or "ontologically" distinct from the prose or scientific formulation in which objects exist, not as solid objects, but as points in a structural pattern which controls them, which subordinates them to the realization of a thesis. A poem has not only this logical structure-meaning, the Determinate Meaning of the poem which is analogous to the prose or scientific formulation, but a texture-meaning as well—a context of many-valued, indeterminate, free and heterogeneous concrete details, which as texture-meaning are significant to the total-meaning of the poem but logically irrelevant to the structure-meaning alone. (Incidentally, Ransom's doctrine of Logical Irrelevance parallels Eliot's doctrine of the Third Dimension, which Eliot makes in his critique of Ben Jonson in *The Sacred Wood*.) The differentium of poetry, Ransom claims in *The New Criticism,* is this texture-structure order of objectivity. The differentium is a metaphysical or ontological one. Poetry is ontology, Charles Maurras writes in his Preface to *Musique Intérieure,* "for poetry strives above all towards the roots of the knowledge of Being." Ransom is primarily a philosopher: he is only incidentally committed to the technical criticism of poetry. He begins with aesthetics as the starting-point of philosophy; the fundamental problem of aesthetics for Ransom, as for Ramon Fernandez, is the problem of Being translated to the plane of the imaginative material of literature and art. Like G. Wilson Knight, whose criticism in *The Wheel of Fire* is (I suggest) of that ontological order which Ransom searches for, the "ontological critic" examines the ontology of the work of art and makes a metaphysical and aesthetic judgment upon it.

The total intention or meaning of the poem, Tate defines in "Tension in Poetry," is its "tension" or organized unity of all the meanings meeting from the furthest extremes of "extension" (abstraction, denotation, icon) and "intension" (concreteness, connotation, symbol). The common feature of all good poems is a synthesis of these two extremes of language. A poem has this quality of "tension" as the ultimate effect of the whole, "and that whole is the 'result' of a configuration of meaning which it is the duty of the critic to examine and evaluate." The aesthetic whole, Tate writes in one of his *Reactionary Essays,* resists practical formulation. The entire meaning of a poem like Marvell's "To His Coy Mistress," for example, cannot be reduced to logical statement or paraphrase. It is the inferior poem, one which comes too close to the "extension end of the scale," that can be wholly replaced by its paraphrase. To paraphrase such a poem, Tate elsewhere remarks, is to scatter it, is to reduce it to something like its originally unrealized condition. Contrary to Jacques Barzun, Tate does not repudiate the validity of critical explication; his own analysis of his "Ode to the Confederate Dead," in "Narcissus as Narcissus," is proof enough. His whole point is that there is no substitute for the poem itself. "We know the particular poem, not what it says that we can restate. In a manner of speaking, the poem is its own knower, neither poet nor reader knowing anything that the poem says apart from the words of the poem." Brooks of course takes the same stand. In "What Does Poetry Communicate?" (*American Prefaces:* Autumn, 1940), he remarks in elucidating Richards's theory of poetry as communication that the poem "is the *only* medium that communicates the particular *what* that is communicated at all. The poem says what the poem says."

Though neither Brooks nor Tate assents to Richards's theory of poetry as communication, both suggest close parallels to the poet-or-reader relation to the poem that is implied in Richards's theory: for him a poem is an organization of experience, a resolution and "balancing of impulses," and the reader gets the same harmony or "ordering of the mind" as the poet originally experienced. Brooks likewise holds that we, as the poet's readers, in a process akin to the poet's exploration of his material, "refabricate from his symbols . . . a total experience somewhat similar, if we possess imagination, to the total experience of the poet himself." And Tate, in "Poetry and the Absolute," suggests a similar correlation: the poem in which perceptions are perfectly realized provides the same experience for the reader as it originally provided for the poet. The parallel formula is Eliot's Objective Correlative. The poem's chain of ideas or events or objects, if they are the "objective correlative" of the poet's particular emotion about them, immediately evoke the same emotion in the spectator. This is indeed the *locus classicus* of modern criticism. It is variously used by Tate, as in one of his reviews of Mark Van Doren (*Nation:* Dec. 18, 1928), and it forms the criterion of John Peale Bishop's judgment on "The Poetry of A. E. Housman" (*Poetry:* June, 1940). Bishop, in this essay, and Brooks, in "The Whole of Housman" (*Kenyon Review:* Winter, 1941), have written two of the half-dozen finest pieces of Housman criticism. Bishop's essay on Housman and his essay on "Poetry and Painting" (*Sewanee Review:* Spring, 1945) represent Bishop as critic at his best. Warren's best critique is "Poetry Pure and Impure" (*Kenyon Review:* Spring, 1943). This essay deserves to be singled out as one of the most important in the whole body of current critical writings.

Like Eliot, Tate and the Southern critics find their standard for great poetry in the 17th Century Metaphysicals, that poetry which joins together widely divergent and conflicting materials in imagery that is functional rather than decorative, achieving thus the desired union of emotion and thought. In their poems image and idea are one; comparisons are not ornaments or illustrations attached to a statement. As Brooks puts it, "The comparison *is* the poem in a structural sense." Using Richards's criterion, Brooks defines metaphysical poetry as a poetry of synthesis and claims for it the "highest order." It is a poetry of inclusion: resolving apparent discords, reconciling the discordant qualities of an experience, including them in the poem. As Brooks points out, the distinction between Richards's poetry of exclusion and his poetry of synthesis parallels the distinction between Ransom's Platonic poetry and metaphysical poetry, and likewise the distinction between Tate's Platonic poetry and his poetry of the imagination. Brooks's *Modern Poetry and the Tradition* is a critical synthesis of this modern revolution in the conception of poetry, a revolution which has consisted partly in a return to the Metaphysicals and consequently in a repudiation of their heretical deviators: the Augustan Neo-Classicist, who regarded metaphor or imagery as a decoration of thought, and the 19th Century Romantics, who discredited wit or irony (the essential quality of metaphysical poetry) and regarded poetry as an elevated way of expressing elevated beliefs. The core of the poem, from this didactic view, is its subject: a Platonic idea or an emotion. In his review of Brooks's book, Tate notes that "the Romantic Movement taught the reader to look for inherently poetical objects, and to respond to them 'emotionally' in certain prescribed ways, these ways being indicated by the 'truths' interjected at intervals among the poetical objects." But as he elsewhere remarks, "no idea is more poetic than another until it is created in poetry; there are no poetic ideas outside the poem." Emotion is not the exclusive subject-matter of poetry. Winters's formula that poetry is technique for dealing with irreducible emotions, which Tate attacks in "Confusion and Poetry" (*Sewanee Review:* Apr., 1930), conceals a modern version of the romantic dogma that poetry is emotion. As Auden says, "abstractions are empty and their expression devoid of a poetic value." And the poet's emotions, these too have no poetic value *in themselves.* In his Preface to Valéry's *Le Serpent,* Eliot observes: "Not our feelings, but the pattern which we make of our feelings is the centre of value."

Eliot's Impersonal Theory of Art, which he elaborated in *The Sacred Wood,* is repeated in scattered instances of Tate's critical dicta. A poem is not a secretion of personal emotions. "The emotion of art is impersonal." For both Eliot and Tate, the emotion or vision obtainable from a poem is to be found in the poem and not in the mind of the poet. Contrary to Coleridgean theory, which has led criticism out of the poem and into the poet's mind, Tate's poetic asserts that the specific poetic element is an objective feature of the poem rather than a "subjective effect." Tate investigates the nature of the poem *as poem;* not the origin of the poem (Herbert Read), nor its effect upon the reader (Richards), nor its value for civilization (Dewey). Tate's stand is poles apart from Read's "ontogenetic criticism" in *In Defense of Shelley,* that criticism "which traces the origins of the work of art in the psychology of the individual and in the economic structure of society." The critic who asserts that he is investigating poetry from the psychological viewpoint is actually leading us away from the fact of art, Tate remarks by way of stating his agreement with Fernandez's *Messages* (reviewed in *New Republic:* Aug. 17, 1927). As Desmond MacCarthy contends, "Literary criticism is concerned with values, not with the psychological origin of such values." For Tate, it is solely the internal organization of the poem that gives the poem its value, not its relation to the mind of the author. As for Eliot, a work of art has a life of its own; the difference between art and its event is absolute. The expression in art of the elements that give art its aesthetic identity and its absolute quality, Roger Fry states in *Vision and Design,* is never identical with the expression of these elements in actual life. The emotions which poems offer are not the "actual emotions" of everyday practical life at all, but specific poetic emotions. This point Belgion makes in criticizing Richards's supposition, in *Practical Criticism,* that there is no gap between them. "Richards misunderstands the nature of the aesthetic emotion: that emotion, not only is different from the emotion we should have if we experienced the poem's subject in actual life, but can be produced without having originated in life at all." Tate attests to this fact in his Preface to his *Selected Poems:* ". . . that, as a poet, I have never had any [original] experience, and that, as a poet, my concern is the experience that I hope the reader will have in reading the poem." We as readers, T. Sturge Moore comments on Valéry, come to poetry not to know what poets feel; "we read poems because they are wholes, composed of harmonized words and meanings which inter-echo symphonically." The specifically aesthetic experience, as defined by Fry, is the apprehension of the formal relations of a work of art. Belgion, in *The Human Parrot,* defines the aesthetic emotion in terms that Tate, I judge, would approve: "The specifically aesthetic emotion is delight in the contemplation of technical ability, as manifested in the result." For Tate these technical and formal qualities of a poetic work are the focus of critical judgment.

Tate's theory of the function of the critic has its parallel statement in the critical writings of F. R. Leavis: their canon derives from Eliot. The critic and the poet have the same objective. The poet probes the deficiencies of a tradition, Tate writes in *Reactionary Essays;* in the true sense of Arnold's dictum that poetry is a "criticism of life," the poet " 'criticizes' his tradition, either as such, or indirectly by comparing it with something that is about to replace it; . . . he *discerns* its real elements and thus establishes its value, by putting it to the test of experience." And the critic, he too "criticizes" a tradition in order to establish a tradition. Always the business of *criticism,* Leavis states in his Preface to *Revaluation,* is "to define, help form, and organize the contemporary sensibility (the traditional mind which lives in the present or not at all), and to make conscious the 'standards' in it." *The critic,* directly or by implication, *deals with tradition.* He deals with tradition, Leavis points out, in terms of representative poets, and with the individual poet in terms of representative pieces of his work. Leavis is at one with Tate's dogma of authority, his rejection of critical relativity, his contention that the critical objective must be informed by a single standard of judgment that allows the reader no choice in point of view or taste. The critic prepares the reader to appreciate the ascendant artists of his time by defining for him "coherent standards of taste and examples of taste in operation; not mere statements about taste." ("The

Function of the Critical Quarterly," *Reason in Madness*) Emulating Eliot, Tate and the Southern critics aim to instruct the reader, to create the *proper* reader.

Their practice follows their theory. The critic's first job is to analyze the structure-texture strategy of the poem, elucidate its intention, dig out the facts and the principle governing the facts, and make comparative judgments about its technical practice. In the manner of Blackmur, Empson, Brooks and Warren, who are unquestionably our most expert readers or interpreters of difficult poetic texts, the critic evaluates the poetic situation: he lets the reader in on the poem's intention and on the critical point of view by which the poem is evaluated. Like Baudelaire, in making a critical judgment Tate and Ransom use a body of principles as a point of reference. Their standards are aesthetic and metaphysical rather than sociological, economic, historical, psychological, or moral. Of all critics Ransom sets the strictest boundaries to literary criticism. The "traditional" critic aims to clarify its center rather than to expand its borders and its scope. In "experimental" critics like Kenneth Burke and Edmund Wilson the aesthetic and metaphysical interests are subordinated to the psychological and sociological considerations; their concern is primarily with the non-resident values, whereas Tate and Ransom's concern is almost exclusively with the resident values in the work of art—the purely aesthetic values. They attend to the properties of poetry as a fine art. Richards protests against the isolation of the aesthetic values and argues for the integration of all values: aesthetic and moral and technical. Auden agrees with this doctrine of the interdependence of ethics, politics, science, and aesthetics. The main difference between them is that where Richards finds his standards for judging a poem in psychology, Auden finds his in sociology. His claim that aesthetic canons are not absolute is diametrically opposite to the claim of Tate and Ransom that the "artificial" division between art and life is necessary and worth preserving. Poetry, Blackmur affirms in *The Double Agent,* "is life at the remove of form and meaning"; criticism has to do with "the terms and modes" by which this remove was made; that is, with the relation between content and form. The aesthetic critic like Tate isolates the poem's meaning in terms of form. The poem is autonomous. It is a water-tight box, constructed with a life of its own, limited by its own method and intention. To assign objective status to the content apart from form is to reduce the poem's meaning to its original state, is to locate it in the historical process. Within terms of this affirmation subject-matter is tested by the criterion of its correlation with the world it represents, the correlations being historical, economic, psychological, or ethical. This Doctrine of Relevance is false. The only relevance Tate subscribes to is that relevance the subject-ideas have to each other within the formed meaning of the work itself. The first job of the critic is to decide in what way the literary work has objectivity. "The function of criticism . . . should be to maintain and to demonstrate the special, unique, and complete knowledge which the great forms of literature afford us." In this principle that the intellect is the foundation of poetry and that the criterion of judgment is a qualitative one, Tate and Ransom are Aristotelian. The Aristotelian method of analyzing the aesthetic object in and for itself is the formalist method of Tate, Ransom, Brooks, and Warren. Our age is indeed an age of criticism. The structure of critical ideas that Blackmur, Winters, Leavis, Empson, Brooks, Warren, Ransom, and Tate have contrived upon the foundations of Eliot and Richards constitutes an achievement in *criticism* the like of which has not been equaled by literary critics in our time or in any previous period of our literary history.

Thomas Wolfe and James Joyce:
A Study in Literary Influence

Nathan L. Rothman

IF STEPHEN DEDALUS WERE EIGHT INCHES taller, and if he shouted his pride and his hungers instead of letting them gnaw at him under his Spartan cloak, he would be twin to Eugene Gant, who is Thomas Wolfe as surely as Dedalus is Joyce. The differences are less significant than the likeness; they rise out of the differences in the two writers, physical, hereditary, and environmental: Joyce, the proud, bitter, introvert, disciplined Irishman, and Wolfe, the lusty, free-spirited, uncontrolled man of vigorous Carolina and Pennsylvania stock. Yet at the roots of their minds they are the same. Inside the large, turbulent frame of Eugene Gant there is the secret, scathing spirit of Stephen.

> Disillusion had come so often that it had awakened in him a strain of bitter suspicion, an occasional mockery, virulent, coarse, cruel, and subtle, which was all the more scalding because of his own pain. Unknowingly, he had begun to build up in himself a vast mythology for which he cared all the more deeply because he realized its untruth. Brokenly, obscurely, he was beginning to feel that it was not truth that men must live for—the creative men—but for falsehood. At times his devouring, unsated brain seemed to be beyond his governance: it was a frightful bird whose beak was in his heart, whose talons tore unceasingly at his bowels. And this unsleeping demon wheeled, plunged, revolved about an object, returning suddenly, after it had flown away, with victorious malice, leaving stripped, mean, and common all that he had clothed with wonder.

Is this not Stephen? It is a description of Eugene Gant, in Wolfe's first novel, *Look Homeward, Angel*. The suspicion, the subtle mockery, the secret mythology, the unsated brain, the stripping of joy and wonder—this is a strange transplanting of that bitter Lokian spirit in the body of one who might well have glowed with the whole, majestic soul of Jove. From the first that kinship was recognized; Wolfe served a glad apprenticeship. Most marked of the books upon his desk was a copy of *Ulysses,* and we find the following in one of the diary entries of young Eugene:

> I was born in 1900—I am now 24 years old. During that period I think the best writing in English had been done by James Joyce in *Ulysses* . . .

Later, in a little book he wrote about the creative process that went into the making of his first two novels, he said,

> Like every young man, I was strongly under the influence of writers I admired. One of the chief writers at that time was Mr. James Joyce with his *Ulysses*. The book that I was writing was much influenced, I believe, by his own book, and yet the powerful energy and fire of my own youth played over, and, I think, possessed it all.

His books, of course, make all such explicit citation of influence unnecessary; I have quoted them to indicate not the influence but Wolfe's conscious recognition of it, his conscious embracing of the greatest literary influence of his time, for as long as he needed it. I think the latter part of his statement just above is quite true and worth noting at every step of his work. The fire of his own youth—and I will say of his own genius—possessed his work throughout. He was never swallowed up by Joyce. He was too conscious of his own strength, of the materials that sprang from his, not Joyce's, life, of the American voice that flowed through him, the inheritor of Whitman as well as of Joyce. Wolfe used all of Joyce that he could, and some elements of Joyce's that no one else had attempted or perhaps understood; yet Wolfe remained always free of purely derivative writing, always indigenous, personal, creative.

The appearance of that first novel in 1929 was a remarkable phenomenon, to be compared, I think, with the appearance in 1855 of *Leaves of Grass*. (I shall have something to say later of Wolfe and Whitman.) It should be remembered that Wolfe's work is not to be regarded as a piecemeal product, as a series of separate and successive volumes, like other men's. That is the way his books were published, of course, but that is not the way they were conceived. It is well known by now that Wolfe planned, from the very beginning, a gigantic auto-

biographic work of at least six volumes, of which the titles and approximate time-periods had already been chosen. In the writing he regarded
them as a unit. He never planned one book, with a start, plot-curve,
finish, but he wrote out of his experiences and passions large blocks of
prose that were sustained upon a tireless, ecstatic level of inspiration,
thousands of words, hundreds of pages many of them among the best
in our literature, torn out of a feverish creative consciousness. The duty
of shaping devolved upon his publishers and editors, in whom Wolfe
was very fortunate throughout. *Look Homeward, Angel* was not only
the first of his novels to be published, but also in many ways the most
unified, the most solidly shaped. For both of these reasons, and because
it was the first revelation of a great talent, it is still regarded by most
readers as their favorite among Wolfe's books. It came to them as no
ordinary first novel, neither tentative nor unformed. It appeared to
spring fully grown from the mind of a conscious artist. It was as rich,
fine, sure, as though he had written it after a long apprenticeship. Dos
Passos and Faulkner had to push forward, to their best work, through a
period of uncertainty and in some ways downright incompetence;
Wolfe began his novels at the peak of power and never left it. The
effort cost him a great deal, as we know. He had to do it that way; he
was wholly possessed by that literary conscience which flays the pupil
as it did their master, Joyce.

The themes of Joyce are everywhere in Wolfe, from *Look Homeward, Angel* straight through. Viewing Wolfe's books as one body of
work, one odyssey of Eugene Gant, we will do well to trace the themes
through the volumes wherever they lead. We note the smaller indications first, the Ulyssean signatures such as Wolfe's phrase about Oliver
Gant's "hot lion-breath of desire," recalling Joyce's phrase, "lion reek
of all male brutes." There are many of the Joycean inversions, such
as this: "Twittered with young bird-laughter, on bank and saddle
sprawled, all of the Bard's personae," or this very familiar image which
seems to come directly out of the consciousness of Leopold Bloom:
"Smiling with imperturbable tenderness Mrs. Selborne thrust out her
heavy legs slowly to swell with warm ripe smack his gift of flowered
green-silk garters." And how startling and stirring it is to come once
more upon "Brightness falls from the air," which we remember in both
the *Portrait of the Artist as a Young Man* and *Ulysses,* or upon such a
fragment of Dedalus-like musing as this:

King Solomon's mines. She. Proserpine. Ali Baba. Orpheus and Euryd-
ice. Naked come I from my mother's womb. Naked shall I return.
Let the mothering womb of earth engulf me. Naked, a valiant wisp of
man, in vast brown limbs engulfed.

More significant are the larger forms and ideas of Joyce, all here and
some of them reappearing for the first time. The stream of consciousness appears throughout in many guises. Its simplest form is most derivative, the associative stream darting from object to object, idea to
idea. The best illustration of this comes early in *Look Homeward,
Angel,* as we follow the thoughts of Oliver Gant, Eugene's father, returning home. He has just been told of the death of an old acquaintance:

In the prime of life, thought Gant. Myself like that some day. No, for
others. Mother almost eighty-six. Eats like a horse, Augusta wrote. Must
send her twenty dollars. Now in the cold clay, frozen. Keep till Spring.
Rain, rot, ruin. Who got the job? Brock or Saul Gudge. Bread out of
my mouth. Do me to death—the stranger——

This will do very well to represent the many such passages devoted to
Oliver Gant. Two observations need to be made about them. First,
these Bloom-ish musings give but one small and far from inclusive
aspect of Oliver Gant, an aspect querulous and fearful. Gant, of course,
was as unlike Bloom as could be, a lusty, storming animal of a man.
Whereas Joyce's Bloom is wholly contained in the conscious stream, for
a whole view of Oliver Gant we must turn to other minds than his
own, chiefly to that of his son Eugene. It is when Eugene is thinking
and speaking of him that the wind of Oliver Gant's wild spirit really
blows. For old Gant the stream of consciousness is an inadequate device, serving at best to add a little weight to the other side, give him
some of the weakness of mortality. This leads us to reiterate what
Wolfe has already said of himself. He employed the devices of Joyce,
but it is plain that his own fire possessed everything he wrote. No device could contain the characters of Oliver or Eugene or Eliza or Ben
Gant; their real and passionate life resides in and springs from the
passionate life in Wolfe.
This is clear again as we observe another use of Joyce's stream, this

time of the long, trance-like, contemplative brooding of Marion Bloom.
Now it becomes a vehicle for the mind of Eliza Gant, Eugene's mother.
She, like Oliver, is realized more fully in the narrative and dialogue of
the books, but there is one large section of writing in which Wolfe has
given her the center of the stage and let her speak, or think, unhindered.
It is called *The Web of Earth* and is part of the volume of shorter
pieces, *From Death to Morning*. I imagine it was originally a portion
of the manuscript of *Look Homeward, Angel*. Eliza is presumed to be
speaking to Eugene, but he is all but silent throughout and her memories and nervous energies impel her restlessly forward and along every
tangent that appears, in a tremendous monologue. It is more successful
than the Oliver Gant stream because it has more in it of the thinker's
essential vigor and mental tone and accent. It is really Eliza Gant,
thinking of her past and her people and of remembered beauties. She is
starting to tell Eugene of a strange portent that came to her once out
of the spirit world; she dramatizes, interrupts herself, interrogates and
answers:

—In the year the locusts came, something that happened in the year the
locusts came, two voices that I heard there in that year . . Child!
Child! It seems so long ago since the year the locusts came and all of the
trees were eaten bare: so much has happened and it seems so long
ago . . .
  'What say?' I said.
Says, 'Two—Two', says, 'Twenty—Twenty'.
  'Hah? What say?'
'Two—Two' the first voice said; and 'Twenty—Twenty' said the
other——

It is more than eighty pages later that she comes back to the opening
phrase:

That was the year the locusts came: it seems so long ago since the year
that the locusts came, and all the earth was eaten bare, it seems so long
ago. But no (I thought) the thing kept puzzlin' me, you know—it can't
be that, there hasn't been time enough for that it was only the year before in January—Lord! Lord! I often think of all I've been through and
wonder that I'm here to tell it. I reckon for a fact I had the power of
Nature in me; why! no more trouble than the earth takes bearing corn,

all of the children, the eight who lived, and all the others that you never heard about—all the children and less married life than any woman that I knew—and oh! to think of it, to think that he should say the things he did—cursin' and tauntin' me and runnin' wild with other women, when he had done it at all, and like the devil when he saw what he had done. Lord! Lord! he was a strange man, a wild and savage man;—Oh! the good, the bad times, all of the happiness and bitter weepin', and there is something now that can't be said——

She relapses now into a peace and tenderness born of all memory:

Lord, boy! What's that I hear now on the harbor? Hah? What say? A ship! —Now it will soon be April, and I must be going home again; out in my garden where I work, the early flowers and the dogwood and the laurel and the lilacs. I have an apple tree and it is full of all the birds there are in June; the flower-tree you planted as a child is blooming by the window where you planted it. (My dear child, eat good food and watch and guard your health: it worries me to think of you alone among strangers.) The hills are beautiful and soon it will be spring once more. (It worries me to think of you alone like this, alone and far away: child, child, come home again!)
O listen! . .
Hah? What is it? . .
Hah? What say?
(Lord God! a race of wanderers!)
Child, child! . . what is it?
    Ships again!

In mood and extension this whole passage, ninety-two pages in length, stems from Marion Bloom's closing solo; this, too, closes a book. Yet the special rhythms and intonations of Eliza Gant are the characteristics that give the passage flow and flavor. (To see how marvellously faithful this is to the actual quality of Eliza's (Mrs. Wolfe's) speech, compare it with a recording made by Mr. John Terry of some of Mrs. Wolfe's spoken reminiscences.) Her tenderness and strength, and the American anecdotage that fills the pages I have not quoted, are the original materials of Wolfe. He needed to borrow nothing but a form, and that only so that he might press his own pattern upon it.

Ulysses is a history given to us largely through two minds, those of

Stephen and Bloom; Wolfe's novels are centered upon one, that of Eugene Gant. There is nothing of Bloom in him, as there is in so many of the derivative studies you will find in modern American writing, in Conrad Aiken, Melvin P. Levy, Nathan Asch, others. And even the Stephen in him is tempered by the exuberant physical vitality that is foreign to Stephen Dedalus. Stephen's physical lassitude, almost enervation, quite shadows the fire of his mind. Gant has a huge virility that lifts the Stephen-mind within him into the sun. This is the contradiction that makes Eugene Gant an even more unpredictable character than Dedalus, less disciplined, reaching higher flights of ecstasy and deeper despairs, more violent of speech, and steadily, as he matures through the books, more assertive of life, more yea-saying as Whitman said yea, and with Whitman's great sea-flow of poetry. But first we search out the essential Stephen.

Early in *Ulysses* Stephen thinks, as he bandies words with Buck Mulligan, ever in defense of his pride, his secrecy, his cunning:

> Parried again. He fears the lancet of my art as I fear that of his. The cold steelpen.

Stephen wages against the philistine world the war of the picador against the bull: light, agile, provocative, inserting the little darts and getting away before the beast knows it is hurt, drawing blood by adroit gestures, sly insertions of the blade, no battle but secret victories. In literary expression this is the attack of irony, satire, and, when skillfully done, the burlesque. Spoken, it is the killing word, the feared lancet. In thought the attack broadens and calls up secretly the heavy bludgeon of burlesque. Stephen wages his war on both fronts. In those early sections of *Ulysses* his tormentors have reason to fear his wit; and his thoughts as they are revealed to us flay with steady acid the society that holds him prisoner. Eugene wages the same war largely upon its silent, secret front. He is not the cold disciplined jesuit that Stephen is by training; he cannot hurl the calculated dart at the precise instant of its greatest effectiveness; he is too emotional, clogged with feeling. Yet inside him the image of Stephen dwells, and along the channels of his thought we come upon the irony, the satire, the destructive burlesque, used as Joyce used them. We will remember, for example, how Joyce used a faithful rendering of the prose of the sentimental two-penny fiction, scarcely heightened since it provides its own burlesque, to give us the color of

Gerty MacDowell's mind, in the Nausikaa episode. And through the mind of the youth Eugene Gant there runs a corresponding stream of images created out of cheap American fiction. In his case he is all too aware of their character; it is not his mind we are beholding mirrored in the stream of this sweet, sloshy fiction, but rather his judgment upon the reading and thinking of his overbearing contemporaries. Like Stephen, he is taking his own silent revenge upon them, as he concocts this orgy of sentimental posturing in the exact verbiage of the dime novel:

"I am going", he said presently.
"Going?" she whispered. "Where?"
The organ music deepened.
"Out there", he gestured briefly to the West. "Out there—among His people."
"Going?" She could not conceal the tremor of her voice. "Going? Alone?"
He smiled sadly. The sun had set. The gathering darkness hid the suspicious moisture in his gray eyes.—
Eugene turned his wet eyes to the light that streamed through the library windows, winked rapidly, gulped, and blew his nose heavily. Ah, yes! Ah, yes!

And so forth. There are dozens of such images scattered through *Look Homeward, Angel,* and in one furious mental outburst toward the end, the images fuse into one huge extravaganza.

"Me! Me! Bruce-Eugene, the Scourge of the Greasers, and the greatest fullback Yale ever had! Marshal Gant, the saviour of his country! Ace Gant, the hawk of the sky, the man who brought Richthofen down! Senator Gant, Governor Gant, President Gant, the restorer and uniter of a broken nation, retiring quietly to private life in spite of the weeping protest of one hundred million people, until, like Arthur or Barbarossa, he shall hear again the drums of need and peril."

This brings us to another aspect of Joyce's burlesque, and we recall his trick of inflation, one word setting off an uncontrollable and mounting series of images that are swollen with detail and finally leave the original concept far behind. The above quotation reminds us of that moment in the Nighttown episode when Bloom's mind, at some provocation, releases a series of fancies in which he is successively Major Bloom, General Bloom, King, Bishop, Pope. It is in the business accompanying the dialogue of this incident that Joyce achieves the effect of incredible nightmare sanity by multiplying his absurd data in business-like fashion:

> (Bloom holds up his right hand on which sparkles the Koh-i-noor diamond. His palfrey neighs. Immediate silence. Wireless intercontinental and interplanetary transmitters are set for reception of message.—Thirty-two workmen wearing rosettes, from all the counties of Ireland, under the guidance of Derwan the builder, construct the new Bloomusalem. It is a colossal edifice, with crystal roof, built in the shape of a huge pork kidney, containing forty thousand rooms——)

Less violent and thorough-going, but in the same mood of satirical inflation is Eugene's inner vision of a singer's closing note——

> Jay's golden voice neared its triumph, breaking with delicate restraint on the last note, into a high sweet falsetto which he maintained for more than twenty seconds. All of the butchers stopped working, several of them, big strong men with grown-up families, dashed a tear out of their eyes. —Somewhere in the crowd a woman sobbed and collapsed in a faint. She was immediately carried out by two Boy Scouts who happened to be present and who administered first aid to her in the rest-room, one of them hastily kindling a crackling fire of pine boughs by striking two flints together, while the other made a tourniquet, and tied several knots in his handkerchief. Then pandemonium broke loose. Women tore the jewels from their fingers, ropes of pearls from their necks, chrysanthemums, hyacinths, tulips and daisies——

There are others of these passages of inflated burlesque, depending for their effectiveness, here as in Joyce, upon their straight-faced presentation of every-day data impossibly massed. And always there are the little spurts of bitter commentary, couched often in satirical phrases, bitterly mouthed:

> Eugene thought of the beautiful institution of human slavery, which his slaveless maternal ancestry had fought so valiantly to preserve. Bress de

lawd, Marse! Ole Mose doan' wan' to be free niggah. How he goan' lib widout marse? He doan' wan' stahve wid free niggahs. Har, har, har! Philanthropy. Pure philanthropy. He brushed a tear from his een.

This is inwit's agenbite, American style.

Closer to the actual tone of Stephen's thinking is another of Eugene's secret mental devices. We will recall Edmund Wilson's apt description of Stephen's mind as a "weaving of bright poetic images and fragmentary abstractions, of things remembered from books—" It is thus that Stephen wields in silence his cold steelpen; particularly in his discourse with Mr. Deasy, with Mulligan and Haines, with the scholars in the library scene, he hurls at them his unspoken fragments of phrase and literary line. There is a large section of *Look Homeward, Angel,* particularly the twenty-fourth chapter, in which Eugene does exactly that, in Stephen's vein. Again we must note that he is younger than Stephen and less intellectual; his poetic images are more apt to be remembered from books than to be the abstractions of Stephen's Aristotelian logic-chopping. But the mood, the method, are the same. All through the chapter there is this counterpoint of mundane dialogue and unuttered poetic commentary:

"Well, if it ain't ole Handsome," said Julius Arthur. He grinned squintily, revealing a mouthful of stained teeth screwed in a wire clamp. His face was covered with small yellow pustulate sores. How begot, how nourished?

Julius took the twist, wiped off his mouth with a loose male grin, and crammed a large quid into his cheek.
He brought me roots of relish sweet.
"Want one, Highpockets?" he asked Eugene, grinning.
I hate him that would upon the rack of this tough world stretch me out longer.
"Hell," said Ralph Rolls. "Handsome would curl up and die if he ever took a chew."
In Spring like torpid snakes my enemies awaken . . ."

They are his enemies who would stretch him indeed upon the rack, the crowd against the artist maverick. They do not fear the lancet of his art—it is not yet sharp enough. He must bear their raillery and answer meekly in their own tongue, inutile upon his lips. But within he draws upon his army of friends, Shakespeare, Drummond, Pope, Words-worth, Milton, Herrick, the German poets, and flings his barbs silently. It is a remarkable and revelatory chapter, and the most Joycean.

*

The satire and the burlesque and the barb are Wolfe, yet they are not the Wolfe we think of, remembering what we have read. Wolfe was a poet. The man and his spirit are most alive for us in all the varied dis-play of lyric power his books afford, stemming alike from Joyce, from Whitman, from his own inspiration. Even the psychological technique of the conscious stream is permeated with the diction, accents, inver-sions of poetry. Whereas the thoughts of Oliver Gant refer us directly to Bloom's mental rhythm, this short passage dipped from Eliza's con-scious stream brings to us again the rich poetic texture of Stephen's mind—

Roofing the deep tides, swinging in their embrace, rocked Eliza's life Sargassic, as when, at morning, a breath of kitchen air squirmed through her guarded crack of door and fanned the pendant clusters of old string in floating rhythm. She rubbed the sleep gently from her small weak eyes, smiling dimly as she thought, unawakened, of ancient losses. Her worn fingers still groped softly in the bed beside her, and when she found it vacant she awoke. Remembered. My youngest, my oldest, final bitter fruit, O dark of soul, O far and lonely, where? Re-membered O his face! Death-son, partner of my peril, last coinage of my flesh, who warmed my flanks and nestled to my back. Gone? Cut off from me? When? Where?——

This is quite transcendent expression; it is not the conscious Eliza who speaks; we have discovered the pattern of her mind in *Web of Earth*. This is not her own diction or rhythm, but those of her son, Eugene, who speaks for her: Wolfe. We are only discovering again that the stream of consciousness offers him at best a limited and strangled ex-pression. It is when we turn from the stream to his fresh use of Joyce's poetic diction, the word as theme, the free poetic passage (swelling, in Wolfe, to great paeans; Joyce's muse is always cool and disciplined), the thematic idea, that we hear the full accents of his voice.

We will recall that Joyce used the word or phrase as motif, in the musical, repetitious‚sense, generally within a passage to unify it and give it a desired emotional tone. Outside this restricted area, his employment of the word-motif is rare; the "agenbite of inwit" comes now to mind as perhaps the sole repeated theme. Wolfe has gone greatly beyond Joyce in this. No writer has worked so powerfully with the evocative echoes and re-echoes of a sounded theme. I want to quote here the passage he set down by itself upon the fly-leaf opposite the opening page of *Look Homeward, Angel.* Its significance cannot be overestimated. It contains the words and themes that are to reappear again and again throughout the books of Wolfe.

. . . a stone, a leaf, an unfound door; of a stone, a leaf, a door. And of all the forgotten faces.

Naked and alone we came into exile. In her dark womb we did not know our mother's face; from the prison of her flesh have we come into the unspeakable and incommunicable prison of this earth.

Which of us has known his brother? Which of us has looked into his father's heart? Which of us is not forever a stranger and alone?

O waste of loss, in the hot mazes, lost, among the bright stars on this most weary unbright cinder, lost! Remembering speechlessly we seek the great forgotten language, the lost lane-end into heaven, a stone, a leaf, an unfound door. Where? When?

O lost, and by the wind grieved, ghost, come back again.

I will not enlarge here upon the sensory beauties of this prose. This is what we mean when we speak of Wolfe's Biblical eloquence, the organ-tone which is not incomparable with the organ-tone of the Elizabethan poet he loved most. What holds us now in the passage is its freight of themes, like seeds that are to sprout through the thousands of pages to come. They are blended here into one emotional chant of spiritual grief and wanting; when we search out its components we discover, first, that searing grief for a dead brother, a remembered hero (which runs also through Faulkner's work, a similar constant vein). "Which of us has known his brother?" The portrait of Eugene's brother, Ben, is to my mind the most poignant element in Wolfe's writing. Alive he is seen as already gone. Dead, he is forever alive in Eugene's mind, the remembered gestures, words, ways. He, most of all, is the cherished image. It is of him that Wolfe cries out always, "O

lost, and by the wind grieved, ghost, come back again!" The words
"O lost," detached, carrying the grief for Ben and for all else that is
gone and mourned, appear again many times; I cannot catalog them
all. "Return! O lost, and by the wind grieved—" Eugene cries again
upon Page 456, "O lost, O far and lonely, where?" upon 522, and on
583, "And Ben will come again, he will not die again, in flower and
leaf, in wind and music far, he will come back again. O lost, and by
the wind grieved—" These are only three. The words sing again
wherever the emotion is once more evoked.

Ben himself is a theme to bind the books together. At a gesture or a
sound the whole body of the narrative must pause while the vision of
Ben rises to haunt us, as, in *Of Time and the River:* "Bitter and beautiful, scorn no more. Ben stands there in the window—" The month
of October, the date of his birth and death, never fails to evoke the
memory:

> For now October has come back again, the strange and lonely month
> comes back again, and you will not return. Up on the mountain, down
> in the valley, deep, deep, in the hill, Ben—cold, cold, cold . . .

These last words are inscribed upon the fly-leaf of *From Death to
Morning,* and the opening phrase, "For now October has come back
again," is the theme of one of Wolfe's most profound and sonorous
poetic passages, with its blending of October, Ben, all remembered, all
lost. I must not carry this further, except to speak of the fortieth chapter
of *Look Homeward, Angel,* in which Eugene, walking in the cemetery
and filled with his emotions, holds ghostly converse with Ben. We have
heard the dead speak in Joyce's Nighttown episode, in James T. Farrell's history of the O'Neills, in Conrad Aiken's *Coming Forth of Osiris
Jones.* It is one of the marks of Joycean influence. Here again the meeting of life and death produces its terrific apocalyptic climax; mortal
emotions and immortal vision flood the pages and bring the book to
its ecstatic close.

So also might we trace that other pregnant phrase, "a stone, a leaf,
a door," through the books. It appears everywhere (see, for example,
the opening story in *From Death to Morning,* called *No Door;* or the
second page of *Gulliver* in the same volume; or page 604 in *Of Time
and the River*), an echoing motif of search and desperation, carrying
now the burden of old Oliver's groping, now the passionate thrust of

Eugene, and always with added weight as the echoes and overtones are multiplied and blended with more and more of the thematic material that Wolfe steadily introduces. It is only such poetic weaving of themes that can produce, finally, the richness and incomparable impact of this brief climactic passage, near the very end of *Of Time and the River*. Eugene's mind is at this moment a cavern ringing with remembered words and voices:

> . . . Garfield, Arthur, Harrison, and Hayes . . . time of my father's time, life of his life. 'Ah, Lord', he said, 'I knew them all—and all of them are gone. I'm the only one that's left. By God, I'm getting old.' . . . In the year that the locusts came, something that happened in the year the locusts came, two voices that I heard there in that year . . . Child! Child! It seems so long ago since the year the locusts came, and all of the trees were eaten bare: so much has happened and it seems so long ago . . . "To keep time with!"—To Eugene Gant, Presented to Him on the Occasion of His Twelfth Birthday, by His Brother, B. H. Gant, Oct. 3, 1912 . . . "To keep time with!" . . . Up on the mountain, down in the valley, deep, deep in the hill, Ben, cold, cold, cold.

Three themes are joined here in grief and memory, the father, the mother, the brother lost. I have already shown the latter two in earlier uses. The words "Garfield, Arthur, Harrison, and Hayes" are the central theme of a story called *The Four Lost Men,* in *From Death to Morning,* a story devoted to the remembered voice of Oliver Gant exactly as *The Web of Earth* is to that of Eliza. As these words reappear now at the head of this quoted passage in *Of Time and the River,* they carry with them the whole aura of emotional content of that story; and just so "the year of the locusts" and "deep in the hill, Ben—" set up in us the accumulated emotion of all the other times we have read them.

All of this is a great, loose application, sprawling across three books, of the tight musical technique of Joyce's Sirens episode in *Ulysses*. That opening passage in *Look Homeward, Angel* is Wolfe's statement of his main themes, later to be developed individually and together in various forms, exactly as the fifty-eight fragmentary lines which Joyce places at the head of his Sirens episode are later deliberately expanded, like theme-fragments first heard in an overture and heard again in the music's full development. Wolfe continues to introduce other themes as he goes along, playing backward and forward upon them and bring-

ing many of them together at last, as above, with magnificently enlarged harmonies—an effect Joyce did not employ. It is a demanding
technique; it demands that we attend as we do to music, hearing all
at once, past and present, and making our syntheses every step of the
way. Beyond doubt it is a successful technique, and especially because
it does not seem a technique at all but a natural way of expression:
poetic, musical, the only possible vehicle for these great mortal emotions.

We return again to the opening inscription: "Which of us has looked
into his father's heart?" This is Wolfe's early statement of a Joycean
motif that has gone untouched from *Ulysses* to *Look Homeward,
Angel*. The theme of paternity is one of the most significant in *Ulysses,*
stemming in its turn from the search of Telemachus for his father, in
Homer's *Odyssey*. (Book Three of *Of Time and the River* is named
Telemachus.) That search, in *Ulysses,* is not the search for a physical
father, but for a spiritual, culminating in the meeting of Stephen and
Bloom at the end of their day. The whole problem of spiritual paternity
here is subtle and engrossing; for the best discussion of it I refer the
reader to the little chapter in Stuart Gilbert's book. It is one of the
great themes in *Ulysses*—indeed the one that serves most to hold the
narrative together and give it direction. The part it plays in Wolfe's
work is less definitive; there were many reasons why Eugene Gant
found more of satisfaction, more of spiritual root, in his physical father
than Stephen Dedalus did in his. Yet there was the same essential
hunger, for a more perfect *omphalos* of the mind, that drove both in
identical search. Reading this in Wolfe's *Story of a Novel,* it may well
seem to us Stephen who speaks:

> From the beginning—and this was one fact that in all my time of hope-
> lessness returned to fortify my faith in my conviction—the idea, the
> central legend that I wished my book to express had not changed. And
> this central idea was this: the deepest search in life, it seemed to me, the
> thing that in one way or another was central to all living was man's
> search to find a father, not merely the lost father of his youth, but the
> image of a strength and wisdom external to his need and superior to his
> hunger, to which the belief and power of his own life could be united.

I do not feel that this was, as Wolfe expressed it, the central legend of
his work, but it was one of the strong currents in it. Like those word-

themes we have been tracing, this spiritual motif inherited in its exact meaning from Joyce appears again and again in varied forms— in the actual dominant theme of the physical father (Oliver Gant himself cries out, "Here, Father! Here!" at the moment of his death) as well as in the symbolic use of the father image to designate the unknown, the desired, the cherished haven. Wolfe uses it so in his evocative sketch, *The Men of Old Catawba:*

> The earth is a woman, but Old Catawba is a man. The earth is our mother and our nurse, and we can know her, but Old Catawba is our father, and although we know that he is there, we shall never find him. He is there in the wilderness, and his brows are bowed with granite: he sees our lives and deaths and his stern compassion broods above us. Women love him, but only men can know him: only men who have cried out in their agony and their loneliness to their father; only men who have sought throughout the world to find him, can know Catawba: but this includes all the men who have ever lived.

This is Wolfe's brooding and impersonal image of the Telemachan search. More direct, more impassioned comes the personal cry, in *Of Time and the River:*

> Shall your voice unlock the gates of my brain? Shall I know you, though I have never seen your face? Will you know me, and will you call me 'son'? Father, I know that you live, though I have never found you.

This is one of the great tensions, in the entire history of Eugene Gant, that remains ever poised in mid-air, pent and crackling. I think it may be said that the whole unbearable effect, which some critics have found in Wolfe's work, of endless acceleration, of curves never descending, is due to this characteristic unreleased tension, of which the unsatisfied father-theme is one looming instance. Whether or not this search must be, in reality, doomed to remain fruitless, Joyce knew that it had to find its ripening in art. At that fatal moment in *Ulysses* when Stephen and Bloom stand face to face an understanding, unuttered then or after, flashes between them, the tension of the whole book is released in a crash of illumination, expressed most temperately by the accompanying crash of masonry. The book leaps into integration. Wolfe failed in this, to create for Eugene Gant what Thomas Wolfe had not known. The great Telemachan theme rises in his books, endlessly, and never finds its resolution.

There are others of Joyce's methods still to be found in Wolfe. You will remember, for example, the nameless, garrulous Citizen, Joyce's man of the street, main spokesman in the twelfth episode of *Ulysses.* This episode has been called the Cyclops, with reference to the Homeric parallel, and with good reason, for see how the Cyclops story is suggested at once:

> I was just passing the time of day with old Troy of the D. M. P. at the corner of Arbour hill there and be damned but a bloody sweep came along and he near drove his gear into my eye. I turned around to let him have the weight of my tongue when who should I see dodging along Stony Batter only Joe Hynes.
> -Lo, Joe, says I. How are you blowing? Did you see that bloody chimneysweep near shove my eye out with his brush?

This lively Dublin Citizen serves to provide one more angle, in vigorous vernacular, from which may be viewed the history of Leopold Bloom; and it is fascinating to observe how often he reappears in the work of Joyce's major pupils. I cannot resist citing, for example, this paragraph from Aiken's *Great Circle:*

> And who should be standing at the bar, eating little-neck clams as usual, but Jitter Peabody, that ruined scion of a noble race, half-shot too as always, leaning with supercilious languor against the bar, his long horse-face flushed with gin, his drooping mustache dripping clam-juice on to his weak chin.
> -Hello, One-Eye!

That salutation rivets the analogy home with finality; it is Aiken's signed tribute to *Ulysses,* although, indeed, Joyce's signature is written on every page of the book. And what of Wolfe? Aiken has decked out Joyce's Citizen in all-too-nice a phraseology, but Wolfe returns him to his original status, in the story, *Only the Dead Know Brooklyn.*

> "So like I say, I'm waitin' for my train t' come when I sees dis big guy standin' deh—dis is duh foist I eveh see of him. Well, he's lookin' wild, y'know, an' I can see dat he's had plenty, but he's still holdin' it; he

talks good and is walkin' straight enough. So den, dis big guy steps up
to a little guy dats standin' deh——"

The same thing is carried out at length in still another story, *Gulliver,*
in which a whole chorus of these earthy Citizens are called upon to
stare, exclaim, jeer, conjecture, upon this outcast from the common
mold. The legend of Gulliver is substituted for that of Polyphemus,
but the method and intent are the same: an oblique view of Gant, such
as Joyce gives in the Citizen's view of Bloom. (Upon page 71 of *Look
Homeward, Angel* there is an early touching upon the Gulliver theme,
referring this time to Oliver Gant.)

Wolfe makes use also of the familiar time-scheme of Joyce's Wandering Rocks episode in *Ulysses*. It is the tenth episode, and named, once
more, after a parallel episode in Homer. In twentieth century Dublin
the rocks are people, crossing and recrossing one another's paths within
the space of one hour. We observe one character for a few moments,
rapidly shifting then to another, then to another, all the while catching oblique glimpses of some of those we have already seen, in the
instant of saying the words or making the gesture that identified them
at first. The characters are placed successively at the center and the
outer fringe of attention, they change places, they are spatially dispersed, they are most often unaware of one another, their thoughts and
movements seem a succession of free and disconnected tangents. But
there at the core is the centrifugal force that holds them together. They
are parts of a picture that is shot with one instantaneous flash of the
lens. The whole point of this tenth episode is that all spaces and lives
are relative parts of one Time history. Time is everywhere at once, and
if we could be everywhere with it, as are God and the writer, as this
episode permits us to be, we could see this history at a glance.

The entire fourteenth chapter which opens Part Two of *Look Homeward, Angel* is devoted to this same technique of telescoped Time, and
the latter half of the twenty-fourth chapter. Both instances are dedi-
cated to exactly the same purpose served by Joyce's episode, to give an
instantaneous, panoramic view of the life of the town—in this case
Wolfe's Altamont. We are everywhere at once, all 'paths cross, all voices
speak; these are the most objective sections in Wolfe's work, always
remembering that even these are written by Eugene. Their indebted-
ness is plain in the way they are arranged, that same sequence of
smaller items introducing the different characters at a fixed point in

time, and is perhaps underscored by a passage such as this, which h
proven to be a kind of Joycean talisman:

> At this moment, having given to misery all he had (a tear), the very
> Reverend Father James O'Haley, S. J., among the faithless faithful he,
> unshaken, unseduced, unterrified, emerged plumply from his chapel——

From Joyce (Father Conmee) to Farrell (Father Gilhooley) to Wolf
(Father O'Haley) we have watched the successive appearances of th
Reverend Father.

It cannot be doubted that Wolfe gave a great deal of thought to tha
problem of Time which Joyce approached in so many ways. The War
dering Rocks technique was one answer, but it answered only the de
mands of actual present time. Wolfe saw that there were two othe
Times to be considered, and wrote of them in that same remarkabl
little essay, *The Story of a Novel:*

> The second time element was of past time, one which represented these
> same characters as acting and as being acted upon by all the accumulated
> impact of man's experience so that each moment of their lives was con-
> ditioned not only by what they experienced in that moment, but by all
> that they had experienced up to that moment. In addition to these two
> time elements, there was a third which I conceived as being time im-
> mutable, the time of rivers, mountains, oceans, and the earth; a kind of
> eternal and unchanging universe of time——

It was from a basic texture of these two Times that Joyce evolved his
Work in Progress (Finnegans Wake). Out of this concept of Time
came the title of Wolfe's second novel, *Of Time and the River,* and to
it are devoted many passages in which Wolfe escapes from the immediate impact of the present and ranges backward into a past both
personal and racial, striving always to encompass them simultaneously
as though they were indeed one immutable and unchanging universe.
Joyce found this unity by receding to the dream world of H. C. Ear-
wicker, but Wolfe sought it in the waking world, in such conscious
drawings-together of all memories as the passage quoted above (v. page
65) and in the actual permanent stuff of the physical world, in the
mountains and rivers themselves, repositories of memory, in the body
of America. And it was in this second way that he found the solution

closest to his wants, turned at last from the methods of Joyce to that other source of which he is inheritor: Whitman.

*

When we discussed Wolfe's failure to bring his Telemachan theme to any climax, we were noting a symptom of the one great gap in Wolfe's art that even Joyce could not teach him to bridge. Wolfe was conscious always of huge insatiable hungers—physical, mental, spiritual —and scarcely knew how to lay upon them the discipline of his mind, and scarcely desired to. In his reading, observing, writing, he yearned gigantically to swallow up all life, all books, all experience, and to disgorge it all, in entirety.

He read insanely, by the hundreds, the thousands, the ten thousands, yet he had no desire to be bookish; no one could describe this mad assault upon print as scholarly: a ravening appetite in him demanded that he read everything that had ever been written about human experience. He read no more from pleasure—the thought that other books were waiting for him tore at his heart forever. He pictured himself as tearing the entrails from a book as from a fowl——
And he would rush out into the streets to find it, be hurled through the tunnel into Boston, and then spend hours in driving himself savagely through a hundred streets, looking into the face of a million people, trying to get an instant and conclusive picture of all they did and said and were, of all their million destinies, and of the great city and the everlasting earth, and the immense and lonely skies that bent above them——
The words were wrung out of him in a kind of bloody sweat, they poured out of his finger tips, spat out of his snarling throat like writhing snakes; he wrote them with his heart, his brain, his sweat, his guts; he wrote them with his blood, his spirit; they were wrenched out of the secret source and substance of his life. —flung down upon paper like figures blasted by the spirit's lightning stroke, and in them was the huge chronicle of the billion forms, the million names, the huge, single, and incomparable substance of America.

Such were the gargantuan ambitions of Wolfe. They would have wrecked the work of any other man, less fit to house them; I think they wrecked his body at last. They were not Wolfe's ambitions solely. You will find them stated by James T. Farrell in his introduction to the Lonigan trilogy in terms more temperate and controlled, and I feel that John Dos Passos, ever since *Forty-Second Parallel,* has been working to set down in a variety of forms the "incomparable substance of America." That Wolfe had more genius than either of them, that his headlong, blasted, writhing flood of words is greater upon every page than their superior discipline, seems incontrovertible to me. Yet he might have wrought greater than he did, if he had only learned to shape his passions to his purposes, not by cramping them but by building forms large enough to conserve and direct his energies. He himself came to see something of this, as when he wrote,

> I actually felt that I had a great river thrusting for release inside of me and that I had to find a channel into which its flood-like power could pour.

This was written after *Of Time and the River* was published, yet there are indications in that book of the beginnings of the channeling, passages and pages wherein the flood-like power begins to converge and flow in one direction. These are the long passages that have seemed so clearly to be infused with the moods and rhythms of Walt Whitman. Let us note here that this is the great distinction which sets the first two novels apart. There are power and beauty and poetry in both, but in *Look Homeward, Angel* it is the poetry of Joyce; I do not find any Whitman in it. Now in *Of Time and the River,* as Wolfe sets about, still unsuccessfully, to curb the torrent, he begins to block out pages of his manuscript and devote them to pure poetic chant—no longer the blind rushing narrative, but now the marginal commentary of, shall we say, the impersonal, racial voice, the all-embracing, the disembodied, the timeless. This is the voice he invokes now to speak for him, and when it speaks we are hearing, for the first time in Wolfe, the accents of Whitman: the great catalogs of times and years and places, names, occupations, men and women, sounds and smells, words and gestures of America.

It may be a directly addressed poem to all of these, five incomparable pages—or it may begin with that familiar lament, "October has come again—" (a time which to him was always inexpressibly dear and painful) and blend then into a panorama of America everywhere as

October passes over it—or he may be sitting in a train, hurtling through the darkness (an experience he celebrates many times in the book) and hears the voices of his forbears speaking out of the ground:

> Who sows the barren earth their voices cried. We sowed the wilderness with blood and sperm. Three hundred of your blood and bone are recompacted with the native earth: we gave a tongue to solitude, a pulse to the desert, the barren earth received us and gave back our agony: we made the earth cry out. One lies in Oregon, and one, by a broken wheel and horse's skull, still grips a gunstock on the Western trail. Another one has helped to make Virginia richer. One died at Chancellorsville in Union blue, and one at Shiloh walled with Yankee dead. Another——

You can hear and feel the pulse of marching iambics, the free line and Biblical sonority. If this is not as plain an echoing of Whitman as can be desired, let us turn to those two ringing pages of names and places at the end:

> For something under our feet, and around us and over us; something that is in us and part of us, and proceeds from us, that beats in all the pulses of our blood.
> Brother, for what?
> First for the thunder of imperial names, the names of men and battles, the names of places and great rivers, the mighty names of the States. The name of the Wilderness; and the names of Antietam, Chancellorsville, Shiloh, Bull Run—
> Then, for the continental thunder of the States: the names of Montana, Texas, Arizona, Colorado, Michigan, Maryland, Virginia, and the two Dakotas; the names of Oregon and Indiana, of Kansas and the rich Ohio; the powerful name of Pennsylvania, and the name of Old Kentucky; the undulance of Alabama; the names of Florida and North Carolina.

Read that whole passage, and hear again, unmistakable, the old Americano himself—"I will make a song for these States." In the very process of writing *Of Time and the River* Wolfe was finding new ground to stand upon, and a fresher vigor was coursing through him. Stephen was dropping from him, a pale, bitter cast of secret thought, and he was joining hands now with the robust, bearded lover. He was looking about with lover's eyes upon the great varied continent of America, looking with affection even into the teeming city and using Walt's own word—"Millionfooted Manhattan." He was going into the streets, among taxis, down into the subway, and looking with tenderness and brotherhood upon the little man, obscure in life, dignified in death, and writing then one of his best stories, *Death the Proud Brother*. And even in the midst of an interpolated section of diary which owes its form to Stephen's diary at the close of the *Portrait* (there is an entry covering two pages, made of broken musical themes, never developed, like those that usher in Joyce's Sirens episode), there are signs here and there that he is coming into the clear——

I am getting a new sense of control—millions of books don't annoy me so much——
Instead of whining, that we have no traditions, or that we must learn by keeping constantly in touch with European models, or by keeping away from them, we should get busy telling some of the stories about America that have never been told——
Never has the many-ness and the much-ness of things caused me such troubles as in the past six months. But never have I had so firm a conviction that our lives can live upon only a few things, that we must find them, and begin to build our fences. All creation is the building of a fence.
But deeper study always, sharper senses, profounder living; *never* an end to curiosity.
The fruit of all this comes later. I must think. I must mix it all with myself and with America. I have caught much of it on paper. But infinitely the greater part is in the wash of my brain and blood.

The intimation of these reflections is borne out by the strong, calm, certainty of the Whitman-like passages, and the broadening note of sympathy and comradeship which appears in many of the tales in *From Death to Morning* and has its final expression in the closing Credo of his last novel, *You Can't Go Home Again,* to which I shall return. Wolfe seemed about to find the balance he sought. He was building his fence. His electric tension was resolving. The problem of Time was finding its answer too, Time was history, was America past and present, all the men and blood and tradition that had seeped into the soil and lived there yet. All of these problems that had tortured Wolfe were being drawn together now; he seemed to be shedding his subjective preoccupations, his frustrate hungers for the unobtainable, his desperate sense of isolation. He was finding his way to an integration from which would have proceeded work beyond our conjecture.

This work did not come to us in *The Web and the Rock*, or in *You Can't Go Home Again;* we shall never see it. *The Web and the Rock* is a good novel for anyone else to have written; for Wolfe it was a deviation. He wrote it to prove to certain critics that he could do the things they said he couldn't. In the chorus of praise that came to him from the day *Look Homeward, Angel* was published, there were the dissenting voices that said he could write only in one vein, only subjectively, autobiographically, about Eugene Gant, that he could not invent, that he would soon write himself out. And of all the critics he read, it was these to whom he reacted most. He was sensitive beyond measure to their cavilling. He smarted, and swore he would disprove everything they said. One of his friends has written of this:

> The suggestions by some of the reviewers that in *Look Homeward, Angel,* so patently autobiographical, he had possibly written himself out, maddened him with a determination to prove to others the faith he had in himself that as long as he might live he could never write himself out. He would "show them too that he could compress, maybe like Dostoevsky", that he could write short stories to conform to "any damned acceptable pattern they wanted". He said he would write a Gargantuan fable for them, without a recognizable person in it, with New York as setting, portraying the struggle of an artist against the attempts of literary people to cheapen and kill him——

They had goaded him into writing for "them," when he should have continued along the path he was finding for himself. The books he finally wrote for them only prove how wrong they were. *The Web and the Rock* and *You Can't Go Home Again* are by no means weak books, but they are built upon concessions to his critics, and they are deflected from the course Wolfe's work was taking at the end of *Of Time and the River*. He dropped, for example, the character of Eugene Gant, and created a new one called George Webber—a shorter man less symmetrically made, with the nickname "Monk" for his stooped shoulders. He endowed Webber with a new history and background; this would show them he could invent! But this was simply not the kind of invention with which Wolfe could function. He started with Monk Webber, but by the time *The Web and the Rock* is half written, by the time Webber is in New York carrying on his battle against the "literary people," all pretense at invention is gone and Eugene is alive again, chafing inside the innocuous disguise. By far the finest thing in the books is the long history of the relations between Webber and Esther Jack; but then Esther is the woman whom Eugene Gant glimpsed for the first time aboard ship, at the rhapsodic close of *Of Time and the River*. The junction is complete here, and that part of *The Web and the Rock* belongs to the Gant history. For the rest, with its abortive attempt to create George Webber, its easy lampooning of literary critics and literary teas, little theater movements, brash publishers (Rawng and Wright), presumptuous intellectuals generally, it all adds up to work any talented young writer could turn out. Wolfe was working with his left hand. There are new characters, plenty of them, but nobody of memorable stature save Esther Jack, who belongs to the history of Eugene Gant, and Foxhall Edwards, who came later into the life of Gant and Wolfe.· "They" had done this for him, impelled the creator of Ben Gant, of Helen and Luke, of Oliver and Eliza, of Horse Hines, Doctor McGuire, Bascom Pentland, Frances Starwick, to waste two novels to show them he could create characters.

Had Wolfe lived it would not have proved a costly deflection, but costly it was because at thirty-eight Wolfe was dead, with his work not done. We feel he knew what that work was to be. It was to Foxhall Edwards that he addressed his long and significant Credo at the close of *You Can't Go Home Again*. In it he reviewed the development of his thinking from the days of early awareness at college to the growing sense of social consciousness that was coming upon him even as he was finishing the pages of this novel.

> There came to me a vision of man's inhumanity to man, and as time went it began to blot out the more personal and self-centered vision of the world which a young man always has. Then it was, I think, that I began to learn humility. My intense and passionate concern for the interests and designs of my own little life were coming to seem petty, trifling, and unworthy, and I was coming more and more to feel an intense and passionate concern for the interests and designs of my fellow men and of all humanity.

This is a weather change in the Eugene Gant we have known in the first two novels. No longer the Byron, the Stephen Dedalus, the wandering Telemachus. His eye now is outside himself, upon men, his brothers. He is seeking for an answer to *their* needs now, not his any longer. He thinks he has it:

> And the essence of all faith, it seems to me, for such a man as I, the essence of religion for people of my belief, is that man's life can be, and will be, better; that man's great enemies, in the forms in which they now exist—the forms we see on every hand of fear, hatred, slavery, cruelty, poverty, and need—can be conquered and destroyed. But to conquer and destroy them will mean nothing less than the complete revision of the structure of society as we know it. They cannot be conquered by the sorrowful acquiescence of resigned fatality. They cannot be destroyed by the philosophy of acceptance . . .

And he closes with the magnificent paean on the last two pages, beginning, "I believe that we are lost here in America, but I believe we shall be found." Wolfe had something else to tell us now. He saw that in the wash of his blood and brain, but also in the wash of human experience about him, were all the meaning of America, Time, Art. He could dip endlessly into these, go on to work upon that huge project, the history of the Gants and Pentlands, go on to wring from this the elements of an American philosophy. His two great novels attest that no one since Whitman has been so well endowed to express it. There remain to us now only some brief sketches of a western journey he made, some posthumous fragments, and the melancholy reflection that seventy-five years intervened between *Leaves of Grass* and *Look Homeward, Angel*. We shall be hugely fortunate if seventy-five years more bring us another such man.

Fantasy in the Fiction of
Eudora Welty
Eunice Glenn

SOMEWHERE BETWEEN THE PROSE FICTION regarded as "realism" and that, on the other hand, which purports to deal only with the inner life of the mind, is the fiction of Eudora Welty; in its method implicating both tendencies and yet, somehow, transcending each. The kind of reality which is not immediately apparent to the senses is described by the late Virginia Woolf as "what remains over when the skin of the day has been cast into the hedge." Miss Welty takes full account of the "skin of the day," even withholding it from the hedge; it is a vital element in her work, for she is not afraid to face and report the harsh, even the brutal reality of everyday life. But at the same time she is fully sensitive to "what remains over." The kernel, with all its richness and germinative power, is there, well preserved; but it is covered by the husk, coarse and substantial.

It is in the inter-relationship of the external and the internal—reality and the imagination—that the particular significance of Miss Welty's method would seem to be. Logic is her background, the logic in the relationship of ideas. The dream, reflecting the irrational world in which we live, goes out to meet it. Sometimes near the beginning of a story, sometimes at intervals throughout it, and again perhaps only at the end, these two worlds become fused; and usually a reconciliation is produced, for both are concurring toward the same end. Instead of serving as an escape from ordinary experience, fantasy brings it into a fuller light and contributes to its interpretation. It is as though the author brought actual events up under a microscopic lens and threw the force of an illuminating mirror upon them. What she shows us could not be seen with the naked human eye; therefore, it appears as improbable. Reality, thus magnified, becomes fantasy.

A microscopic vision such as this, naturally, involves careful focusing; and within the limits of the short story, which is Miss Welty's chief medium, it is understandable that much exclusion is necessary. Her characters, representing ideas as they do, cannot be fully realized as individuals *per se*. She leaves that to the novelist, whose scope is larger, and to the writer of short stories who is concerned primarily with the portrayal of character. She is not interested, in her short pieces, in telling us everything about a character; instead, she selects only such material as will suit her needs. Deliberately fixing her boundaries, like those of a picture frame, she arranges the elements within a particular area of experience that will fit into the frame and produce a harmonious result.

In her concern with theme, however, Miss Welty does not succumb to a mere manipulation of her characters, like puppets, for the representation of ideas. Her people are real individuals, even when they may seem to be only caricatures. They are never oversimplified, though, from the standpoint of art, they may exist in the smallest sphere. This remarkable achievement is undoubtedly due to the author's power of discrimination; her keen psychological insight—her understanding of the subtleties of human behavior.

Miss Welty is very much interested in abnormal behavior and treats it with deep discernment. But her mentally deficient and particularly her mentally ill individuals consistently show traits that are commonly regarded as normal. Thus they symbolize insane persons living in an insane modern world. Out of their crazed brains, however, there always emerges some rationality, some sanity: the backfire of the inner life against prevailing disorder. Many other types of "unfortunates," as well, in Miss Welty's stories exemplify this tendency to assume individual dignity, from an inner direction. There are members of racial minorities, the economically oppressed, shut-ins, and various individuals in the grip of social forces. Little Lee Roy, a Negro man in the story, *Keela, The Outcast Indian Maid,* does not wish or need the reparation offered him for a terrible wrong. Partly because of their utter lack of comprehension of the intricate reason for this, those who have done him the wrong are the ones who suffer; they are their own victims. In the beautiful story, *A Worn Path,* the nurse at the clinic becomes aware of a barrier, the nature of which she is unable to explain, between herself and Grandma, an old Negro woman. Similarly, *A Visit of Charity* reveals a Campfire Girl's helplessness on the occasion of a dutiful visit to an Old Ladies' Home. Then there is the half-witted girl, in *Lyly Daw and the Three Ladies,* who is superior to misdirected efforts to help her. The well-meaning but patronizing ladies are pathetically unable to cross the imponderable distance between themselves and the girl; to grasp her real needs.

In all of these and in many other stories of Miss Welty the conventional pattern is rearranged and the people appear in new positions. Those who are seemingly defenseless become superior; while those who are tangibly superior become the really unfortunate, because of a more important deficiency within themselves. They are inevitably turned back upon their feelings of guilt.

Thus, Miss Welty shows us the individual pitted against modern society—a diseased society, which finds its reflection in distorted minds and lives. But the individual's conscious, or perhaps more often unconscious reaction to a mad world is one of defiance. At the most unexpected moments those who would seem to be in total despair manage somehow to rise out of it. The pathos of the heroine in *Why I Live at the Post Office,* who is a victim of painful self-consciousness and the will to be imposed upon, is balanced by something in her that exults; she strikes back. So does Little Lee Roy, and Lyly Daw, and Grandma; the frustrated old maid in *Clytie,* who walks upon the street looking at faces and for beauty, and finds it in the face of a child; and the heroine in the story, *Livvie,* who has her own way of ascendancy.

The neuroses that result from the individual's inability to reconcile himself with society are thoroughly realized in Miss Welty's characters. She writes of those whose lives are circumscribed by corruption, many forms of it—triviality, malignity, vulgarity, snobbery, self-pity, bitterness, power mania, and human cruelty that cuts deep. But her superior technique relieves her work from many of the faults common to fiction which attempts to deal with bare reality. She escapes the mere spreading of grossness and evil before your eyes, and asking you to weep, or approve, or to conclude that human nature is hopeless. Nor is there in her work the slightest hint of collusion with characters who exemplify symptomatic wrongs; an impression which is so often obtained from realistic fiction, in spite of the intentions of the author. Miss Welty is, indeed, far removed from any trace of such slackness or negativism; or tender indulgence, so easily resolving into soft sentimentality. Her tolerance is one that is more magnanimous, superseding that which is remiss. For it is apparent that Miss Welty believes that there is such a thing as individual responsibility; and also that conscious volition is a quality to be taken into account, if not the core of human existence—a sane human existence.

Miss Welty's knowledge and attitudes can only be realized, however, in terms of her art. Her transcendence of bold sensationalism and of slackness, on the one hand, and hardness and restricted moral teaching, on the other, is inherent in the structure of her stories. Tone is controlled with sureness and delicacy. Her diverse shadings in tone, the shifts, the blending of two or more tones together, and the complexity —all do wonders with the material. It would be simplifying the matter to say only that she has a qualifying irony; but that lies over it all: toughness continuously controls, where otherwise pathos would get out of hand, and bring ruin. Her blade of satire cuts through human evil with unfailing sharpness; and she adds her scalding humor; as well as an enviable compound of compassion and just condemnation. The result is a totality, that refuses to be stricted to any one conventional attitude.

Miss Welty often employs the grotesque for evoking a sense of the horror of evil. Intensified, magnified into unreasonable proportions, the baseness of the everyday world confronts the reader, whose first impulse is to revolt: at the humiliation of Little Lee Roy when he is forced to eat live chickens and drink their blood, for the amusement of spectators; at the highly symbolical jeweled hat pin as it enters the ribs and pierces the heart of its victim, in *The Purple Hat;* at the spectacle of the old maid drowning herself in a barrel of rain water, her feet sticking up ludicrously, in *Clytie;* at the morbid river-dragging party in *The Wide Net;* and at the stone man, pygmies and twins in a bottle, of the traveling freak show, in *Petrified Man.* Unlike Poe, Miss Welty is far removed from conjuring scenes of horror for its own sake. She uses it for a specific purpose: to make everyday life appear as it often does, without the use of a magnifying glass, to the person with extraordinary acuteness of feeling. Her fantastical characters become actual persons; her incongruous events those that are taking place every day. As in Thomas Mann's novel of the grotesque, *The Transposed Heads,* gruesomeness sharpens the sense of social and individual distortion.

Symbols achieve much of the meaning in such stories. In *Petrified Man* the little stone man symbolizes the pettiness, hypocrisy, all the shallowness in the lives of the beauty parlor women in the story. Formidable and hard, the stone is their obdurateness, their death-in-life. The jeweled hat pin is the flashing, steely substance that represents lurking, criminal passions. Symbols like these are strongly reminiscent of some of those used by Nathaniel Hawthorne: in *Ethan Brand,* for example, where the leaping flames of the lime-kiln, the fiendlike facial expression, the fearful peals of laughter, and the snow white skeleton crumbling into fragments, characterize Ethan's "Unpardonable Sin."

The story, *Old Mr. Marblehall,* is one of the best examples of Miss Welty's unique device in interweaving fantasy and surface reality. Each world, the real and the imagined, impinges upon the other, without obtruding in the actual sense. Both are so real to Mr. Marblehall that he has lost the power to distinguish them, one from the other. And in terms of the story, they are not to be distinguished: at certain points they become one and the same thing, even while maintaining their separate identities, because their end is the same. This coalescence takes place in Mr. Marblehall's mind, particularly when he catches on, ". . . he thinks, to what people are supposed to do. That is it: they endure something inwardly—for a time secretly; they establish a past, a memory; thus they store up life. . . ." His is a soul obsessed with terror (he even reads *Terror Tales*), to be treated with the ironical indulgence, or pity that one might bestow upon a crazy world. But out of his chaotic mind streams some logic that gives him hope. He speculates upon the future, ". . . upon some glorious finish, a great explosion of revelations." Roderick Usher, in Poe's story, is without such an outlook; he is *completely* enveloped in fear; he realizes his terror, but, unlike Mr. Marblehall, lacks the vision that would give him relief. Mr. Marblehall's "castle in the air," like that of Dickens's character in *The Poor Relation's Story,* in his *only secure* "castle."

Death of a Traveling Salesman, a more powerful and subtle story, demonstrates the same technique, with some variances, and a slightly different resolution. Mr. Bowman comes to terms with reality in an incident which reveals a whole lifetime of experience to him, the sort of which he feels that he has been cheated. The realization in him of his estrangement from humanity is enormous. It comes with such violence of impact that he is stunned—to death. The story is a superb study in autosuggestion, that resulting from an individual's inability to clear his complexes, to cope with the real world. In the story, *Powerhouse,* also, a privately constructed world clashes with reality and brings it into focus. *A Piece of News,* though a slighter story, illustrates a similar method. The method is general in Miss Welty's stories—that is, reality inevitably collides with the imagination—but these are mentioned merely because of a very noticeable closeness in the technique employed.

All of the stories that have been referred to, with the exception of *The Wide Net* and *The Purple Hat,* are to be found in the volume entitled *A Curtain of Green.*[1] In a later volume, *The Wide Net,*[2] Miss Welty moves, for the most part, in a slightly different realm. The imagination has fuller play; there is less of the actual world, except by implication; more of the dream. In no sense are these stories farther from life; on the contrary, they seem to be closer to the very heart of life. But in almost all of them the setting is strange and unearthly. *A Still Moment,* the most poetic of them all, has a distinctly legendary flavor. It concerns three persons who at the same moment come across a snow white heron in the woods: the evangelist, Lorenzo, riding in the wilderness, crying for souls to save; Murrel, the bandit,.who too wishes to solve the.mystery of life, but by laying hold of men and murdering them; and Audubon, the student, who seeks only radiance and beauty for his art. For one brief moment the snowy shy bird lays quiet over them and unburdens them of their furious desires.

There is a marked similarity in the theme of this story and that of Hawthorne's *The Minister's Black Veil;* there is also a likeness in method, particularly in the conjunction of fantasy with actuality, and the use of symbols. The veil is Hawthorne's symbol of mystery. By hiding his visage the minister hides the secret from the world. In trembling at the sight of the veil, the people tremble at the manifold mystery of their own lives. But Miss Welty's story finds a really remarkable parallel in method in Hawthorne's *The Artist of the Beautiful.* In *A Still Moment* the three characters, like Virgil at the moment of his death, discover the meaning of life; with the disintegration of their separate purposes (which, after all, were the same, with different methods of pursuit) they gain a common insight into the mystery they sought. "As he [Audubon] had seen the bird most purely at its moment of death, in some fatal way, in his care for looking outward, he saw his long labor most revealingly *at the point where it met its limit.* (Italics mine) This is the experience of Hawthorne's artist, Owen Warland, ". . . who leaves half his conception on the canvas to sadden us with its imperfect beauty, and goes forth to picture the whole . . . in the hues of heaven." Also Lorenzo, fearing death more than anything, and yet managing to

[1] Doubleday, Doran and Company, 1941.
[2] Harcourt, Brace and Company, 1943.

escape it by ". . . turning half-beast and half-divine, dividing himself like a Centaur . . . ," finds a counterpart in Warland, who felt ". . . an anxiety lest death should surprise him in the midst of his labors; whose "anxiety," as Hawthorne adds in a generalization, "is common to all men who set their hearts upon anything so high, in their own view of it, that life becomes of importance only as conditioned to its accomplishment. So long as we love life for itself," he adds, "we seldom dread losing it." Hawthorne could have said this concerning Miss Welty's theme, so identical is it to his. (Miss Welty would not have made the generalization.)

Most striking is the resemblance in the use of symbols in the two stories: the heron in Miss Welty's and the butterfly in Hawthorne's. "It was as if three whirlwinds had drawn together at some center, to find there feeding in peace a snowy heron. Its own slow spiral of flight could take it away in its own time, but for a little it held them still . . ." So, the butterfly "had there been no obstruction . . . might have soared into the sky and grown immortal. "The various effects of the heron and the butterfly upon those who observe them are also interesting in comparison. In Lorenzo the bird incites awe and reverence: ". . . nothing could really take away what had happened to him . . . its beauty had been greater than he could account for . . ." As to Murrel, his faith in the innocence of travelers and the knowledge of ruin is shaken; he knows now that there is something outside his grasp. Audubon, because of his quest for beauty, comes nearer than they to appreciating it; but he knows that it has not ". . . been all his belonging . . ." The butterfly causes Robert Danforth to say: "That goes beyond me, I confess. There is more real use in one downright blow of my sledge hammer than in the whole five years' labor that . . . Owen has wasted on this butterfly"; and the butterfly droops its wings at his touch. The child who looks at it knows more of its mystery than any of the others, besides its creator. Yet he compresses it in his hands and the mystery of beauty flees forever from the "small heap of glittering fragments." Owen, knowing all of its mystery, can look placidly at what to the others is ruin; the symbol means nothing to him, now that he has achieved the beautiful and made it perceptible to mortals. There are some apparent differences in the way the symbols are used, and in their intended meaning. But at this point Hawthorne and Miss Welty seem to come closer together in specific meaning *and* method than they do elsewhere.

The accident of similar theme and method in particular stories of Hawthorne and Miss Welty, however, seems worthy of attention only for what it indicates: a more general resemblance, which goes much deeper. Throughout the work of the two is a startling similarity, which can come only from related caliber of mind. You feel them striving toward expression of the same values, and finding methods of achievement that are closely kin; Hawthorne, to be sure, more explicit, using more care to make his meaning unmistakable, sometimes intruding in such a way as to damage the structure; Miss Welty leaving more to the discernment of the reader, accomplishing meaning so completely *through* structure that there is little possibility of reducing it to a simple statement, or to any statement at all. But the same preoccupation with the deepening of the ego is there, in both of them; the same effort to discover an equilibrium between inner and outer experience; the same concern with a full recognition of self and the consequent integration with the Universe; the same consciousness of the unutterable loneliness of man: although in the latter Miss Welty comes nearer being a twin of Melville. The Hawthorne who created Ethan Brand would have felt completely at home while reading Miss Welty's story, *At the Landing,* which in its characters effects a realization of the mystery of love that seeks wisdom, but finds that the complete vision is always hidden; that one must remain lost in wonder, because of the lack of ability ever to penetrate another's complete being. Hawthorne's story is concerned with wisdom without love; but the same prevailing kinship of theme is there.

However, Hawthorne would probably have liked *The Robber Bridegroom*[1] best of all of Miss Welty's work, because of its greater supernaturalism, closer approximating of idea with image, its more faithful use of material objects as tokens. In *The House of the Seven Gables,* as Miss Welty does in this tale, Hawthorne varies the key, going from realism to supernaturalism, and back again; although *The Robber Bridegroom* better succeeds in reconciling the two. Hawthorne's novel also vacillates from tragedy to comedy; while Miss Welty's shows less variation but more complexity in this sense. In the latter, serious meaning *comes through* wit. The tone is one of mock irony: you see the characters as ridiculous, while at the same time you are appalled at their evil. This skillful control of tone relieves the tale from the somberness of *The Scarlet Letter,* where only one tone is maintained.

[1] Doubleday, Doran and Company, 1942.

It is in *The Robber Bridegroom* that Miss Welty's fantasy has its fullest reach. Whereas many of her short stories are in the nature of parables, some partaking of the nature of allegory, this longer tale is more purely allegory, in its greater consistency in the representation of ideas by characters. Yet it goes beyond an allegory like *Pilgrim's Progress,* where the pattern is more obvious, the meaning cut in straighter, sharper and simpler lines. Structure in *The Robber Bridegroom* is infinitely more complicated: ideas and characters are interwoven in a system that ingeniously reveals meaning. In its satire, as well as its subtlety and complexity, it is much closer to *Gulliver's Travels.*

Yet the characters in *The Robber Bridegroom,* as in Miss Welty's short stories, could never be said to exist *only* for the conveyance of ideas. Indeed, they are thoroughly realized as individuals; for in the larger expanse that is here, there is more room for a complete presentation of characters. In fact, the story may be said to possess three distinct levels. First, the mere surface, which itself comprises an entertaining and interesting tale that could be read (and probably has by many) as a story of horror and mystery. There is the strange and exciting wilderness setting, and the romantic and gruesome happenings, in the medieval manner. Bandits capture young maidens and whisk them away on their horses to huts in the woods, where they engage in idyllic and sometimes strange lovemaking. People wrestle with ghosts, who suddenly appear on pathways in the forest, and sometimes turn out to be willow trees! Someone is hidden in a trunk for days, and cries to be let out. And they slice off one another's heads at the slightest provocation. A second level is the story of the characters as such, and much value could be obtained by the reader who never got beyond that level.

The real significance of the work would be lost, however, by the reader who failed to get to what we shall call the third level; for that is where the richest meaning lies, and where the power of Miss Welty's artistry shows to greatest advantage. Each of the characters, some to a larger extent than others, tends to embody certain general traits of humanity at large. Jamie Lockhart, the chief protagonist, has a double role in life—one as a bad, ruthless bandit, the other a respectable, prosperous merchant. His purposes are many and complex; as are his deeds. He has the "power to look both ways and to see a thing from all sides." The mixture of good and evil in him—the cunning, the treachery, brutality counterbalancing the kindliness, the wisdom, the humaneness—is, without saying, universal. But, more particularly, the dualistic nature of his

character symbolizes the conflict between idealism and realism, the neuroses that result from modern man's inability to attain his ideals. In-
terestingly enough, Jamie manages to free himself, by refusing to feel
any guilt: he will not discriminate between right and wrong. He permits no one to ask of him *what* he is; *who* he is becomes all that is important to him. He determines not to recognize evil as a part of himself; it is, to him, merely something that he has been caught up into,
and over which he has no control. In his imagination he keeps his personal *self* inviolable, and in that manner comes to terms with reality.
Clement, one of his victims, is a sort of Don Quixote, caught in his own
trap. Clement's wife, Salome, a catlike creature, having suffered great
loss and cruelty, has nothing left in her destroyed heart but ambition,
which she exerts in her domineering treatment of Clement and Rosamond (whom she hates but also seems to love). She even commands
the sun to stand still and dances in order to make it obey her. The
convincing force of the story is in the juxtaposition of the rough-and-
tumble and grotesque life in the wilderness with the conventional, the
real; and the harmonizing of the two. The beginning is in the realm of
the actual; there is reversion to it at intervals: and at the end the
sense of reality is restored, when Jamie and Rosamond settle in New
Orleans, and there is a shift of scene to the streets of that city. Yet the
magic and dreamlike quality of those surroundings, where "beauty and
vice and every delight" are hospitable to one another, repeats the nature
of the wilderness, and ties the actual world with the dream world.

Miss Welty's exploration of the adult mind is closely allied to her
extraordinary penetration of the mind of childhood. Like Franz Kafka,
she seems to regard the relationship of childhood and the dream as very
near; since the dream has childlike qualities. Her reproduction of the
sensibilities of childhood has a decidedly Proustian quality. In the little
but exceedingly dimensional story, *A Memory,* she brings the whole
world of impressionable childhood up against the adult world, with all
of its sordidness. The child, estranged from adults, can look upon them
only as observer and dreamer. Out of the wisdom she possesses, intensified by love, she constructs her own vision of it. A story entitled *The
Winds* also is an illustration of the author's acute insight into the perceptions of children, with all of the implications. Nothing seems omitted
that would illuminate their inner minds.

This skill in getting inside the minds of her characters, in establishing
motivation from within, is a very essential part of Miss Welty's tech-

nique. In this connection, she is a master in implying inner states
mind by physical description. In *Death of a Traveling Salesman* the
are such subtle strokes as these, which transfer the intangible to tl
tangible: "People standing in the fields now and then, or on top of tl
haystacks, had been too far away, looking like leaning sticks or weed
. . . the stares of these distant people had followed him solidly like
wall, impenetrable, behind which they turned back after he had passed
And, ". . . When that was done she lit the lamp. It showed its dal
and light. The whole room turned golden-yellow like some sort
flower, and the walls smelled of it and seemed to tremble with the qui
rushing of the fire and the waving of the burning lampwick in its fu
nel of light." In such a way as this the portrait of the salesman's mir
comes through; description has a definite function, and is not ju
tacked on for purposes of decoration. And in the same story one com
across such arresting similes as this: "He could not hear his heart—
was as quiet as ashes falling." Or a metaphysical figure like this on
"In docility he held his eyes stiffly wide; they fixed themselves on tl
woman's clasped hands as though she held the cord they were strur
on." Miss Welty's work is liberally sprinkled with such striking poetr
and the poetizing in each instance is identified with the characters;
assists in revealing the state of their thoughts and feelings.

Miss Welty's primary interest in theme is easily confused with mor
intention; and there an important distinction should be made. Only l
a consideration of her method does it become apparent that she is n
interested in enforcing any moral "truth"; or in exhortation—far fro
it—to any particular line of conduct. True enough, her characters a
clear symbols for basic ideas. But by means of the attitudes that a
taken toward the characters any moral purpose is subdued. The read
is required to take full stock of the context; in this way the resolutic
cannot appear as simple. The moral conviction, when and if it come
does so through the process of the story; which is to say that it is realiz
in the experiences of the characters, and the reader draws his own co
clusions, without direct assistance from the author. In the story, *Asph
del,* for example, the reader, while he is horrified at Miss Sabine's dor
ineering cruelty to innocent people, feels also the tragedy of her life ar
the necessity within her for wreaking vengeance upon others. In S
lome, as well, is a demonstration of the same psychologically basic trut
This—and, as we have seen, it is representative of the ideas in Mi
Welty's stories—is not really a moral, but a truth upon which there

no necessity for the reader to agree or disagree. It is generally recognized among mature and thoughtful readers that any inflicting of wrong is due to an inadequacy within the wrongdoer, and that he is likely to suffer more than his victims; so, without disputing it, the reader will concede that it is a question that is worthy of serious reflection. He may judge that his own reflection, or someone else's, is more fruitful than the author's; but in this case the author would have no objection; Miss Welty, like any other of like caliber, would be ready to admit that she is only a fellow explorer.

But the fiction writer has more opportunity than those using other writing mediums, to make his idea convincing and alive. Tension, a necessary device for this accomplishment, in Miss Welty's fiction takes the form of conflict between the real and the imagined. Fantasy, therefore, serves as an agent in making the conflict more dramatic, in *rendering* the idea. The same device is recognizable in much of the work of Hawthorne, who works out his ideas in terms of structure, although not with the craftsmanship that in every instance comes up to Miss Welty's. *The Birthmark,* among others of his stories, comes to mind as an illustration of his method of presenting a basic truth, not a moral. For, though Hawthorne is closer to Puritanism as an institution, and perhaps in spirit, almost the same could be said of him in answer to a change of moral intention as can be said of Miss Welty. Both are sensitive to a distinction between right and wrong—not, of course, the conventional or puritanical standards, even though Hawthorne in some instances does come nearer the latter. Although we are more concerned with their similarity in method, a conclusion of Henry James seems applicable to a clarification of the moral purpose of both: "There is, I think, no more nutritive or suggestive truth than that of the perfect dependence of the 'moral' sense of a work of art on the amount of felt life concerned in producing it." The reader of Eudora Welty can entertain no doubt concerning the amount of "felt life" that is in her work.

It is her profound search of human consciousness and her illumination of the underlying causes of the compulsions and fears of modern man that would seem to comprise the principal value of Miss Welty's work. She, like other best writers of this century, implies that the confusion of our age tends to force individuals back upon conscience, as they have not been since the seventeenth century; for in the intervening centuries, values were more clearly defined, behavior was more outwardly controlled. Miss Welty's prose fiction, like much of the poetry and fiction of this era that seeks to explore the possibilities of the imagination, is comparable to the rich prose of Sir Thomas Browne; and reminiscent of the poetry of the seventeenth century.

Franz Kafka precedes Miss Welty in an analysis of the backgrounds of abnormal human behavior and an understanding of the psychology of the feeling of guilt. He, too, was concerned with modern man's ambivalence, with the potentialities that are within him of dispensing with the rationalizations, the impotence of will, and the laxness that grow out of a diseased society. And a general impression gained from his work, as from that of Miss Welty, is that it is the world that we regard as actual that is irrational; that the positions are reversed—the actual world becoming a dream and the one created by the imagination the only reality.

Miss Welty's distinction, then, is rather in her method: one that, as we have observed, effects a reconciliation of the inner and outer worlds in a particular way. Kafka, too, uses fantasy, but not in detail as does Miss Welty. The contrast in the style of the two is another matter; suffice it to say here that Miss Welty relies more upon fantasy, by it implying much of the factual; while Kafka, at least in his short stories, does the opposite. Miss Welty employs fantasy to reveal the heightened consciousness of man, and relates it to surface reality. The individual, even in his irrational state, becomes rational and capable of choice. The effect is one that is compelling, and rare in modern literature.

For all her strange and dreamlike settings, Miss Welty never stray far from the Natchez Trace, in Mississippi, her home state. Which in itself is evidence of the sense of reality that she conveys. She observes a Bird Festival in a Negro church in her home town, Jackson, and describes it in non-fiction.[1] Yet the piece is as steeped in fantasy as some of her fiction. She has caught the tendency of man to dream, to build a world of his own, and, without violating reality greatly, used it as a device in fiction. Actuality is placed on the plane of the dream; and thereby a more perfect realism is attained.

Her characters are thoroughly Southern—in temperament, customs and speech. Yet they transcend any geographical limitation. She is concerned with Southern traditionalism only in respect to the values which it seeks to conserve; and only, apparently, as those values relate to people anywhere, in any society.

It would be presumptuous to attempt to place a final evaluation on

[1] "Pageant of Birds," *New Republic,* October 25, 1943.

e work that Miss Welty has done thus far (incidentally, she is still
ung and is still writing); as though that could be done for any in-
ividual reader, except by himself. But a key to some of its treasures
ay have been furnished by Schopenhauer in these sentences: . . .
This is worth noticing, and indeed wonderful, how, besides his life in
ē concrete, man always lives another life in the abstract. In the former
e is given as a prey to all the storms of life, and to the influence of the
resent; he must struggle, suffer, and die like the brute. But his life in
e abstract, as it lies before his rational consciousness, is the still re-
ection of the former, and of the world in which he lives . . ."

Robert Penn Warren, "Provincial" Poet

William Van O'Connor

THE POETRY OF ROBERT PENN WARREN can best be studied as the esthetic expression of a mind in which tradition and the forces destroying tradition work in strong opposition to each other—ritual and indifference to ritual; self-knowledge and indifference to or inability to achieve self-knowledge; an inherited "theological" understanding of man and the newer psychological and social understanding, illustrated perhaps in the religious concept of evil and the liberal belief in man's ultimate power to control "evil" forces. There are two major pulls at work in shaping his idiom, the older belief in a morally integrated human being and the naturalist's belief in a being formed by ill-understood forces. The former pull expresses itself in a body of poems, and in some of his prose as a provincial homogeneous and consistent view that in another age might have achieved the epic proportions we associate with poetry as vision, the latter pull expresses itself in fictional characters of a low order and in a poetic idiom of a considerably less imaginative vitality. These conflicts of course are not peculiar to Warren, except insofar as he is a Southerner and feels and sees these conflicts more sharply. This exception is significant because in terms of it not only Warren's poetry, but a considerable part of that of the Southern School, can be more readily characterized.

The Southern writer has been raised in a world that inherits a love of rhetoric. Traditionally Southern statesmen have been orators. A society emphasizing social rituals and manners requires a kind of reverence for words to adequately express sentiment and feeling. The dregs of this rhetoric remain the stock in trade of the grass roots politicians. The Southerner generally does not shy away—to the extent the Northerner does—from a use of language that is something more than bare statement. The Northerner, with his conditioned respect for *practicality* and getting-to-the-point is more likely to possess a far greater reading than

92

speaking vocabulary and to associate anything more than simple expression with ostentation. The Southern writer inclines toward rhetoric at his own artistic level. But he likewise feels the pressure of a more universal distrust of rhetoric, a matter-of-factness in speech and writing. He has the alternatives of putting his rhetoric into the mouths of fictional characters, a fairly frequent device, or of justifying his rhetoric in terms of emotional and intellectual tensions, in which instance the term rhetoric must be used without the usual connotation of over-emphasis. In this latter instance the Southern poet is frequently at an advantage. His free expression is not inhibited at its source.

In *Cass Mastern's Wedding Ring* Warren easily reproduces the rhetoric one expects of the mid-nineteenth century when he has Cass Mastern write in his journal:

> . . . Then the tears can only prove that sentiment is no substitute for obligation, if the second, then they only prove the pity of the self is no substitute for wisdom. But she shed the tears and finally lifted her face to mine with those tears bright in her large eyes, and even now, though her tears were my ruin, I cannot wish them unshed, for they testify to the warmth of her heart and prove that whatever her sin (and mine) she did not step to it with a gay foot and with the eyes hard with lust and fleshy cupidity.

Yet the prose style of the setting of Cass Mastern's entries is in a style that might have been created by any of a number of fairly facile and capable novelists. But few such novelists could so easily approximate the language that an historical Mastern might have written, and this Warren does frequently and apparently easily. It is in the idiom of the journal entries and letters of the Civil War period. It is not our idiom and we are capable of a burlesque of the sentiment and the style. Set in its proper context, however, the passage is moving because it is justified by the moral fervor and intensity of the character who is made to state it. If the same situation were to be handled by a Northern contemporary writing for a sophisticated audience, the situation itself —not the moral implications and their consequent effect on the character—would be emphasized. The language seems exaggerated to us, in part because we are used to seeing similar situations handled in terms of their psychological and social, rather than moral, implications. It may not be beside the point to note that "Fundamentalists" in the Christian faith doubtlessly are proportionately far more numerous in the South than in the North. In this the Southerner is closer to his antecedents than the Northerner. Even those who have set aside belief in the supernatural hierarchy are inclined to see moral values in more absolute terms than their Northern contemporaries.

The Southerner, in addition, is closer to the language of his grandfathers. He feels less under the necessity for creating a *modern* idiom to treat those matters that relate to everyday events and beliefs simply because he is not so keenly aware of being different from his forebears. Civil War letters, journals and studies are likely to be treasured parts of the family library in the Southern home. The average Northerner is unconcerned with who, if any, among his forebears fought in the Civil War. Only a few feel even an academic interest in understanding those a generation or two before them. The Southerner feels that the ante-bellum world which was destroyed, perhaps irrevocably in all its major aspects, possessed values and a way-of-life in which the needs of the whole human being could be more readily satisfied than they can be in our industrialized society. He looks readily to his past and is not so eager to cut himself off from his cultural antecedents. Language was a part of the tradition of graciousness. Rhetoric was necessary to men to whom politics was the accepted goal of secular achievement. Except insofar as the Southerner feels the universal pressure to foreshorten speech and check its emotive force he is likely to continue to use it in a manner similar to that of the forebears he admires on other scores.

The more basic set of pulls in Warren's poetry is that between his work as a provincial artist and as a serious scholar and an aware modern. Doubtless he would, with his metaphysical preoccupations alone, have inclined toward obscurity of the esoteric kind demanded by his insights. In his erudition and knowledge of cultural history another dimension is added to his obscurity. Both metaphysics and erudition served to make difficult the matured idiom of *11 Poems on the Same Theme*. In his earlier work, *Thirty-six Poems,* the erudition was germinal only and less apparent. In his *Selected Poems* the development of his thought and idiom can be seen with some clarity and probably would be even more apparent if he had not chosen to exclude some of his earliest pieces.

The language of the Southern poet has been subjected to the twists and pulls of a society violently in transition. Because the South has reacted more slowly in its shift from a "theological" to a "sociological" society one cannot infer that the impact upon the idiom of an extremely sensitive Southern poet is less than that upon his Northern contemporaries. If anything, his idiom is more directly influenced. Most Northern poets (with the notable exceptions of those who have completed the anti-religiosity arc of the liberals and are now looking for a faith that can be expressed in theological rather than in social terms) are genuinely indifferent to such problems as the relationship of modern moral uncertainty to the dissolution of dogmatic and doctrinal faith. This faith was a part of the "organic" society that is the central consideration in the writing of the foremost members of the Southern School.

Doubtless no such sharply defined dualism as this of the provincial artist and aware modern exists in Warren's mind but two such positions must be posited if we are to understand his idiom. First, we have such provincial poetry as Jesse Stuart's *Man With the Bull Tongued Plow*. Stuart writes within his provincialism, at home and at ease with it, even though he may lack Warren's perception and finely conceived artistry. And he writes of a people who for the greater part are untouched by the anarchic forces that are changing the character and mind of more thoughtful Southerners. Much of Stuart's work is comforting to read, but it offers the comfort of nostalgia. In Warren, particularly in his early work, we get the *feel* of a society (an achievement the provincial Southern writer seems more inherently capable of than the less deeply rooted Northerner), the Kentucky farmhouse, peopled with the old who hold unquestioningly to their way of life and the young who are sensitive to an *odd oldness* in their environment, the hound whimpering in its sleep, the old horse in the pasture, and the mountains that hold exhilaration for those who trek along their sides and occasion to think upon the history and the character of one's home country. In a sense, Warren's earlier poetry is more provincial than his later poetry. Eventually, travel and study afforded him a chance to understand his beginnings. Learning and more serious thought begin to merge with the simplicity of his provincial scenes and stories. Sometimes the bare bones of thought stick out from a poem which in the work of the younger Warren would have been structural, inherent in the situation—but less thoughtful. Even the exquisite "Bearded Oaks" —this of Louisiana rather than Kentucky—is disturbed as self-sufficient art by the attached observation—

"We live in time so little time.
And we learn all so painfully,
That we may spare this hour's term
To practice for eternity."

The mature Warren is not as much at home in the world of his later poems as he was in the world of his early poems, even though paradoxically he may be a greater artist in them. He has a great gift and he has used it well—but he is no longer completely at ease in his provincial world. He questions and remonstrates with himself. He searches for "definition." Like Eliot and others in the foremost line of English poets he sometimes feels the need for speculation in an all but purely abstract realm. The esoteric words of his scholarship and his subtle insight into cultural and intellectual history are sometimes joined in poems more nearly philosophical than provincial.

We might infer from a frequently quoted passage from Eliot—The ordinary mind ". . . falls in love, or reads Spinoza, and these two experiences have nothing to do with each other, or with the noise of the typewriter or the smell of cooking; in the mind of the poet these experiences are always forming new wholes . . ." that the speculative mind and sensibility in our world feels desperately in need of new syntheses. In his essay *Pure and Impure Poetry* Warren reduced the concept of "tension" in poetry to a moral as well as an esthetic test. What does the poet really believe? Does he really know in each instance what he believes? Has he reasoned his way, through using the thought processes available to him as a poet, to his belief? If his poetry has "dynamic tension" his perception and imagination will have served to prove his belief. His belief will have been earned in that each image will have been tested in its relation to the central "statement" of the poem, in relationship to other images and in terms of an ever ironic intelligence. The comforting generalization is unlikely to find its way into the poetry written by one holding to such esthetic principles. The contemporary poet who is constantly "forming new wholes" from the data in his experience does so because he feels impelled toward self-knowledge in an age whose lack of self-definition is one of its chief characteristics. The provincial writer might incline toward such an esthetic for purely artistic purposes. Warren inclines toward it for the additional reason that he is only partially at home in a provincial society and is impelled to intensive exercises in self-knowledge when he considers his relationship to the outside world.

Allen Tate has stated the central view of the Southern writer who in transcending his provincialism is yet able to maintain a hold on it and, to an extent, to live within it. "Humanism, properly speaking, is not an abstract system, but a culture, the whole way in which we live, act, think, and feel. It is a kind of imaginatively balanced life lived out in a definite social tradition." The Southern writer who is aware of this "humanism" is content to be a provincial. It does not follow that he is blind to the limitations of his way of life or indifferent to other ways of life. Moreover, in maintaining his provincialism he is in slight danger of becoming either of the modern integers, the economic man or the political man. "The responsibility of men is for their own welfare and for that of their neighbors; not for the hypothetical welfare of some fabulous creature called society." The provincial writer, whatever his political theories, is unlikely to forget the nature of the human being. Certainly, if the ideological conflicts of this war teach us anything one inference might be that a too restrictive and neatly patterned society, born of neat theorizing, is "unrealistic." The people within such a society or people outside of it will destroy it. The state planners, webbed in their intricate meshes, truly forgot to study individual men, to study their neighbors before they studied the "fabulous creature called society."

The poetic imaginations of Langland, Milton, and, to a lesser extent, Blake, were able to function within the Christian Vision. A reader's understanding of Christianity was qualified, enlarged and *renewed* in terms of the imaginative constructions these poets conceived. The reader became even more at home in a world already understood in terms of the symbols and dogmas of the Church. But this Vision is no longer sufficiently vital to allow of a universal orientation within it. The "visions" of individual poets are personal and usually offer little hope of any general acceptance. The provincial society, however, offers as a partial substitute an orientation of a secular kind.

In lieu of a vision of existence which would serve to explain man in his relation to the universe the Southerner has a provincial view which at least explains, or indicates, the relationship of man to his immediate community. The Southern community is homogeneous, even though evolving in terms of 20th century socio-economic pressures, in a way that the Northern community generally is not. There is a more profound

sense of the Christian faith (though with occasionally strange aberra-
tions and a gradual lessening of its hold), local history, acceptable manners, the ancestral home, and the family. The locale, the setting, the
characters and the themes are at the artist's hand. If he accepts these
things with little awareness of the pressures affecting them, his art may
be vital but have little more than local interest. If the locale and situations are used by an artist with a critical awareness of the historical
forces at work as well as with the personal sympathy and understanding which only a native can possess to an adequate degree, he is likely to
present not a community but humanity. The provincial artist in this
position will not be reduced to a delimited and non-critical view of his
world. And he will be at an advantage over those artists whose *milieu*
inclines them to look at societies in the light of a more generally abstract
understanding.

Forces in the modern world, thus far observable at least, militate
against the likelihood of Warren's poems ever cohering into the large
imaginative fusion we call a vision of life. This limitation he shares
with all contemporaries who cannot return with Eliot to the vision of
Christianity and who yet are unable to participate in any large universally acceptable belief in which one's imaginative, esthetic, rational,
moral and religious views and insights merge, mutually sustaining and
explaining one another. His inability to participate in a universally acceptable ontological view inclines him toward the naturalistic view,
which unfortunately has yet to offer any symbols around which a fully
satisfying faith might adhere.

Mark Van Doren has made a comment on modern poetry that
relates peculiarly to Warren. "Poetry," Van Doren says, "is fiercely
moral." Dante made it clear that the great bulk of mankind is neither
good nor bad—a fact he, as a poet, took for granted. But the modern
world has found "poetic news in the discovery the world is a waste land.
It always was." Poetry should pause to note boredom and *ennui* "but it
should only pause. The rest of the journey is through Hell and Heaven.
The modern poet scarcely gets started on the long road, in the great
subjects. This is because he shares the common delusion that Hell and
Heaven are far away. They are here or nowhere. But we do not think
they are. And in a sense we are right. We have lost the theology which
placed them for us, and have not found another which can place them
again."

The theme of Warren's poems and novels is, apparently, that the man who is *whole* maintains a balance between the imaginative or religious faculties and the rational faculty. The esthetic of an overly rational world we have come to call naturalism. In terms of the philosophy behind this esthetic the solutions to our problems are now held to be social, rather than theological, and soluble. Possibly the most powerful of Warren's poems is the theological *Original Sin: A Short Story*. It partakes of the faith still inherent in the provincial world in which he grew up, even though it exhibits not a "provincial" faith but a religious sense that transcends the substitute faiths in politics or mechanics of our time. Yet one is hard put in our mental climate to keep one's self from succumbing to these faiths. If a balance is more easily held in a provincial society one might do well to remain a provincial—at least until that day when deinstitutionalized men voluntarily—and with reason—find a belief that gives sustenance to the whole man. In which event, we will have a newer and more profoundly meaningful provincialism.

The naturalists deal with an eviscerated man, a shadowy figure without motives and without purposes—a Billie Potts. The naturalists for the most part are no longer aware of certain needs: a hunger for religion, a life of the imagination—a life of carefully balanced esthetic and ethical values arising from a society of individuals that recognizes itself as a community in the thousand and one ways in which men give comfort to one another. The South, despite its many and stubbornly held-to weaknesses, approached the homogeneity, the provincialism, in which such a society is possible. For a Southerner with Warren's sensibility to write, even experimentally, in the idiom of the naturalists indicates a dualism which is difficult of explanation. Obviously enough Warren has not overtly espoused the naturalistic mode of thought. *The Ballad of Billie Potts* is his commentary on those who reject father and family, on those who reject the way of their society. It is ironic then that this commentary should be done in the naturalist idiom: for historically naturalist forces have served to disrupt societies similar to the one in which Warren has been reared. It is as though Warren had chosen to speak under the banner of the group he is attacking.

Possibly Warren through his academic training and wide knowledge has been too profoundly touched by the anarchic forces of the world outside and within the South. Or perhaps this is not so much a criticism of Warren as a criticism of his society. Provincialism of the kind we have seen in our South may be closer to its end than many would like to believe.

The Southern Quality
Herbert Marshall McLuhan

THERE IS A SENSE IN WHICH AT LEAST literary and artistic discussion may
benefit from the advent of the atom-bomb. A great many trivial issues
can now, with a blush, retire from guerrilla duty and literary partisans
can well afford to cultivate an urbane candor where previously none
had been considered possible. Perhaps Malcolm Cowley's recent appraisal of William Faulkner may be viewed as a minor portent of even
happier events to come. *La trahison des clercs* may come to an end since
the atom-bomb has laid forever the illusion that writers and artists were
somehow constitutive and directive of the holy *zeitgeist*. In colossal sky-
letters the bomb has spelt out for the childlike revolutionary mind the
fact of the abdication of all personal and individual character from the
political and economic spheres. In fact, only the drab and deluded
among men will now seek to parade their futility and insignificance in
public places. This is more than the very vigorous and very human
egotism of artists and writers is prepared to swallow. It was one thing
to indulge in the lyrical megalomania of being a "revolutionary" writer
when mere political affiliation absolved one from a too strenuous artistic
discipline and assured reputation and audience. How easy it was then
to concoct or to applaud a plastic or poetic bomb designed to perturb
the unyielding bovines, and, at the same time, to feel that the metaphysics of human welfare were being energetically pursued.

It is quite another thing to look around today. The destructive energy
postulated by the revolutionaries is here, and it is vastly in excess of any
available human wisdom or political ingenuity to accommodate it. Of
course, Marx had always pointed to the revolutionary process as technological rather than political or literary. His austere concept of "man"
and the universe was rigorously monistic and technological—a perfect
expression of the cynical sentimentality of an era. Like the affirmations

of Calvin and Rousseau those of Marx are rooted in the negation of the human person. But technology hath now produced its master piece. The Brick Bradford brains of modern laboratory technicians, the zanies of big business, fed on the adventures of Tarzan and detective thrillers, have finally given adequate physical form to the romantic nihilism of nineteenth century art and revolution. Every human cause has now the romantic charm of a "lost cause," and the irrelevance of proposed human ends is only equalled by the likelihood of the annihilation of human beings. Even the "lost" cause of the South begins to assume intelligible and attractive features for a great many who formerly assumed that it was more fun to be on the side of the big battalions. In fact, the "Southern cause" is no more lost than that of the present-day left-wingers, whose literary production, for that matter, has been dependent on the creative effort of men like Hopkins, Eliot, and Yeats, whose own allegiance was in turn given to the seemingly most forlorn of causes.

Perhaps the point of this can best be illustrated by the case of Henry James, whose current vogue is by no means related to a commensurate improvement in the general level of literary discrimination. A primary postulate of James's world is that it enjoys an enormous material ascendancy with its consequent euphoria. Correlative with the elaborate and tenuous sensibility of his created world there is the even more elaborate structure of abstract finance, and the ethereal technology which that finance called into being. Wherever this abstract structure exists and triumphs James can manipulate his puppets, for both are completely inter-animated. It is no accident, of course, that in this area feminine life should be dominant and luxuriant, and masculine beings timid and meager. It is a big, safe nursery world on its material side. There are no financial worries. (Almost everybody in his novels is a tourist, forever engaged in a pilgrimage not from this world to the next but from one part of the Old World to the next.) But the moment James steps beyond the confines of this abstract materialism, as he did once, he is helpless. The eye of the "restless analyst" grows dull and evasive. It sees nothing. Gone are all the familiar and, to him, indispensable groupings of human motives and energies. It does James no harm to smile at his chapters on the South in *The American Scene*. They force him to show his hand, a very strong hand, though not so strong as he thought it.

Henry James belonged to a society suffering from the last stages of elephantiasis of the will. In fact, he could bear to contemplate only its peripheral products—dominant women and effete men. The pivotal figures of the Jamesian *ethos* are never obtruded in his work—the morbid tycoons whose empty and aimless wills served a power-appetite as lovely as a tapeworm's. This is not for a moment to suggest that James is complacent about these remote figures. His composure in the presence of the diabolical, his "quiet desperation," produces the maximum tension in his work—its co-ordinates are clearly theological, delicacy of nervous constitution being both the means and sign of grace. (The eighteenth century had earlier substituted lachrymose sensitivity for sectarian religious enthusiasm.) And yet, that society was riddled with negation and timidity. A philosophy of action is always bankrupt of thought and passion, and "nothing is more timid than a million dollars." Against the lurid background of such an *ethos* there is *bathos* rather than *pathos* emergent in Lambert Strether's exhortation in *The Ambassadors:* ". . . it doesn't much matter what you do in particular, so long as you have your life. If you haven't had that what *have* you had? . . . Live, live!" A society held together by a tense will and evasive bustle can never produce a life-style with all that implies of *passion*. It can and does produce abundant tourists, museums, and houses like museums. And with these James is completely at home.

For, after all, a "business civilization" (a contradiction in terms), with its elaborate subterfuges and legal fictions, produces equally intricate and subtly aimless characters. Such a society requires endless action and hence *motivation* of its members. And *character* is strictly constituted by motive. *Passion* constitutes character only negatively. The "lover the madman and the poet" only become characters in the degree to which the ruling passion conflicts with another passion, or with some rational end. Likewise, *passion* makes for the tragic in art and life just as *character* tends toward satire, comedy and the play of manners. The sharp division between these two worlds is, for example, the heart of *Wuthering Heights*—the Earnshaw-Linton clash being an analogue of the modern world's intolerance of passion, thus forcing passion into the monstrous outlaw forms which occur in Faulkner, as well as in the Brontës. As Lockwood symbolically says to Mrs. Dean, who is the narrator of *Wuthering Heights,* when she tries to put him *into* the story: "I'm of the busy world and to its arms I must return. Go on. Was Catherine obedient to her father's commands?"

Passionate life does not produce subtle characters. Heathcliff is less complex than Edgar Linton. And the nature of simply agrarian society, for example, is such as to produce men who are primarily passionate in the strict sense. They understand the severe limits of mere human motives and habitually *feel* the fatality of the larger forces of the life that is in them as well as outside them. A sense of fatality broods over the memories and loyalties of such a people. Character in passionate societies is consequently simple, monolithic, and, when occasion requires, heroic. There is unconscious irony, therefore, in James's stricture: "I caught the wide-eyed smile of the South, that expression of temperamental felicity in which shades of character, questions of real feature, other marks and meanings, tend always to lose themselves." This hardly exhausts the passions of the South, but it provides a comment on James's own characters. Had they chosen to live passionately, the restless analyst would not have been interested in them. When James's world did try, with its head, to go passionate and dithyrambic, D. H. Lawrence took over. But not even Lawrence could make a Heathcliff of Edgar Linton. Passion obliterates differences rather than makes them, as the Civil War illustrates. Witness the removal of deep economic and class divisions, both sectional and political as a result of that conflict. And the primarily non-introspective and passionate character of Southern life speaks from every product of Southern writers. At the same time that this passion defines the Southern writer it baffles the Northern critic, who is of purpose all compact. But this is to arrive too quickly at the problem.

To the merely rationalist and revolutionary mind of the social "planner" or engineer there is never any way of grasping the nature of politics or of art. Rilke makes the same point as Eliot in *Tradition and the Individual Talent:* "Add to this that neither can I in any respect imagine the artist, obedient, patient, fitted for slow development as he is, among the insurrectionists." However, the true traditionalist will always agree with the revolutionary on the facts. But only the traditionalist can be radical. He isn't content merely to cut the shrubbery into new shapes. The *essential* impatience and rebellion of the New England mind disqualifies it for political and artistic functions, so that the defection of Henry James and T. S. Eliot was a trauma necessary to the preservation of their talents. It was not primarily the meager texture of the American scene which attached them to the English aristocracy and the Anglican Church. On the other hand, it is worthy of prime consideration that the Southern man of letters, while always feeling a considerable affinity for English and European tradition, has never felt any

need to expatriate himself either in the nineteenth or twentieth century
Whereas the Northern writer in the twenties was engaged, as Malcolm
Cowley says, in discovering that "people in Dijon and Leipzig and
Edinburgh were not very different from people in Zenith and Gophe.
Prairie"; and while he was spending his main energies in defying the
old lady from Dubuque, the Southern writer on the other hand was no
tortured by this need for revolt. One reason for this striking divergence
of attitude may be indicated by an observation of W. B. Yeats. The
quality which he isolates and contemplates in his own experience is
variously present in all Southern writing of the present day, just as
clearly as it is absent in the world of Henry Adams and Henry James.

Considering that Mary Battle received our thoughts in sleep, though
coarsened or turned to caricature, do not the thoughts of the scholar
or hermit, though they speak no word, or something of their shape and
impulse, pass into the general mind? Does not the emotion of some
woman of fashion, pass down, although she speak no word, to Joan with
her Pot, Jill with her Pail and, it may be, with one knows not what
nightmare melancholy to Tom the Fool? . . . . . Was not a nation, as
distinguished from a crowd of chance comers, bound together by this
interchange among streams or shadows; that Unity of Image, which
I sought in national literature, being but an originating symbol?

From the moment when these speculations grew vivid, I had created
for myself an intellectual solitude, most arguments that could influence
action had lost something of their meaning. How could I judge any
scheme of education, or of social reform, when I could not measure what
the different classes and occupations contributed to that invisible commerce of reverie and of sleep, and what is luxury and what necessity
when a fragment of old braid or a flower in the wall paper may be an
originating impulse to revolution or to philosophy?

It would be easy to show an identical awareness with this of Yeats in
The Fathers, So Red the Rose, Night Rider, or a dozen more novels. It
is the theme of Donald Davidson's *Attack on Leviathan,* and it is the
product of a profound political and social passion—a common attitude
to a common experience. Behind this passionate vision there is, of
course, a major human tradition which did not originate in the South,
any more than the totally non-political and "theological" solitude of the

characters of Henry James is rooted in a tradition that originated in New England.

To grasp the implications of this passage from Yeats, as of the preceding one from Rilke, is to see the specific disease of modern "politics." Whereas Yeats passionately and humbly sets himself to watch and listen for the hints and promptings of a corporate wisdom far richer than his merely individual perception can invent, the social planner arrogantly identifies his own impulses and perceptions with social good. Contrast with Yeats's awareness of the nature of culture the *ad hoc* note of Van Wyck Brooks when he says that we need "a race of artists profound and sincere" who will bring us "face to face with our own experience and set working in that experience the leaven of the highest culture." That Kaltenborn tone would be recognized anywhere as that of a pedagogic engineer. Moral fervor is made a substitute for patient thought and perception, and good intentions become the excuse for enslaving men for their own good. Perfectly analogous with Brooks's engineer-culture is Sinclair Lewis's proclamation in his Nobel Prize speech: The aim of the American writer should be "to give to the America that has mountains and endless prairies, enormous cities and lost far cabins, a literature worthy of her vastness." The pulps have taken care of that order.

As Guizot put it: "Even the best revolutionaries have a vain confidence in themselves, and in all they think and all they desire, which urges them to rush head foremost along the path they once have chosen . . . Modesty is a great light; it keeps the mind open and the heart ready to listen to the teachings of truth." And it is precisely this kind of intellectual modesty which is to be found disseminated throughout the social comments of Southern men of letters, a freedom from that note of political rectitude and absolutist contempt for the person which is inherent in the "progressive," for whom things and persons are just so much energy to be harnessed for virtuous purposes.

Just how much of the latent insurrectionist and moral aggression of the social planner lurked in the make-up of Henry James emerges amusingly in his contact with the South. In his tour he has never once to make his perpetual Northern complaint about "the air of hard prosperity, the ruthlessly pushed-up and promoted look worn by men, women and children alike." On the contrary: "I was to find myself liking, in the South and in the most monstrous fashion, it appeared, those aspects in which the consequences of the great folly were, for extent

and gravity, still traceable." In other words James senses some dangerous depravity in his own admiration for the cultural vestiges of an alien
and defeated nation—the "great folly" being the presumption of a people in having established a mode of life distinct from the North. It is as
though a too successful missionary were for a moment to see a com-
mercialized China through the eyes of a Coomaraswamy. But complacency soon returns. James had a basic respect for success which could
never forgive failure. The Southern cause was in his eyes *predestined*
to fail. Therefore it was damned.

Something must be said at this point to place the divergent traditions
of North and South in a wider historical frame, if only to relax some of
the factional tensions which develop whenever representatives of these
dissenting parties begin discussion. Something of the scope of the human issue is finely caught in Tate's poem *Aeneas at Washington*. The
Civil War and the Trojan War merge:

> Stuck in the wet mire
> Four thousand leagues from the ninth buried city
> I thought of Troy, what we had built her for.

It is no mere attempt to glamorize the defeated South by hinting that
Negro slavery was like the rape of Helen, a wrong avenged by an army
backed by superior force and calculating guile. It is rather Tate's very
Southern feeling for the mysterious unity of history and art alike, which
blends these events. Homer's Greeks are actually endowed with the
prosaic virtues and vices of the active life. The Trojans are given all the
sympathetic qualities of dignity, pathos, and romance. The wrath of
Achilles is a passion which is first turned against the Greeks and then
against the Trojans. This passion which is the decisive force and the
dramatic pivot of the poem, when omitted alike by the medieval versions and by Shakespeare in *Troilus and Cressida*, provides a remarkable analogue of Civil War itself.

But what is important, for the moment, is Tate's sense of the historical dimensions of the Southern attitude. (It occurs equally in John
Peale Bishop's *The Burning Wheel*.) A merely commercial society (like
Carthage) has no historical sense and leaves few traces of itself. (In his
research into the origins of American technology Siegfried Giedion
was astonished to encounter an almost total absence of records or models
of early activity in major industries. Ford, for example, while spending

millions on his museum, has no records of the initial *production* process of his firm.) Jefferson, on the other hand, shows, like Aristotle, a strong historical sense concerning the material and intellectual factors which govern the development of societies. William Gilmore Simms, well in advance of the Civil War, displays an historical perspective and even nostalgia for the early South Carolina, that South which frankly and often too boastfully claimed for itself the glory that was Greece and the grandeur that was Rome. A perfectly justified insistence, however, on direct connection with the taproot of classical humanism and Ciceronian *humanitas* and eloquence occurs in every kind of Southern writing from the time of William Byrd of Westover to the present.

Now these claims were never made in the North. Moreover, the reason why New England never laid claim to Ciceronian and Erasmian humanism is abundantly clear from the evidence gathered by Perry Miller in *The New England Mind*. The author of *Jurgen* feels historical affinities of life-style which enable him to move easily and unchallenged among classical myths and medieval legends with a sense of continuity and contemporaneity which is marred only by a self-protective whimsy. But Henry Adams's gropings around Chartres, "stirring the cold breasts of antiquity" with worshipful awe, provides merely the spectacle of artificial respiration. However, this is a sight entirely acceptable to the academic mind when it would simulate a passionate perception which it cannot feel. In a word, Perry Miller's research presents us with a dialectical mind in seventeenth century New England, just as John Dewey represents the same mind today. Two things most important for an understanding of the quarrel between North and South are not shown by Miller: first, the violent European opposition of the humanist to the dialectical mind in the sixteenth and seventeenth centuries; and, second, the age-old quarrel between these minds in fifth century Athens, twelfth century France, and fourteenth century Italy. This is not the place to provide such an historical picture. But were the New England mind as capable of perceiving its own roots in the dialectics of Abelard and Ockham (striving to settle the problems of metaphysics, theology, and politics as though they were problems in logic) as the South has been able to feel and to focus its own forensic tradition of Ciceronian humanism, then some qualifying modesty might have gotten into the dispute a lot earlier.

In short, the trouble with the New England mind has always been its ignorance of its own history. It has always assumed that it was Mind *per se,* rather than the fractious splinter of scholastic tradition that it is. Once Ramus had welded Ockham's theories into a tool of *applied* theological controversy, he and his followers laid about them heartily. Ramus was strictly interested in the fray, not the weapon. However, that dubious weapon was the main intellectual equipment that the Cambridge divines brought to Harvard during the time James I and Charles I had made life intolerable for them by favoring the patristic or humanist party at Cambridge.

The tool of Ramistic scriptural exegesis proved very destructive of Scripture, naturally; for it was rationalistic and nominalistic. That is, it *made* all problems logical problems and at the same time destroyed *ontology* and any possibility of metaphysics, a fact which accounts for the notorious aenemia, the paralyzing skepticism of New England speculation. Already in the seventeeth century Harvard had designated *technologia* as the true successor of metaphysics—an absurdity, with all the practical consequences, which is piously perpetuated at this hour by Dewey and his disciples. For this mind there is nothing which cannot be settled by *method.* It is the mind which weaves the intricacies of efficient production, "scientific" scholarship, and business administration. It doesn't permit itself an inkling of what constitutes a social or political problem (in the Burke or Yeats sense) simply because there is no *method* for tackling such problems. That is also why the very considerable creative political thought of America has come only from the South—from Jefferson to Wilson.

For the Ciceronian program of education, as outlined in the *De Oratore* of Cicero (and no less in *Il Corteggiano* of Castiglione) looks primarily to man in his social and political aspect. In fifth century Greece this had been the aim of the Sophists, whose work we know through the hostile medium of Plato. Cicero received it *via* the great Stoic tradition, and having consolidated and exemplified it, provided the Church Fathers with their charter of Christian education which held the field undisputedly until the time of Anselm and Abelard in the eleventh and twelfth centuries. (It is only recently that Gilson has shown that until the twelfth century the tradition of classical humanism is unbroken, unabridged, and unchallenged in the Church.) Scholastic theology was the anomalous innovation, not the characteristic mode of Christian theology.

Against this background, the humanistic reaction of a John of Salisbury or a Petrarch against what they called the barbaric dialections (the

Goths and Huns of the Sorbonne) is, like the similar reaction of Erasmus, Colet, More, the reassertion of the central classical and Christian humanism against an upstart party of vermiculate disputationists. Unfortunately for simplicity of subsequent retrospect, the two intellectual parties in theology (the humanists or patrists and the schoolmen) were not split in accordance with the Protestant-Catholic divisions. Both Protestant and Catholic camps were in turn divided. Each had its partisans of patristic and scholastic theology. (The *ratio studiorum* of the Jesuits attempted to combine both modes.)

The great dispute within the Anglican Church under Elizabeth was over this question. And it was of the greatest possible significance for the cultural and political future of North America that the patristic party finally won out in the Church of England—a victory celebrated by the sudden flourishing under royal patronage of patristic eloquence in Andrewes, Donne, Crashaw, Taylor, and King. This victory finally settled English Public School education in the Classical grooves of linguistics, history, and manners, and just at the time when the Episcopal Church early gained social and political predominance among the planters. The Ciceronian program of education, because of its social prestige and utility, was readily accepted by all—even by the Presbyterians who in the North pursued very different modes.

Wherever this classical and forensic education spread, it carried with it the full gentlemanly code of honor, dignity, and courtesy, since that was inseparable from the reconstituted program as it was propagated by Castiglione, Sidney, and Spenser. It was no mere archaeological revival. It had the full vitality of medieval chivalry and courtly love in every part of it. However, seventeenth and eighteenth century England saw such a powerful upsurge of the trading spirit that its gentlemanly code was swiftly modified. Duelling, obviously, is not compatible with commercial equipoise, nor middle-class comfort. In the South there was very little of the trader's self-abnegation about personal honor, and no curtailment of the full Renaissance flavor of the gentlemanly code. In fact, with the strong Celtic complexion of Southern immigration (Scotch-Irish) there was, if anything, an intensification of the cult of personal honor and loyalty to family and patriarch.

In such a society, uniformly agrarian, possessing homogeneity of education and population, the aristocratic idea was democratic. It is obvious, for example, that Jefferson's concept of democracy would have every man an aristocrat. The prevalence in all classes and places of the aristocratic idea was, of course, out of all proportion to the number of planters who could incarnate it with any degree of effectiveness. It certainly got into Whitman. But there need be no mystery about how a small yeoman farmer could overnight, almost, blossom out as an aristocratic planter. It was altogether less superficial and comic than the way in which Thomas Arnold of Rugby plausibly transmogrified the sons of grocers, mechanics, and patent medicine quacks into haughty young bloods. The vigor of the aristocratic idea in the nineteenth century South probably explains how Poe, alone of his age, forecast the effect of the machine on the forms of human life, on the very notion of the person.

One main condition of aristocratic life was present in the South and not in the North—personal responsibility to other human beings for education and material welfare. (A Carnegie or a Ford, like a bureaucracy, molds the lives of millions without taking any responsibility.) Perhaps even more decisive, at any time or place, in the creation of the aristocrat is *absence of private life*. To live always in the presence of family and family servants subtly changes the most average of beings. Formality becomes a condition of survival. Moreover, to represent one's family first and oneself second in all social intercourse confers a special impersonal character on human manners and actions. A social code will always emerge very swiftly under such conditions. And where there is a code, all classes will share and interpret it for themselves in the way in which Yeats has shown in the passage quoted earlier. Striking evidence of this occurs in Faulkner's *Light in August*. Joe Christmas the octoroon lives and dies by a code which is never mentioned but which is perfectly defined by his own *tenue* as well as by his relations with the other characters in the novel. Clearly an "outlaw" only because he lives among lawless folk—that is, among men and women of endless conniving average confusion, ordinary egotism, and avocation— he acquires by his detachment and suffering a weird dignity in his full acceptance of fatality. No shadow of mediocrity, vulgarity, or self-pity ever falls on him. He judges nobody, but all the rest are judged by his proximity.

> He nothing common did or mean
> Upon that memorable scene.

In a world of private lives, skeptical ambitions, and cynical egotisms, the aristocrat or the man of passion is helpless. In a world of merely material appetites his role is to suffer. That is why the world portrayed in the novels of the South is one of violence, passion, and death. Joe Christmas is a genuine symbol in the proper sense of being occasioned by an actual and particular spiritual condition—not just a Southern but a universal human condition today. And this power of symbol-making is not possible for those who conceive of the inner life as being in a perpetual state of flux. For they are incapable of separating spiritual from physical objects. By a rigorous contemplation of his own local experience, Faulkner has moved steadily toward universal statements.

Probably no more discriminating evocation of all the facets of such a society has ever appeared than *The Fathers* of Allen Tate. In that novel the dominant character of George Posey (peripheral Southerner of unstable poise), who had "the heightened vitality possessed by a man who knew no bounds," explains more than a library of sociological investigations:

> I should say that the Poseys were more refined than the Buchans, but less civilized. I never saw a letter written by George Posey; he must have written letters, but I cannot imagine them. In the sense of today nobody wrote personal letters in our time: letters conveyed the sensibility in society, the ordered life of families and neighborhoods. George Posey was a man without people or place; he had strong relationships, and he was capable of passionate feeling, but it was all personal and disordered, and it was curious to see them together: the big powerful man of action remained the mother's boy. What else could he have been? What life was there for him in the caverns of the Posey house? What life was there for him outside it? That was what, as I see it, he was trying to find out.

The Ciceronian ideal reaches its flower in the scholar-statesman of encyclopedic knowledge, profound practical experience, and voluble social and public eloquence. That this ideal was perfectly adapted to agrarian estate-life with its multiple legal problems and its need for direct (republican) political representation is obvious to anybody who has considered the South. Moreover, within such a society, literary ability is quite naturally drained off into legal and political channels, to say nothing of highly developed social conversation. So that in assessing the intellectual quality of such a life one is obliged to turn to semi-public documents and the correspondence of people like Washington and Jefferson.

But since the defeat of the South it may be asked whether the Ciceronian program has any further relevance. That question is usually put
in a hostile manner by people who regard Ciceronian humanism as inseparable from feudalism or slavery. One abrupt way to answer it
would be to say that whereas the Ciceronian humanism of the South
represented the main current of European and Western culture, the
technology of the North (with its epiphenomenal art and *belles lettres*)
was built on the most destructive aberration of the Western mind—autonomous dialectics and ontological nominalism. The fact of the matter
is that one phase of the Civil War is being fought over again in the
North today. President Hutchins is merely the most vociferous member
of a large party which is embattled against the dialectics and educational technology of John Dewey and Sidney Hook. All the old features
of the quarrel have re-emerged. Hutchins wants education for citizen-
ship in a limited society, whereas Dewey wants education for a functional absolutist society—absolutist because the society rather than the
person is constitutive of value. Hutchins wants encyclopedic training;
Dewey wants training in methods and techniques—know what *vs.*
know how. That the "cause of the South" is quite independent of geography needs no urging.

An answer to the question about the value of traditional Southern
life and education could, however, to some extent be based on a scrutiny
of present-day letters in the South. If some quality or characteristic ex-
cellence has emerged in current Southern letters not to be duplicated
elsewhere, some testimony or exploration of human experience not attempted by others, then some sort of "answer" to the hostile critic will
have been given. For the historian's question—what the South was—is
included in the question: what is Southern literature today?

Meanwhile, it is worth pondering the plight of many Southern writers
whose works are hooted, or admired for the wrong reasons, in Northern journals. In this respect the position of the Southern writer is not
unlike that of an Irish writer forty years ago. When a Galway country
editor saw in a London paper that an Irishman had just produced a
book about the people of Galway in which at last even the Irish might
see the irremediable if picturesque depravity of their stubborn race, with
its impractical and morbid brooding over the wrongs done by Crom-
well, then the Galway editor would denounce the Irish traitor to his
readers. All Irish writers were soon hated in Ireland as wretches who
had sold the misery and poverty of people for a price in the Sassenach

market. It was partly this which made Joyce so bitter about the old sow
that eats her own farrow. But in the present condition of the centralized
publishing and marketing of books in New York and London there is
no escape from this stultifying situation. What is more natural than
that provincial newspaper editors should be more concerned about
what a Northern critic says than what he himself thinks about a Southern book? The Northern critic holds in abeyance his habitual moral
aggression just as long as he feels sure that a Wolfe, a Caldwell, or a
Faulkner is ripping up the South in a manner which squares with
Northern convictions.

It has already been suggested that the Southern writer does not feel
impelled to technical experiment as other writers simply because he
doesn't think of art as a means to *épater le bourgeois*. For good or ill
he has never been of the ardent Kreymborgs and Millays who

lust uncomforted
To kiss the naked phrase quite unaware.

—an ecstasy which seems to have been reserved for Joyce in *Finnegans Wake*. The South, on the other hand, may be said to have confronted Philistia in 1861.

Again, letters in the South enjoy a degree of autonomy not envisaged
by those who have pitched their wares into the cause of revolt. Literature is not there conceived of as "an inferior kind of social will" as in
Axel's Castle. In fact, it may be one weakness of Southern writers as
writers that they are so concerned with living their own lives that they
resist that absorption and annihilation which is expected of the modern
writer. The gentlemanly code in a Byron works also in a Thomas
Wolfe to produce a rebellious man but a conventional artist. Moreover,
the Southern writer shares most of his experience with the majority of
Southerners, who never have heard of him—there is not the split between educated and "uneducated" which occurs in an atomized industrial community. In conversation, the Southerner delights to report,
without condescension, the fine remarks and shrewd perceptions of
quite illiterate folk. But the main reason for this solidarity is the universal acceptance of a passionate view of life. Not only is there no fatal
division between educated and uneducated, but there is not the familiar
head-heart split of the North, which became glaring in Europe and
England in the eighteenth century. The South escaped that because it

had no sizable urban trading class until after the Civil War. So it has been able to preserve to a degree the integrity of thought and feeling much as we find it in Conrad and the Russian novelists of the nineteenth century, with whom recent Southern novelists have a strong affinity.

The passionate and tragic sense of life as opposed to the life of multiple and divergent purposes is already discernible as a basic life-style long before the Civil War, as the work of Poe strongly testifies. The ominous sense of fatality which was already haunting that life comes out in all his work, and nowhere more strangely than in *The Man Who Was Used Up,* which may have inspired Ransom's *Captain Carpenter.* And today the moral aggression of *Uncle Tom's Cabin* has been more than cancelled by the great popularity of *Gone With the Wind* in the North. Even so crude a work as Margaret Mitchell's caught something of the style and passion of the South in a way which compelled a wide response. The power of a life-style to mold future imagination and life is incalculable where the spectacle of mere brute power is stupefying. The chivalric South, it has been said, wanted the whole horse, whereas the North wanted only to abstract the horsepower from the horse.

But the huge material achievement of a Boulder Dam evokes another kind of "passion" which it may be well to look at here. There is the passion of a civilized person for whom action is repugnant or unthinkable unless the whole man is involved; and there is the passion or suffering of the little sub-men, the Hollow Men, of Dos Passos, Fitzgerald, and Hemingway. In all the Civil War novels, whether Young's, Tate's, Stribling's, or Faulkner's, the characters are full-size, social beings, because in 1860 men still counted. Not only war but the causes of war, and the problem of evil, both in individuals and societies, are frankly faced. So the South met physical destruction but never felt spiritual defeat at all. However, spiritual defeat came to the North within a few decades. The characters of Hemingway are men of pathos in the limited sense only—they are pitiable, clown-like dwarfs. Their actions have no context. They go to wars they don't understand. Their love is despair. Their speech is little more than a grunt or a *hausser des épaules.* There is no problem of evil and no tragedy in this world because there is no human dignity nor responsibility.

It is the same in Fitzgerald. We are not given any work-a-day motives or actions in *The Great Gatsby* because it is, in its way, a tale of passion. There is no introspective analysis. But the figures are Hansel-and-Gretel-like. Pathetic, irresponsible waifs, subjects of the Emperor of Ice-Cream, whose little interlude of life is played out on the Great Rock-Candy Mountain. One thinks of Gershwin's "Do, do, do what you done, done, done before, baby" as being at the same level as Fitzgerald's "gold-hatted, high-bouncing lover." Ironically, the little submen of the great cities best express their own sense of helplessness by means of Negro-music. While ostensibly setting about the freeing of the slaves, they became enslaved and found in the wailing self-pity and crooning of the Negro the substitute for any life-style of their own. They destroyed or rejected the best things in the South and took the worst. Even the characters of Erskine Caldwell are free at least from self-pity. Contrast the pseudo-innocence of the people of Hemingway and Fitzgerald with the frank perception of Faulkner:

> She was a waitress. . . . she was slight, almost childlike. But the adult look saw that the smallness was not due to any natural slenderness but to some inner corruption of the spirit itself: a slenderness which had never been young . . .

One of the most persistent naïvetés of Northern criticism of the South has concerned the Southern representation of genuine human evil and tragic violence. It has been supposed again and again that this feature of Southern literature was not a vision of human life but just the natural result of a bad conscience about impenitent Negro-baiting or general political backwardness. That is part of the legacy of Rousseau in the doctrinaire North. As Philip Rahv says of Henry James, he "was always identifying his native land with innocence and 'simple human nature,' an idea which his European critics have not found it easy to swallow." There is never any historic sense any more than there is any innocence, where this illusion of innocence prevails. A passage from Faulkner's *Absalom, Absalom!* may help us to see the contrast:

> It was a summer of wistaria. The twilight was full of it and of the smell of his father's cigar as they sat on the front gallery after supper until it would be time for Quentin to start, while in the deep shaggy lawn below the veranda the fireflies blew and drifted in soft random— the odor, the scent, which five month later Mr. Compson's letter would carry up from Mississippi and over the long iron New England snow

and into Quentin's sitting-room at Harvard (It was a day of listening) too—the listening, the hearing in 1909 mostly about that which he already knew, since he had been born in and still breathed the same air in which the church bells had rung on that Sunday morning in 1833 and, on Sundays, heard even one of the original three bells in the steeple where descendants of the same pigeons strutted and crooned or wheeled in short courses resembling soft fluid paint-smears on the soft summer sky.

To this as exegesis one may append Tate's remark: "The Southerner can almost wish for his ease the Northern contempt for his kind of history; he would like to believe that history is not a vast body of concrete fact to which he must be loyal, but only a source of mechanical formulas." For the pragmatist there can be no question of a passionate and loyal contemplation of history. For him it is explicitly an armory from which he draws the weapons to advance whatever conviction he may, at the moment, entertain.

Why has it never occurred to anybody to consider the reason why every Southern novelist is a teller of tales? This is true not only of Poe, Simms, and of even Mark Twain, but of Katherine Anne Porter, Mildred Haun, Andrew Lytle, Ellen Glasgow, John Peale Bishop, William Faulkner, Caroline Gordon, T. S. Stribling, Stark Young, and James Branch Cabell. The tale is the form most natural to a people with a passionate historical sense of life. For in the tale, events march on, passing sometimes over and sometimes around human lives. Individual character is interwoven with the events but is subordinate. That is why the Southern novel is, at first glance, so very deficient in the portrayal of human character. As Lacy Buchan, the narrator of *The Fathers,* says: "I have a story to tell but I cannot explain the story. I cannot say: if Susan had not married George Posey then Susan would not have known Jane Posey and influenced her." This sense of the fatality and impersonality of events would be upset at once by elaborate character analysis. Instead of sharply defined motives, therefore, and clear-cut frames around people, their individual potential, the charge of spiritual energy that is in them, is indicated from time to time as the narrative proceeds: "He was a hatchet-faced, impassive young man, quite honest —said my father—of the small-farming class for generations: if he never entered our front door, we never entered his simply because we were not wanted." The impersonal social code which permits a formal expression of inward emotion makes it quite pointless for people to interpret one another constantly, as they do in most "realistic" novels. There is thus in the Southern novel a vacuum where we might expect introspection. (It is quite pronounced even in *Huck Finn.*) The stress falls entirely on slight human gestures, external events which are obliquely slanted to flash light or shade on character. Thus John Erskine notes that a sharp difference between the scouts of Cooper and Simms is that Cooper insists that the success of his scouts is dependent on skill and character whereas Simms makes the success of his a matter of happy circumstances, irresistible as Cuchullain's luck. There is a world of difference in life-style here which holds for all Southern writers. The work of Thomas Wolfe, for example, partakes fully of this character, except that in his experience the impersonal attitude born of formalized social symbols, which finally left each person entirely locked up in his own passionate solitude, was intolerable:

> He understood that men were forever strangers to one another, that no one ever comes really to know anyone, that imprisoned in the dark womb of our mother, we come to life without having seen her face, that we are given to her arms a stranger, and that, caught in that insoluble prison of being, we escape it never, no matter what arms may clasp us, what mouth may kiss us, what heart may warm us. Never, never, never, never, never.

Wolfe has all the passion without any of the formal means of constraint and communication which make it tolerable. He was a Southerner by attitude but not by tradition. Thus he stretches himself dramatically over that abyss of personalism which is the negation of every civilized agreement and effort. The same can be said of the frantic puppyism of the early Byron. But Byron had the energy and luck to achieve a quite impersonal poise, finally; and Wolfe might very well have done the same, in time. By contrast, in Stark Young, emotional intensity focusses sharply in the shape of a house, a room, or the movement of hands. "They were long hands, white and shining . . . As a child I used to watch her hands and used to think she lit the candles by merely touching them." There is nothing here for the analytical mind to seize on. Here is rather the "skill of the interior mind to fashion dignity with shapes of air." Once the social symbol of an interior order of intense personal life has been evoked for contemplation, the writer passes on without comment. Mr. Young's deep sympathy with Italian society (one recalls his fine appreciation of Dusé) is as natural as Bishop's for France or Andrew Lytle's for Spain. It is clear that De Soto, the conquistador in *At the Moon's Inn,* is no mere historical figure but the symbol of some personal and contemporary pressure: "We went for days and weeks at a time lacking any society, and what we had was of men of our own calling, silent and contemplative men given at moments to passionate action."

The teller of tales like these may provide a great deal of conventional description, as a Lytle or a Faulkner does. Description of physical environment is after all of prime importance to the author of passionate narrative whether Scott or Poe, Wordsworth in *Michael,* or Twain in *Huck Finn.* It is a major means of controlling emotional response, as the first page of *A Farewell to Arms* illustrates. In Southern writing external nature is usually a major actor or player in the narrative, as for example the heath in Hardy, the sea in Conrad, or the river itself in *Huck Finn.* But for all that, the Southern story-teller takes a great deal for granted in his readers. He assumes a large stock of common experience and a set of basic attitudes which make the surface simplicity of Southern fiction rather deceptive. The surface complexity of Henry James is less difficult in a way, because James is forever explaining everything. One has merely to be patient. That is because his people are elaborately motivated *characters,* not men of passion. There is really no paradox in the fact that intensely self-analytical and introspective people are the ones for whom endless action is the only catharsis, while passionate natures are not at all self-analytical yet seem to be broodingly contemplative and lazy. In *The Beast in the Jungle* James has finally this to say of the life-long esthetic calculations of John Marcher: "No passion had ever touched him. . . . He had seen *outside* of his life, not learned it within, the way a woman was mourned when she had been loved for herself; . . . he had been the man of his time, *the* man, to whom nothing on earth was to have happened."

In contrast, Caroline Gordon's *Aleck Maury, Sportsman* says at the end of his life:

"I sat there until nearly midnight and during those four or five hours I engaged, I imagine, in more introspection than in all the rest of my life put together. I knew suddenly what it was I had lived by. . . . I had known from the first that it was all luck; I had gone about seeking

it, with, as it were, the averted eyes of a savage praying to his god. . . .
Delight . . . I had lived by it for sixty years. I knew now what it was I
had always feared: that this elation, this delight by which I lived might
go from me . . . Well, it had gone and it might never come again. . . .
When I awoke in the morning—and I believe this is the strangest thing
that has ever happened to me—I had a plan. . . . I would set myself
definite problems: . . ."

Passion at an end, Aleck, as it were, becomes a "Yankee" overnight.
Tate refers to this sort of planned, lost life:

> Think of tomorrow. Make a firm postulate
> Of simplicity in desire and act
> Founded on the best hypotheses;
> Desire to eat secretly, alone, lest
> Ritual corrupt our charity.

The whole history of this Northern confusion is in a line or so of Ander-
son's *The Egg:* "She was a tall silent woman with a long nose and
troubled grey eyes. For herself she wanted nothing. For father and myself she was incurably ambitious." A more viciously disintegrating
formula is unimaginable.

What has been said so far may serve as a means to get a reader into
some intelligible relation to Southern literature. However, it cannot
properly be said to be an introduction to the numerous writers themselves. The reason for stressing what all Southern writers have in common, rather than their individual notes and idioms, has been to draw
attention to the nature of that civilized tradition in which they all share.
That is why it may not be amiss to conclude these observations by pointing out some further interests shared by Southern writers as a result of
their passionate attitude to life. In none of them is there any discernible
effort to evade the very unpleasant limits and conditions of human life
—never any burking the fact of evil. Perhaps Wolfe is, in this respect,
least satisfactory of all:

Health was to be found in the steady stare of the cats and dogs, or in the
smooth vacant chops of the peasant. But he looked on the faces of the
lords of the earth—and he saw them wasted and devoured by the beautiful disease of thought and passion. . . . The creatures of romantic

fiction, the vicious doll faces of the movie women, the brutal idiot regularity of the faces in the advertisements, and the faces of most of the
young college men and women, were stamped in a mould of enamelled
vacancy, and became unclean to him.

The sense of belonging to a great chain of persons and events, passive
yet responsible, is everywhere in Faulkner: "I seem to have been born
into this world with so few fathers that I have too many brothers to
outrage and shame while alive and hence too many descendants to bequeath my little portion of lust and harm to death; . . ." Likewise in
John Peale Bishop:

> This is my blood, my blood that beats
> In blithe boys' bodies
> And shall yet run (O death!)
> Upon a bright inhabited star.

Equally in T. S. Stribling: "Through what obscure channels his blood
had flowed since that distant hour in his father's barn. . . . It was like
strangling a python at night . . . the chain of wrongs and violence
out of which his life had been molded . . ."

"Blood" is, of course, a symbol as well as a fact in Southern writing.
It is intensely related to the loyalty to historical fact, tradition, family
name. As Cabell says: ". . . one trait at least the children of Lichfield
share in common. We are loyal. We give but once; and when we give
we give all that we have." Symbolically associated with this passionate
blood loyalty in all Southern fiction goes its disease—the shadow of in-
cest, the avarice of the affections, as St. Thomas calls it. While it may
suggest great Ph.D. possibilities, it is actually very complex and, artis-
tically, symbolical. In no instance is it sentimentally exploited, as in
Ford, the dramatist. Rather, in Tate, Stribling and Faulkner, it is inci-
dental to the tragic fatality of the larger theme.

Inseparable from the profound acceptance of the destiny of one's
blood and kin goes a contemplation of death which pervades all Southern writing. It goes always with the passionate contemplation of transient beauty, as in the light poise of Ransom's *Blue Girls:*

> For I could tell you a story which is true;
> I know a lady with a terrible tongue,

Blear eyes fallen from blue,
All her perfections tarnished—and yet it is not long
Since she was lovelier than any of you.

The conqueror worm haunts Cabell's *Jurgen:*

Nessus tapped with a forefinger upon the back of Jurgen's hand.
"Worm's-meat! this is the destined food, do what you will, of small
white worms. This by and by will be a struggling pale corruption, like
seething milk. That too is a hard saying, Jurgen. But is a true saying."

Finally, there is basic in any tradition of intellectual and social passion
a cult of feminine beauty and elegance. A feeling for the formal, civ-
ilizing power of the passionate apprehension of a stylized feminine elegance, so obvious in Southern life and letters, stems from Plato, blossoms in the troubadours, Dante, and the Renaissance Platonists, and is
inseparable from the courtly concept of life. There is a strong secular
vein in this tradition, despite its affinity with some forms of Christian
mystical expression, which was excluded entirely from that branch of
scholastic speculation which flourished in New England. Perhaps no
further explanation of the bearings of this matter need be given than
to say that in this, as in so many things, Southern writers are at one with
Yeats in his vision of things:

The cloud-pale unicorns, the eyes of aquamarine,
The quivering half-closed eyelids, the rags of cloud or of lace,
Or eyes that rage has brightened, arms it has made lean,
Give place to an indifferent multitude, give place
To brazen hawks. Nor self-delighting reverie,
Nor hate of what's to come, no pity for what's gone,
Nothing but grip of claw, and the eye's complacency,
The innumerable clanging wings that have put out the moon.

The South Falls In
Robert B. Heilman

To speak of "The South" is to commit oneself to a special, almost esoteric, subject, as if one's materials are of a uniqueness that exacts quite
particular microscopic equipment and a carefully sandpapered awareness that old saws don't hold here. To talk about some other region
might mean that one would have to be alert only for variations in stress,
for reshufflings of the old familiar sociological deck, with about the
same number of cards and the same promise or shadiness as the game
at home. But for the South, no; here one crosses frontiers, contends with
forces subtly alien, and measures a human spirit not quite accountably
transmuted. That, at any rate, is the conditioning assumption, perhaps
hardly articulated, of onlookers hard and soft.

It is ironic, of course, that the different being has so often been readily
defined even by observers who insist upon the difference. The sense of
difference often fails in its duty of warning them that if they are to
achieve their objective they at least need special instruments to detect
the concealed emotional drift that can at length effect a shocking deviation from course. But the ready definers sail ahead, and in them we
can see the sense of difference operating in two ways: when it goes
only skindeep, it means novelty, the stimulus of an exotic which is not
too demanding, the charms of a change of scenery; when it cuts deeper,
its meaning can quickly range from condescension to fear and hostility.
At both levels the definitions have, most of them, the deceptive simplicity that comes from business-like despatch in making difference
intellectually and morally manageable.

I

There is the simple popular South, the tourist South, the South of
movie and melody—the "romantic" South of moon and magnolia, of

colonel and julep, of devoted darkie and easy living, of a lush amorous-
ness in which the passionately pulsating and the fiercely gentle are re-
freshingly compounded, all against a backdrop of ordered terraces
culminating in a tenderized super-Monticello. To count the grains of
sand framing this calendar-art mirage is beside the point. For in its
relations the mirage takes on a measurable reality. In its purely practical function it is the secularized Venus couched languidly above the
bar—the aphrodisiac which catalyzes the profitable commerce between
the Pilgrimage Week ladies and the prodigal tourist lusting for the
lovely that can be hired for the weekend. It is a phenomenon, of course,
which has its parallels from Carlsbad to a thousand beds where Caesar
slept. The mirage says next to nothing about the South; on the other
hand, it does say something about the optical equipment (1) of those
who assert its reality and (2) of those who recognize it as mirage but
are indignantly sure that southern critics are themselves taken in by it.

The latter provide interesting research materials. They are the ones
who really cannot make head or tail of modern southerners who feel
that pre-1861 southern life was given form by values whose loss is serious for all of us; by what they cannot understand they are outraged;
they define the outrage, and restore a sense of understanding, by the
embarrassingly simple theory that the apologists of the earlier South
are mirage-struck—colonels *manqué,* a bit thirsty, yearning to lounge
languidly through decadence, and occasionally up to the mild exercise
of thwacking the niggers that happen into range. Perhaps no other adverse judgment could so obtusely miss the tough realism of the best
contemporary southern minds—a realism that, as it gets into fiction, for
instance, produces in the same distant observers who cry "Mirage!" a
contrary reaction, a horrified shrinking, as if idyll-mongers could also
affect a horrid coprophagy. And not only to miss the realism—which is
nothing more than an unflinching search for durable values, especially
in what by the general consent of any given moment is an unlikely
place—but to mistake it for escapism: this is a considerable obstinacy.
What this tells us about the distant observers is that their modes of
judgment are dangerously inflexible, so much so that they find it more
congenial to rely on doctrinaire preconceptions than to risk the revisions
which consideration of an unforeseen argument may demand. They
have long known what the Old South was; he who sees something
different has hallucinations. When, as so often, it is liberals who prac-

tice this intellectual leatherneckism, one must regret the spreading abroad of another confusion, and one that is hardly necessary.

Again, the romantic mirage-South is meaningful insofar as it is a widespread American dream, widespread enough to be persistently nourished by outsize doses of paracodeine from Hollywood and the fiction-millers. What it does is show the country at sentimental reverie: and what we see is degraded contemplation and an alarming kind of phony spirituality. "If we can nourish so beautiful a vision, we aren't so bad after all." This fostering of a papier-maché Paradise may also, insofar as it is a non-southern phenomenon, have at its core certain elements of the expiatory, though it is an easy and corrupting penance to pay off the defeated in such neon glory. The South seems, at times, to be moving toward the role of a Troy that had, until the seventeenth century, a special seat in European imagination; but only a burlesque can be produced by a public consciousness that will take Rhett for its Hector—any day. Actually, potential expiation dwindles into defense mechanism, and a hard trader may very well try, without recognizing the process, to ward off petrifaction by cherishing a few soft spots— such as apparent affection for the charming and easy-going and really not very dependable South.

II

These are some of the considerations called forth by the popular one-dimensional picture of the South. When the sense of difference sinks in to where it really bites, the resultant portraits appear in harder lights. The "scientific" spirit assumes that climate produces some special brand of mortality, with stagnant bloodstreams that quite remold character. But climate is one thing that it is safe to be relativistic about. At the other extreme from such determinism we find the voluntarism which proposes that the South renovate itself by act of will, instituting this or that improvement that the neighbors regard as beneficent. Let it forget the past and live in the present; let it pull itself together, work harder, and get over being poor; let it take a good deep breath of modern air and get rid of poll-taxes, sharecropping, and race-prejudice —for the past, indolence, indigence, and sociological circumstance are the sole bars to the universal pursuit and probable achievement of happiness. Well, voluntaristic proposals for someone else's reform are rarely acted upon with the despatch that a wholly rational state of affairs might call for, and, failing to demonstrate its free will by following

alien prescriptions for soul-saving, the South has had its difference constantly described in quite uncompromising terms.

By millions of readers of Westbrook Pegler it is regarded as prejudiced. By millions of customers of the manufacturers of labor-saving
devices it is regarded as lazy. By millions of residents of states where
unemployment is unknown only in wartime, it is regarded as lament-
ably poor. By the most solidly Republican sections it is regarded as having a wholly senseless devotion to the Democratic Party; by the most
solidly Republican sections it is also regarded as having sold out to the
Democratic Party for a mess of pottage of incredible depth and diame-
ter. By millions of constituents of legislators who voted funds for the
use of Dies, and millions of neighbors of the gentry who encourage the
useful public services of O'Daniel and Bilbo, the South is excoriated
for sending demagogues to Congress. By millions of readers of the
Saturday Evening Post it is regarded as intellectually and esthetically
sluggish. By readers of the liberal press it is regarded as doctrinaire,
hyper-emotional, and unintelligibly satisfied with itself. By millions of
readers of best-sellers and subscribers to book-clubs, it is regarded as
unsophisticated, at best quaint and at worst susceptible to dictators. By
millions of graduates and foster-children of Columbia Teachers' College it is regarded as spiritually backward. By those who have found
God out, the Bible Belt is regarded as gothically addicted to enthusiasm
and, still worse, as being the uncurious slave of illusion. By those to
whom fate has entrusted the norm, the South is known to be regret-
tably abnormal. As two untraveled non-southerners, members of the
intelligentsia—of different ages, sexes, and points of view—have said,
with easy assurance of immunity to the graver human perils, "The
South does things to people."

What is worse is that people are doing things to the South: it has
at last begun to overhear its critics and to nibble at the apple of conformity.

III

To the new knowledge into which the South has bitten we shall return after a brief search for likelier images of the present reality.
The standard brands of criticism, it is clear, are no more applicable to
the South than to other sections, or are beside the point, or dissolve in the
light of fact. Take the legend that the southerner is touchy, inordinately
sensitive to criticism, aggressively defensive about everything southern.

We might argue that any section which has been the recipient of as much adverse criticism from self-satisfied neighbors as has come to the South could only become touchy. We might argue that sensitiveness expresses an awareness of imperfection which is spiritually safer than a complacent conviction that one has come justly and triumphantly into Canaan. But the compelling fact is that outside the South one finds everywhere an equal sensitiveness, often growing into a vast, though unrecognized, self-distrust: "boosters" are saints, "knockers" accurst; Chambers of Commerce and "public relations" experts shout the glories of Megalopolis and Freedom Corners; in these shrieks of praise we hear not merely the voice of uncertainty but a positive dread of reality, an effort to drown out whispers that possibly all is not well. Finally, with regard to the blanket defensiveness attributed to southerners: they pull the blanket over themselves only at levels where it is not critically significant. What the outsider might observe, if he were less sure of how things go, is that the most uncompromising critics of the South are southerners—uncompromising because they are concerned with the fundamental spiritual well-being in which outside critics rarely show any interest at all, and because they must face not only incomprehension abroad but the hostility of ignorance and privilege at home. In them one finds neither flabby local pride, nor laziness, nor sentimentality—nor faith in socio-political panaceas.

Another rather common allegation is that southerners are clannish, stick together defiantly, hate outsiders. But anyone who has observed a mixed southern community can see that where choices are possible it is not geography but intelligence and character that determine associations. The outsider bent on profits does not fight a solid South; he is soon bosomed among the home-grown exploiters. The minority concerned with ideas and arts are not slow in finding common ground that transcends latitude. But the most fascinating phenomenon is the speed and the minimal margin of error with which the carpetbagger mentality and the Ku-Klux mentality, whether in business or education, identify each other and forge the unbreakable bond. It works like a chemical reaction, and out of it boils, as a by-product, a dark hatred for individuals of courage and distinction, a hatred which is far more powerful and dangerous than any intersectional dislike and suspicion ever were.

It is not our business, however, to compile a new Pseudodoxia Epidemica. This brief notice of conventional judgments suggests a para-

doxical truth: that the devoted southerner is not at all devoted to everything and everybody southern, and that his devotion may express itself
—and prove itself—by the severest criticism. Here we have a clue to an
understanding of the South: that it must be sought in the paradoxes
in which, in the end, human identity is rooted. Perhaps the general
sense of the differentness of the South signifies merely that the essential
paradoxes are closer to the surface and more visible to the common eye
than those of other sections where a less broken historical continuity
has made possible a morphological leveling-off, a handier suppression
of the contradictions, the counter-turns, the eruptions which are humanity's answer to professional simplifiers with easy generalities.

Of the paradoxes which the South offers to the observer, perhaps the
most fundamental is that observed by Donald Davidson: that the South
keeps a nostalgic eye on its birthright but at the same time hankers
after the fleshpots. It faces, indeed, the perplexing problem of trying to
harmonize the fleshpots and the Lares and Penates in one master-
scheme of interior decoration. Unlike idle, neurotic women, who add
antiques to their basic Grand Rapids equipment, the South starts with
antiques, to which it is indeed devoted; but it is today finding the
Grand Rapids finish more and more seductive. Again, there is on the
one hand an almost Oriental ancestor-worship, so compelling that it
seems at times to let the present exist only as an echo of a resounding
past; and on the other there is a sheer love of the up-to-date which must
be very encouraging to exporters of the up-to-date. The one part of the
country that is conscious of a specific past longs for the "modern" and
goes consciously after a streamlined industrialization that elsewhere
was not quite so expressly planned. On the right there are the various
material and emotional phenomena popularly summarized under the
easy term *backwardness* (a state which may or may not be of spiritual
advantage); on the left, an expanding devotion to "progress," which
of all the intangibles receives the most explicit, insistent acclaim—at,
for instance, the Conference of Southern Governors. Beside a trium-
phant "progressive" education which progresses even faster than in the
North and which has been rushing school systems off into a life of sin
as fast as they are born, there are the Bible Belt's obduracies with respect to secular knowledge (it is worth noting that the Belt has com-
pensatory psychological immunities which most of the outer world
pitifully lacks: its suicide rate must be the lowest in the nation). Sectarian schools with rigidly delimited curricula flourish across the street

from booming colleges of commerce and engineering. But a general weakening of piety and spirituality is partly camouflaged by an energetic, bustling ecclesiasticism which must be the envy of clergymen closer to Greenland's icy mountains.

Again, there is on the one hand a degree of illiteracy greater than that of any other part of the country; on the other, a highly disciplined literacy from which springs some of the most complex and subtle of modern American literature. The South produces a Margaret Mitchell and a Robert Penn Warren, a Dorothy Dix and a William Faulkner. Various southern states make relatively generous—some even lavish—grants for education; yet in general they commit the funds to gentlemen of such spectacular mediocrity that their antics give one the impression of watching parvenu poor whites on a gaudy holiday. Perhaps where nature is prodigal, even a continuously talked-of poverty cannot inspire thrift with its hard corners; looking at evidence of a minor but possibly symbolic kind, one sees in the South few of the out-of-date but carefully shined and preserved and long-used cars that are fairly abundant elsewhere in America, but instead either bright new cars or else not-old cars that have been worn hard and are ready to die young. Perhaps a healthy indifference to the materialities of existence? Perhaps a habit of living hard, keeping nothing back, running through capital when it is available? Perhaps some not consciously recognized incapacity for restraint? Southern undergraduate bodies show a marked inhospitality to restraints, and especially to subtler forms of discipline; yet against this there is a special southern passion for military training and for military schools hardly equaled elsewhere. The same undergraduate bodies exhibit a collegiate languor of notable amplitude— "southern laziness," no doubt; yet against this there must be set, as a distinguishing quality of certain students, scientists, intellectuals, and writers, an exceptional capacity for and devotion to intense, unremitting work. The offspring of laborers can hardly be made to work; the apologists of an old leisure-order hardly rest from work. Among the undergraduate bodies as already described—the products of bad schools and the victims of fuddled educators who treat students like political constituents—the educational problem is well-nigh hopeless; yet from just these bodies come saving individuals of extraordinary abilities who, without being wide-eyed, have an intense desire to know and master and produce that carries them beyond the conventional borders accessible to the youth of more sophisticated areas where the general level of academic achievement is higher. John Peale Bishop has remarked that once in the South old men customarily laid down their Horace beside their bourbon. To judge from the universities, most of their grandchildren lay down their comics-book beside their coca-cola. Yet somewhere among them, it is likely, are our best hopes for another Catullus or Juvenal or Lucretius.

In "southern pride" there is another nucleus of contradictions. At its finest it means an awareness of an achieved way of life, of beliefs courageously fought for, of the unpopular validity defended against success—that is, of an aristocratic stability in the best sense of the words; but that pride has been contorted by a century of exacerbation, and perhaps even more by the late Faustian corruptions which stop at no regional boundaries. With rare exceptions the modern self-esteem misses wholly the best justifications for solid pride—the distinguished work of artists, writers, and thinkers who include some of the best critics in the country. In fact, that South has such a habit of casually exporting talent like raw materials that it is as difficult to find a southern intellectual or poet at work on his native soil as it is to buy choice strawberries in Louisiana or choice peaches in Georgia. Nor is the man of insight who sticks to the native soil likely to have any attention paid to his insights; he is the archetypal prophet scorned; he finds that his fellow-southerners in need of prophecy turn to local money-lenders or to seers who, drifting in from elsewhere to teach or administer or exploit, seem hardly to sustain an export-import balance in human quality. Losing sight of its proper nourishment, pride feeds itself on material things of no qualitative significance—roads, buildings, excesses of population. To change the terms somewhat: beside or beneath a self-assurance often considered characteristically southern there are evidences of diffidence and uncertainty. The diffident and the uncertain, lacking the guidance of men of talent, seek firm foundations in the most obvious, and hence most deceptive, places. They admire office and never question that the office makes the man. They worship bigness. Universities—and even their graduate schools—keep counting enrollments and measuring the size of the "plant." Hence there is little discrimination among bignesses. One university, for instance, spent money with equal abandon to buy a music school with distinguished teachers, and a quarterly with distinguished editors and contributors, and a football team with distinguished players. It had a trinity of Rocks of Ages until finally it decided that the third was really the soundest cornerstone after all.

A perverse pride is that of the southerner who scarifies southern indolence, lauds northern energy, debunks the Old South, and welcomes Progress with the enthusiasm of a hotel-greeter. Bobbing equally anchorless across the bay of opinion is the anxious neo-southerner, *né* elsewhere, who is in a loyal fever about "southern problems," announces his devotion to the life graceful and charming, laments the loss of faithful "country niggers" and assists in keeping their sulky city cousins where they belong. One such convert, scarcely dry from his sacramental immersion in a S'wanee-Jordan, has proposed that southern libraries should be such that southerners can do all their graduate work in the South because only thus can they be adequately fitted to lead in the solution of southern problems. He forgets, then, to refrain from leading; and he hardly regards certain southerners who have a pretty good grip on southern problems despite the disadvantage of having been educated, not only not in the South, but not even in America. In the academic analogue of such enthusiasm we find the paradox of southern history: though in the South there is, inevitably, an exceptional, sensitive awareness of the past, the formal study of that past seems in certain universities to be almost the private scholastic vocation of midwesterners.

IV

Of such contradictions as these, which are far from exhaustive, he who would define the differentness of the South must take account. Such a synthesis, which is beyond the scope of this paper, may point beneath the cloak of differentness to familiar human patterns; indeed, the further beneath the merely sociological we look, and the closer we come to moral and spiritual issues, the deeper the tendency of diverse regional problems to coalesce. But that closeness of paradox to the surface which makes the paradox perceptible to the laity and leads them to consider the southern reality particularistic, has another meaning: as a cultural characteristic it evidences a considerable spontaneity and unself-consciousness. What is happening now, however, is the replacement of spontaneous, even haphazard, existence, by a conscious, rational, planned program; and rational management means the flattening out of special modes and features, which contribute to vital contradictions, into a smooth regularity designed by the fashion-sense of the majority.

After long indifference to a barrage of critical club-blows from abroad, the South, as we have said, is now listening to the serpentine voice of its critics, who say, "Be like us, and rejoice"; it has bitten into the apple of conformity; it has become self-conscious and put on the fig-leaves of standardization; it has fled its naked individuality. It proposes—the vocal sections, at least—to become modern, progressive, industrial, urban, scientific, rational; and here is the heart of its problem. In abjuring differentness, perhaps the South leaves little that could be defended as an Earthly Paradise, yet it must depart with far greater misgivings than those which assailed the proto-exiles from Eden. For them, an unchosen proscription was meaningful: nemesis proved the godhead, fierce penance vindicated the system of beliefs, and ultimate salvation still beckoned. But upon its entry into the World, the South goes by choice (unless, taking a Spenglerian view, we consider it driven by historical necessity); it takes off a hairshirt and bids farewell to antique gods; nothing beckons except the well-to-do neighbors on the North Side. For the first parents, the rough Wanderjahre validated faith; for the South, a swift trip on the best concrete highways means, in the realm of faith and belief, a revolutionary gamble in which nothing is certain.

As a "backward" area by suddenly coming "forward" recapitulates a half-millennium of the cultural cycle, the temporal compression of conflicts heightens the possibilities of explosion or schizophrenia. It may be, of course, that the South has already made so many secret concessions to progress that it will have little nostalgic anguish and internecine struggle. Yet the very paradoxes we have noted imply that not all southerners march expectantly through the gilt archway whose attendant spirit is the Zeitgeist. If they who hold back can keep from being crushed by the leveling-out process, they will illuminate the real problem for the marchers, who otherwise will be a long time in seeing it straight. But it is in the light of that problem that the South will now come to seem more and more familiar, for the problem is embodied in the question that experience asks all of us: what shall we believe? How shall the spirit be nourished? The South is accepting the answer of the majority, and it will have, along with the majority, to make the great pragmatic test.

And having embarked on this perilous adventure, the South may

surely expect, from certain distant but attentive observers, a congratu-
latory pat on the back for having disavowed an apparent failure of
nerve.

V

When the South puts on sameness instead of difference, several interesting but perhaps not wholly foreseen consequences may follow upon
the change. To the outer critics who have long lamented its alien status
and who can now in some sort celebrate a triumph, the converted South
may, paradoxically enough, bring unsuspected discomfort; and yet at
the same time it may do a service more substantial than the flattery of
imitation.

For in the standard hostile criticisms of the South there are, we may
conjecture, two layers of meaning which rarely show through the familiar surface. In one respect, which is hardly likely to be surmised by
the critics, the criticism has elements of the defensive; and conversely
the criticized aspects of the South are themselves implied criticisms of
a different cultural mode. All nonconformity is a moral judgment, and
the South can only have been hated by the conformity which it did not
espouse. The South is lazy, the critics say: laziness is a criticism of
puritanical energizing. The South is poor: poverty is a criticism of the
profits which have assumed divinity. The South is backward: backwardness is a criticism of the get-ahead-and-devil-take-the-hindmost religion. The South is emotional and violent: emotionality and violence
are a criticism of the calculating spirit. And so on.

So then we have had, at least in part, a pleasant irony: northern
critics, in their onslaughts on the South, are seen to have been engaging,
with the most innocent self-deception, in a bit of extra-curricular, but
nonetheless sturdy, self-defense. But may there not also be another,
more piquantly ironic possibility in their critical fluency? Besides indirectly defending their own *modus vivendi,* have they not also, perhaps, succeeded in keeping their inquiring eyes away from themselves?
For any attack on an outside entity or mode of life is often found, upon
inspection, to constitute a partial way of avoiding a too realistic view
of oneself. In the dogma of difference lurk some rather special ad-
vantages for the psyche: by permitting the devotion of all faculties to
being honestly outraged by, and to scolding, the different, the dogma
does make it possible for the dogmatist, albeit such an objective never
enter his consciousness, to neglect somewhat the problems at home.

Xenophobia does, after all, substitute a reassuring telescope for a possibly disturbing microscope. Anti-alienism is like war: it is a boon to a distraught humanity eager to reduce the tragedy of life to melodrama. War comforts man by deluding him with the conviction that he is facing reality when in fact it permits him to get by with the facing of a simpler, secondary reality—that of physical survival. It validates the easy psychology of melodrama, by which all evil is across the water, and all is sound at home. This is no inconsiderable benevolence. Then peace relentlessly brings back the tragic burden of facing the primary reality, that of spiritual survival; here man cannot escape looking directly at himself. As long as the South was all different, and therefore inferior, and in need of reform, it was pretty comforting: it had the essential virtue of every No. 1 Problem—that of permitting the student to assume that all is well with himself and that to create a general, free-for-all Paradise he need only export, possibly at profitable rates, a modicum of that wellness. Problem No. 1 was, ironically, a double boon.

But when the South declares peace, gives up difference, and decides to be like the North, the North—or at least some quite articulate segments of it—may have, alas, to step out of a zestful and tonic melodrama, however well-meaning, as hero, it may have been. To change the figure: the South tells its physician, in effect, that it has a complete supply of all his pills. All that may be left for him to do is to heal himself—an awesome assignment. Perhaps the South, with ironic graciousness, will hold onto the race problem long enough to save the doctor from an immediate plunge into total introspection. But in the main the South is solidly in the World; it will not long be poor and lazy and backward; to the critic who risks travel, it will soon make things seem like home, all right—with better stores, hotels, services, and the like. But all the soothing and flattery will have their price. For will not the most convenient scapegoat be gone? Will not the reforming spirit, though nostalgic for foreign lands, have to undergo all the rigors of repatriation?

This is the ironically unsuspected discomfort that the New South may bring to the North: depriving it of the reassurance of a distant, unmistakable, and surely conquerable enemy, and making it face—unless it can find another whipping boy—a subtler and more elusive and ever-present foe who will never surrender. But the discomfort bittercoats an essential service: for it is surely a needed good to have to face oneself instead of turning one's ameliorative instinct loose among safely foreign corruptions and failures.

It is possible that even in the scapegoat stage the South has caused some of the missiles fired at it to ricochet and even locate vulnerable spots in the triggermen. One thinks of the dismay and indignation aroused by the recent use, here and there, of the concept of original sin or radical evil; Irwin Edman, for instance, indicates his persuasion that we face not evil but medicable evils—slums, dictators, wars, worms —a position rather typical of the anti-absolutism of our era. But do not the liberal pluralists, those tireless pursuers of the evils that beset us all, prescribe a single good for the South? And do they not think, after all, that original sin is about the only way to account for the unregenerate state of the South? For slavery? For post-slavery negrophobia? If these are simply misdirected goods, or simple ailments, one sees few signs of medication; the southerner is simply beaten over the head—as if, oddly enough, even moderns were trying to scare out the devils of which he is possessed. And the tougher-minded southern fiction, assuming that some of its reviewers may be considered representative, springs, if not from original sin, at least from original nastiness or radical disagreeableness.

One must suppose, too, that the prescription of modern improvements for the South is rather illiberally dogmatic, and that there is a quite unpragmatic petulance in the attacks on southerners who have their hesitancies about the improvements. One must suppose further that the proponents of the rational mastery of life do not altogether rationally master these hesitancies about improvements. It ought not to be needful to conjecture that the hesitancy does not mean a positive love for, let us say, outside lavatories. Probably no southern conservative will feud against inside plumbing. But he is rather likely to insist that it will not save souls. He and a few of his fellows, who are suspected of radical intransigence, or what we might call radical reaction, have a vestigial concern with souls and hope not to see corporeal suavities mistaken for techniques of salvation. They will not seriously object to sanitation, which Mr. Edman, we may assume, believes will put down quite a number of manageable evils; but it is not, they suspect, of sacramental efficacy.

We are, however, going to have a vast amount of sanitation, and other improvements. The main reasons for the exhorting or contemning of the South are on the way out, and we may anticipate, surely, a proportionate rise of neighborly viewing with pride. Yet even such new kindliness, if it come, may warm the heart of neither giver nor receiver: there is, after all, an ironic irrelevance in either scorn or admiration for the new cultural voyage. For there are no first-class passages in the boat in which we are all traveling through the not wholly trustworthy waters of our century. Time may show it to be Charon's boat, or, if we are more fortunate, that other boat which, under angelic guidance, comes swiftly from the east to the mountain at the opposite pole from Jerusalem.

Myth-Makers and the South's Dilemma

Louis B. Wright

No region in the United States has created so many legends about itself—and had so many created for it—as the South. The very word carries with it a multitude of connotations and scenes, romantic or realistic, pleasant or unpleasant, according to one's personal temperament and prejudices, but often utterly at variance with facts, historical or physical. At the present moment that region is the focus of a new wave of myth-making, and this crop of legends and beliefs may have tragic consequences for the efforts of men of good will to achieve just relations between Negroes and whites in the land below the Potomac.

During the last decade, an army of writers from both sides of Mason and Dixon's line rediscovered the South as a locale and a theme for their efforts. Authors of poems, plays, short stories, novels, sketches, biographies, autobiographies, travel narratives, and even cook books have capitalized upon the growing popular interest in the South. This interest is prevailingly romantic, but it is not romanticism that takes pleasure in the legendary South of Thomas Nelson Page. This latest interest finds its deepest satisfaction, not in the fragrance of magnolias but in *fleurs du mal,* in the clowning bawdry of Erskine Caldwell and the exotic perversions of William Faulkner. Sometimes the new romanticism appears in the garb of "historical" fiction, as in Howard Fast's *Freedom Road,* or in a problem novel that purports to be realistic, as in Lillian Smith's *Strange Fruit,* but the setting is actually in operaland and the characters, for all of their simulated realism, are abstractions in allegory. Indeed, Miss Smith herself declared in the *Saturday Review of Literature* (February 17, 1945) that she thought of her book "as a fable about a son in search of a mother, about a race in search of surcease from pain and guilt—both finding what they sought in death and destruction"—which is not precisely what most readers thought they saw in *Strange Fruit*. The "realism" which many readers discovered was in inverse ratio to their firsthand knowledge of the book's milieu. To a resident of Brooklyn the scenes and people were "typical of Georgia," though that resident had never been farther south than Jersey.

That *Strange Fruit* presents a sort of inverted pastoral romance as old and as unreal as *Daphnis and Chloe* is obvious, even if Miss Smith had not given us the hint in the *Saturday Review*. But many an outlander reading the story is certain that North Georgia is a region where every white boy lusts after irresistible Negro girls; where these eager youths engage in erotic dalliance until overtaken by Envy, Jealousy, Revenge, and Hate (personified by libidinous Baptist preachers, anemic white girls, vengeful Negro men, and assorted specimens of poor whites). The dénouement of this type of inverted pastoral must inevitably be a rousing revival ending in a lynching at which a good time is had by all (except, of course, the victim and his terrified brethren). Having sacrificed a black scapegoat to Jehovah, pious Southerners feel refreshed in spirit and return the next day with new zeal to their normal adulteries and meannesses.

Although the literary Columbus who discovered this profitable Otherworld has been lost and forgotten in the fog of reviewers' superlatives, many a writer has found treasure by following in his wake. Illicit love, orgiastic religion, and sadistic murder are ingredients in a sure-fire formula certain to elicit from the more advanced reviewers adjectives like "fearless," "beautiful in its terror," "provocative," "daring," "sincere," and "realistic." Southern authors, and would-be authors, discouraged by an accumulating pile of rejection slips, at last discerned that crinoline romanticism was out, but that a hangman's noose and a faggot would work a charm. Once having realized what the customers wanted, the writing profession, both North and South, got on with the job of production. For a while Southern violence rivaled the popularity of strictly professional murder mysteries.

There is a strong suspicion that pioneers in the genre started out by travestying certain of the North's treasured notions of Southern backwardness. William Faulkner, for example, has pulled his public's leg on more than one occasion. Telling a tall tale of horror amused him, but the serious reception of his fiction as social documentation must have caused the author to speculate cynically upon human credulity. The darker purlieus of Mississippi are the nominal settings for his best stories, but the actual realm that he describes is the world of Gothic romance.

Gayer in spirit than Faulkner, Erskine Caldwell has written Rabelaisian tales of Tobacco Road, a community more easily found on the vaudeville circuit than on the map of Georgia—its alleged locale. When Mr. Caldwell visits the back country out of Augusta, he may believe that he is seeing Tobacco Road, and he may think that the farmer at the country store, carefully spitting across the porch, is Jeeter Lester, but he is deluding himself. Jeeter's nearest of kin are the descendants of Joe Miller. The characters of Tobacco Road are denizens of the jest books.

Perhaps some of the latter-day romantics have come to believe in the reality of their characters and their settings. It would not be surprising if Mr. Faulkner, Mr. Caldwell, or any of their recent successors, should convince themselves that the characters in their books, the actions and the scenes, are typical of the South. Edgar Bergen, we are led to believe by his press agent, thinks of Charlie McCarthy as an animate being. In the same way, some of these writers apparently forget that they too are merely ventriloquists giving words to automatons in a puppet show.

Whatever the authors may think of their work, most readers outside the South accept the fictional pictures at face value. The tremendous popularity of Mr. Caldwell's playful obscenities, on the stage and in book form, have given a fixed idea to thousands of people who imagine the South as a land of subnormal buffoons, amusing at a distance, like Pappy and Uncle Rafe in Paul Webb's *Esquire* cartoons. Thousands of others, who feel deep indignation over discrimination against the Negro, have acquired equally fixed ideas from other books which picture a sinister South, malevolent and cunning in its cruelty.

A Southern writer, traveling recently between New York and New Orleans, sat opposite a Wave, a college girl from New York, getting her first glimpse of the South. To her the small towns through North and South Carolina, Georgia, and Alabama were precisely the desolate towns she had read about, towns where, as H. L. Mencken once declared, a lynching supplied the place of a merry-go-round and furnished the only diversion and excitement. The run-down houses along the right-of-way and the shiftless people reminded her of Jeeter Lester and his household, as she had seen them in the theater.

She was convinced that the books she had read were not only realistic, but photographically true to life. She could not believe that the South consisted of anything better than what she now saw as the train flashed by. When she discovered that her traveling companion of the moment was a Southerner, she expressed curiosity about the dreadful folkways of the country. "How many lynchings have you seen?" she finally asked. When the reply was "None," she looked incredulous and suggested that the speaker must have led a sheltered life. "Don't they usually have lynchings after the summer revivals?" she persisted. To the reply that in five years as a newspaperman in the South, no lynching had occurred in the speaker's fairly wide area of operations, she looked more than a little doubtful. "Of course you Southerners always rationalize your attitude toward the Negro."

The logical sequence of that observation was not crystal clear, but it has become a cliché and a conventional phrase in the party line—a fragment in the new mythology which insists that Southern whites propose to keep the Negro in physical, intellectual, and spiritual peonage. When Southerners treat Negroes well, they are "rationalizing their guilt complex," or they want to "rationalize an exaggerated ego" which makes them "contemptibly patronizing" and anxious to retain feudal vestiges of patronage toward inferiors. If they try to explain the economic reasons why social progress has been so slow, they are "rationalizing the *status quo*." If they point out that the heritage of hate left by Reconstruction must not be unearthed again, that view is simply a "rationalized interpretation of history." In the eyes of left-wing reformers, the Southern white finds himself damned if he does and damned if he doesn't. And the Southern Negro leader who tries to approach the problem realistically is equally damned, for he is "rationalizing his own fears and timidity." The new mythology feeds on fiction and finds its "scientific" dogma in the jargon of psychology and not in the realities of historical or observable facts.

In a shrewd appraisal of the social implications of a batch of new novels, Brainard Cheney recently remarked in *The Sewanee Review* (Winter, 1945): "Since the early nineteen-thirties we have had many novels from a cult which, having now given up the Communist party line, has veered, when it has come South, toward a new line in the race problem. I would call the members of this cult, the Prophets of a New Past, the past being overhauled to meet the specifications of some immediate political pressure. Their obvious aim is to increase the force of their socio-political doctrine. . . . The peril brought to us by the

Prophets of a New Past exists less in their aims than in the disarmed credulity of a 'socially conscious' public. By disarmed credulity I mean public ignorance disarmed by information without understanding . . ." Mr. Cheney's statement, with all that it suggests, deserves thoughtful reading by every person anxious to aid the Negro.

The Negro is in greater peril today than he has been in a generation, and for a large measure of that danger he must thank do-gooders whose zeal is equaled only by their lack of wisdom. Race tension is steadily growing more acute. Mutual tolerance in the South that promised so much in understanding a few years ago is disappearing. Southern liberals who hoped and believed that the end of economic and political discrimination against the Negro was in sight are now in despair. The demagogue who thrives on racial hatred has received a full arsenal of fresh ammunition supplied by well-meaning intellectuals, and he is making the most of it. The tragedy that has overtaken Southern whites and Negroes is vividly described in *The Virginia Quarterly Review* (Autumn, 1942) by John Temple Graves, himself an earnest advocate of Negroes' rights. Social scientists who have devoted their lives to bringing about understanding and fair play between the races are at their wits' end. Some of them believe that the problem has been made insoluble as a result of the hysteria engendered by extremists on both sides of the controversy.

By cultivating the myth that Southern whites do not want amelioration of the Negro's condition and have no intention of permitting it, by insisting that the South is inhabited by a generation of moronic poor whites scarcely capable of self-government, by magnifying the belief in atrocities and crimes against the Negro committed as a deliberate policy by Southerners, by maintaining that all the Negro's problems can be solved if the country is sufficiently "aroused," by naïvely believing that social reform can be accomplished overnight by fiat of the national government, reformers are creating an atmosphere of suspicion and hate that has already set back social progress in the South a generation. And the result has fateful implications for both whites and Negroes, not only in the South but everywhere.

Racial peace in the South, and the permanent achievement of the Negro's rights as a free citizen in our democracy, are dependent upon mutual respect and goodwill in the region where white men and Negroes must dwell together. A few years ago that dream seemed to be materializing. The old battle cry of white supremacy, which had kept many a demagogue in office since Reconstruction, had lost much of its potency. Southern liberals could no longer be smeared when they demanded justice for all men regardless of race. The educational base was broadened. Negro schools, in many instances, were brought up to the standard of white schools despite the financial burden upon poverty-stricken states. Provision was made for the professional education of Negroes. Public health was improved. The administration of justice was watched more closely to prevent discrimination against Negroes. Vigilantism and lynching almost disappeared. Even Jim Crowism was slowly changing. Although the South still clung to the theory of segregation, the question could be debated without violence. That in itself was a step forward. Time was on the side of the Negro, and the most intelligent white leaders in the South were abetting time.

That is not to say that the South had suddenly turned pure and had washed all the spots from its racial garment. More than its share of fools has always plagued the country below the Potomac, and none has trumpeted his folly louder than the Negro hater. Some of these remain to shame the white race and trouble the Negroes. They have their full share of blame for keeping the embers of hatred alive. But even in the period immediately after World War I, when race tension mounted for awhile, Ku Kluxism, as a movement against the Negro, found small support and soon died of anemia. Although disgraceful incidents occurred and no one was yet ready to herald the racial millennium, the South was not complacent and public opinion seemed firmly intent upon adjusting balances that had been weighted against the Negro.

Then the war came, and with it an insistent demand that Americans solve their own minority problem before talking too glibly about democracy in the rest of the world. Logic was on the side of the reformers, but government, democratic or otherwise, is not a result of pure reasoning. Democratic government comes by growth, slow growth, and social justice is not a matter of government decree. The Negro press in the North, and white protagonists, screamed for an "all or nothing" solution of the Negro problem—immediately. In their violence against segregation and other injustices, the reformers were indiscriminate, intemperate, and inaccurate. Ignoring the tremendous social gains of this generation, they pictured the South as a realm of mean-spirited fascists, and they hysterically called upon the federal government to take action now. Every reformer had his own prescription, but most of them believed that the remedy was political—and apparently easy. Just pass a law. What law was another matter. Many innocently believed that a law eliminating the poll tax was the prime solution, but others had various legal substitutes. The refrain that ran through all the clamor was that force could accomplish at a single stroke what time had failed to complete.

The insistence upon absolute democracy now, and the naïveté of reformers about the ways and means of attaining the millennium, have alienated the majority of Southern white liberals and the wisest of Southern Negro leaders. After all, they have some respect for the gains already made, and some knowledge of the workings of practical politics. Mindful of Aesop's dog, they do not want to lose the bone they have by grabbing at the reflection in the pool.

As the violence of controversy has mounted, the lunatic fringe of rabble-rousers in the South has improved the opportunity to stir up the poor whites—the Negro's bitterest enemies. But the poor whites are not the only ones who will jettison liberal racial legislation if the North attempts another "force bill." The South is fundamentally the most conservative section of the country. If the Negro pins his faith on radical pressure—especially Northern radical aid—his cause is lost. Upper-class Southerners will then make common cause with the poor whites against what they both will believe to be the common enemy. And conservative Southern Democrats will find an ally in conservative Northern Republicans who have latterly espoused states' rights. German experience in occupied territory ought to prove that not even military power can effectively compel social compliance where majority opinion is solidly united against it. Hate, bigotry, murder, and chaos can result, but social and political progress stop when raw force begins. That knowledge, born of experience when the South was also an occupied territory between 1865 and 1877, makes thoughtful Southerners tremble at the implications of expedients suggested by those to whom the South is a theory and not a complex region of resourceful human beings.

Perhaps much reading hath made the theorists mad. At any rate, they draw conclusions from one another's books and multiply myths which confuse the issues. Every third novelist has become an authority on social relationships, politics, folkways, and mores in the South, though he may never have escaped the sidewalks of Brooklyn. Literary critics devote their columns to the further simplification of a world they know not. To the writing profession, the problems of the South have a moral solution. Everything is clearcut. There are no lights and shades. Justice, they believe, will reign as soon as white consciences are sufficiently aroused. With that spirit of crusade, authors are carrying their torches high. But they have generated more heat than light.

The literary crusade today is not unlike that conducted by abolition writers in the period between 1830 and 1860, and the emotional effect is following a pattern tragically similar. Then, as now, the demand was for an all-or-nothing solution. William Lloyd Garrison in the first issue of the *Liberator* in 1831 announced his determination to procure "the immediate enfranchisement of our slave population," and he asserted with the vehemence of an Old Testament Prophet that he did not intend "to think, or speak, or write, with moderation." Southern writers were not far behind Garrison in the violence of their replies, and soon invective supplanted reason as section was arrayed against section.

The abolitionists, of course, were morally right. Slavery was an abomination, as political and social discrimination against the Negro today is an abomination, but the conditions which the abolitionists described with so much emotion were not the conditions of fact. They created an imaginary South in which the hands of planters dripped with the blood of black slaves. The New England clergy, few of whom knew anything about the South at first hand, described it as a land of moral and spiritual degradation, a slave civilization controlled by tyrants, in contrast to the freedom-loving North. The Reverend Horace Bushnell, of Hartford, Connecticut, one of the more temperate preachers, delivered a sermon in 1854 which described the South as a weak and degenerate section, devoid of literature or learning and even the capacity for these accomplishments, a section notable only for belly-cheer, harangue, and low political trickery. That this picture of the South was typical of the propaganda carried on by the clergy has been amply documented in a dissertation at the University of Chicago by Chester Forrester Dunham.

Professional writers in the North were equally clear as to their duty, and fully as positive in their knowledge. Humanitarians like Whittier, Lowell, and Harriet Beecher Stowe, whose knowledge of slavery was for the most part abstract, taught that compromise with this great moral wrong was wicked, and those who counseled moderation were compounding a felony. After the sensational popularity of *Uncle Tom's Cabin,* an imaginary South became more vividly real to Northern readers than the slums which they experienced visually every day.

Abolitionist writers succeeded in creating a set of fixed ideas, in both

North and South, which had a tremendous influence in preventing a peaceful solution of the slavery question. Placed on the defensive, Southern preachers and writers in their turn equaled—if possible—the intemperateness of the abolitionists. Gradually, between 1830 and 1860, the Southern press and pulpit convinced their public that the North's attack on slavery was an attack on the South itself and upon white civilization there. Southerners who hated slavery came to believe that emancipation by Northern force would be the first step toward turning over the South to the Negroes. Rich whites and poor whites, regardless of economic and social status, believed they had to unite in common defense. That settled conviction welded the South together in 1861, and the persistence of the belief in the North's desire to destroy the white South explains the enduring strength of "white supremacy" as a political issue. So violently did Southerners reply to abolitionists that they convinced themselves and the North—and some historians of the present generation—that war was the only solution. Once emotions on both sides had crystallized, perhaps war was inevitable.

War of course hastened the end of slavery, but if reformers had had the patience to attain that end peaceably—as Great Britain achieved emancipation in the Empire—the Negro would have been saved from later years of hardship and humiliation. And the South would have been spared a grinding poverty that for three generations has prevented adequate education and social advancement for both whites and blacks. The Civil War, which emancipated the Negro, did not solve the problem of how he was to live in peace and justice with his former masters. The follies of punitive Reconstruction and the occupation of the South by Northern armies, made up in part of recently recruited freedmen, left a heritage of hate and suspicion of Northern motives that will endure for generations.

Of late, it has become fashionable among certain writers to insist that the South has deliberately cultivated legends about the horrors of Reconstruction to excuse its continuing discrimination against Negroes, that the Southern view of Reconstruction is merely a rationalization of its desire to perpetuate racial injustice. It is becoming an article of faith that the trouble with Reconstruction was its mildness, that Lincoln's healing policy was foolish, and that the real hero of the period was Thaddeus Stevens, Lincoln's and the South's inveterate enemy. If Stevens' policy of rule by Northern bayonets had only been continued, the millennium would have dawned and the South would have had, presumably, a thousand years of peace and justice, in which the poorer classes, white and black, would have lived in harmony and happiness. That is the implied thesis of Mr. Fast's *Freedom Road,* and it is held as gospel by leftist dialecticians. As Mr. Cheney points out, the doctrine of democracy by bayonet sounds suspiciously like the credos of Herr Goebbels, but apparently that inconsistency can also be reconciled by dialectics.

The new mythology, having relegated Lincoln and his policies to the dust bin, is even more severe upon Rutherford B. Hayes and the liberal Republicans of 1877, who recalled troops from the South. That action, the legend has it, was the result of a slick horse trade between Northern capitalists and Southern aristocrats. For the sake of commercial exploitation of the South, industrialists sold the Negro down the river and delivered him into the hands of his oppressors. This interpretation overlooks the fact that reactionary members of the Republican party opposed the new policy, and that liberal Republicans like Carl Schurz, who had taken the trouble to make a personal investigation of conditions, led the agitation for a restoration of civil power to the South as the only means of insuring the rehabilitation of either Negroes or whites.

The new interpretation of Reconstruction is typical of a school of moralists who would disregard traditions and folkways dealing with the race problem in the South. They would disregard them because they have convinced themselves that traditions have no validity—and perhaps no strength. These conclusions are based, not on facts and realistic observations, but upon the theory of what society in a given area and time *ought to be.*

By ignoring history, and by twisting and distorting historical and contemporary facts in the interest of special pleading, the new mythologists are creating an unreal world in which they will find equally unreal answers to social problems. An imaginary South more vivid than truth itself already exists in thousands of minds. A terrible danger exists for the country as a whole, and for the Negro in particular, because so many sincere people will predicate the actions they advocate on fictitious ideas which they believe to be true.

The manufacture of myths is taking place on all levels, and gathers momentum with each new accretion. In addition to writings which get into print, the present morbid interest in the South is producing an unwritten folklore which achieves fantastic effects. Howard W. Odum has listed hundreds of tall tales in his *Race and Rumors of Race*. Rumor-mongers have been busy during the past four years. How many of the tales have been set in motion by enemy agents, not even the F.B.I. can guess, but some of the agitation clearly bears the mark of homebred or imported fascism. Some of the stories have their source in old abolition-ist propaganda. Professional South baiters, leftist idealists, and ardent humanitarians, pitying the plight of the Negro, find it easy to believe the worst of the South. Professional Southerners on various social levels also contribute to the growing legend. One will relate in a drawing room romantic stories of Negro retainers and feudal patronage in his old home, while another will make the eyes of his tent-mates pop with yarns of lynchings by the dozen, or of horsewhipping Negroes because they wouldn't say "Sir" and tip their hats to every white man. South-erners not only have an affinity with Baron Munchausen, but they also possess a regrettable capacity for supplying the information which the audience expects. If outlanders circulate absurd libels, Southerners themselves supply much of the documentation.

Once a legend has achieved vitality, any bit of evidence, however far-fetched, will help to establish its truth. One strand from the beard of Mahomet preserved at a shrine will make a faithful pilgrim believe all the legends of the Hegira. Travelers in the South are fully as credulous. A young teacher from Chicago, for example, driving with his wife down a street in a Tennessee town, very nearly ran down a Negro. When the driver stopped, the Negro raised his hat politely instead of swearing, as the Chicagoan had expected. But ever since this teacher has boiled with indignation against the South. He firmly believes that the Negro's action was evidence of humiliating servility and fear of white men. No amount of argument will convince him that provincial Southerners, white and black, retain certain old-fashioned manners. That the Negro's conduct was a simple reflex of natural courtesy, and that a white man might have acted the same way, are beyond belief. The legend was so real that this single episode proved to an otherwise scholarly temperament that Southern Negroes all live in constant terror and must tip their hats even when being run down by the white man's juggernaut.

The new legends about the South have acquired such vigor during the past few years that they are creeping into scholarly works and promise to become a part of historical dogma. For example, Gunnar Myrdal's *An American Dilemma*—a work which commands every man's respect for its sincerity and earnestness—loses much of its value because it swallows whole an amazing number of myths and half-truths. No amount of statistics and factual evidence will be able to eradicate "knowledge" cemented into place by the emotions.

The attainment of justice for the Negro in the South, as well as in other parts of the country, is an end that everyone ought to desire. That achievement will require cool-headed wisdom on the part of both whites and Negroes throughout the nation. The surest way to disaster lies in an emotional approach to the problem. Hysterical utterances and misguided actions have already so stirred emotions that there is less likelihood of understanding between North and South today than at any time since Reconstruction.

An atmosphere of hate and distrust unparalleled since the period preceding the Civil War has developed. In this milieu rumor-mongers and myth-makers displace sober scholars and become prophets and soothsayers. The grimmest irony of all is that the Negro, the unhappy theme of controversy, is likely to suffer longer and more tragic humiliation than he might otherwise have expected. But he will not suffer alone. The white race, North and South, will be involved in his ruin.

Being by ceaseless motion
Perpetually transformed,
Cold as the depths of ocean
And yet by friction warmed,

Until I forgot my name,
Forgot the friends above,
And in time's dark well became
The piston plunge of love.

Sea

Brewster Ghiselin

This handful of ocean water clearer than glass
Is like the mind at morning when it lies
Still in the palm of sleep, before it feels
Its forces shoreward combing the green eelgrass,
Fuming sand from the seaground, marshalling a myriad
Glimmering fishlights to mote the glory of the sun.
Even under the cornices of the Poles
The ocean lidded with twilight, dreams monsters,
Hot whales, and the cold creatures that are mostly water—
But all are issue of the dust. The clear
Water here in my hand is full of dust,
Dissolvings of life and death: powder of fire
And sea-born earth returned to the using sea.
And used, will banner the tide with long algae
And thousand every drop with diatoms,
Will star and urchin, will lion the bald rock.
The sea lion sleeks its face in the kind sea.
I too, the shoreling man, have not forgotten.
Scatterings of skull with the shards and shattered shells
Of the headland lie with their kind. Out of the sea
That fed it, the domed abalone colored with calm
Of westward morning on the ocean; out of the sea
The skull that was gilled in its mother's belly; out of
The sea of sea-born mind the shell-like shard
Rippled on the rim by man's benthonic thumb.
And once far inland in a humming room
I saw my love undressed to the bone before me,
And in its lattice cage, that undersea
Creature, her living heart, dancing its tide.
I will go down to the ocean when I am dead,
Will ocean my ash, marry my dust to the water
That thought of us. For I see that we are the ocean
Walking the land with feet of the dust. We are use:
As much as the sea worm coiled like a stone snake

In the tidal pool, crested like ancient Mars,
A clouding of the crystal of the sea.

And I have not forgotten how the shark rolls
Feeding, while the kind sea sluices his smile,
Nor the killer whale's brief breath, hot pluff of fog
Stinking of flesh. With eyes brine-blurred I have seen
A bag of jellied death in the undersway.
And I have smelled carrion on the high hills.
O long snore of the fortress going over
With snouts that will rootle in the flesh of cities!
The brass-bright dolphins of the cerulean mind
Lie by the cannon, fettled for our thought
Whose smoky flaw pushes them where we will.
Slowly the buzzards circle to decision;
Heavying, they drop, bouncing like injured airplanes
Beside the heap the hot sun cooks for them
And the maggots dolphining in the dust.

II

When armies walk, sometimes in the dry of the earth
Their wheels smoke dissolution like a banner
Before them flown or after or candled high,
The flaunt of all their trackless history,
Their powdery past, their secret yet-to-be.
And like that banner slacked along the waves
Is the mortal stain rolling upon a coast
Of rainy storm. Mix of the cloudy land
With roil of nameless slime and chyme of weed
And sea worms' houses crushed, riffles and churns.
In that chaos the pride of death is downed
Like a streamer that has floated awhile.
And any swimmer in the finishing chop
Will feel his joints smoother with fear, may feel
His courage warm his throat like frosty mint
While dark under his breast the glidings suck.
For there, below him, the filled ditch of sleep.
Therein no coming gleams. What treasures pearl
The bottom of the waves? His dream shall fathom.

But in the dawn his soul swims back to him,
With hands like fins and seadepth eyes staring
And lips that drink the brine. Perhaps it swam
In circles in the deep. Perhaps it found
The floor-end precipice, and looked and looked.

From that old landend that keeps Dana's name
But not the shape he found in his century,
Pale sift simooms in summer; in the winter rains,
Conglomerate comes down and an earth stain—
And sometimes flowers. All round it the busy sea.
No silence trembles in those bouldered halls
We dare in calm but the sea's silken fret.
We hear the crumbling of a century,
Or an eternity. But when we shake
The fires and shadows from our eyes and climb
Over the cliffs, we find some things that came
Out of these crumblings: sage, and pointed grass,
And sometimes flowers. There sometimes the octopus-eyed
Rattlesnake glides in the leisure of his venom,
His scales whispering; a beetle prints
His stipple in the dust. And a clawed creature
Standing with dangling hands stares at the south
Rolling the midday waste of riding fires.

I have walked in a vineyard by the cliff
And break of the long land over the long
Monotonies: there eating the ripe grapes
I have held remembrance in my ears:
When I lay down for sleep by the gray shade
Under the vines, my face against the dry,
I heard a sound like bees. Till my love came
Walking against the light, and shaded me.
This was that afternoon when first I traced
Her lineage to the foam, while her hair flowed
Like summer wind over her throat and mine.
We wished never to die. By the grape's blood,
The too-lush tendril clipped, the aphid crushed,

The steady vanishing of the water's flash;
By shapes and vanishings: shapes, vanishings . . .
We heard salt rushings on the prow of land.
Lying as if in sleep, perhaps we slept.
And heard planes, drummings shaking the floor of sleep.

III

What shapes are rising in the earth? Windwaked
They walk on the hills, or in tall columns on
The talus plains, hurled up a stairless height,
Hang . . . trackless. . . . The ropes of chaos wind
And unwind over the world: atomic ghosts,
Blown leaves of lost letters of embassy
Bleached of their use, blind increment far drawn.
Is not all blown into those sucking wells?
I have seen the fieriest moment of a life
Fading, gold smear upon the mind, sea-shine
In the sludge of night, along the edge of sleep.

How many cry, If it were really so! ,
If these were not sea fruits with tight juices
The air will dry to a difference. O if we too
Were not the thing we are, then we might be
Like idols that need not fear the rainy jungle,
Stilled in some sweet unequaled attitude
Timelong like stones. So we inherit those
Brown nomads of the rusty-colored earth
Who heaped hard walls, their new Jerusalem,
Precious shelter, out of the way of time.

It is long since first the sea sent up beyond
Its margin ambassadors to the courts of death,
To the stand and stillness germinal unrest
In shells of form, creatures of earth but also
Of the waves' vagaries. Breathers of change,
How did they learn to love the unflowing rock
And found their houses there? Why do they choose
The heresy of stone? Even where they hide

They hear the cry wiser than hope mounding in,
And run to pray in their dry citadels
Against their breath, their blood, and the ways of their dances.

                                    •

Beautiful is the body of the brown world,
Idol out of the blue vague of the sea.
Great plains are under the oiled hooves of riders,
Morning breezes trample the scent of grain
To the red hills with the passes blue among them,
And clouds beyond are watching the unknown earth
Their shadows stain. And no wall of an ending,
Only the halt in the dusk by the poppy fires
And dawns of discovery under a setting star.
What is my life before me? How shall I say
Except that I feel the horizons under my breastbone?
We race all day in the open world till evening
And when the embers click and the acid crickets
Are loudening we lean to our sleep. And at last descend
The valley of home, trample the heels of memory,
The ash we scattered to the morning star.
O dry sound of our hands then on the walls
At morning as we stroke the doorframe thought!
Beautiful to us therefore the winds' violence,
The lifted modulations of the dust,
The dry hills that are called everlasting
Vague in the veils of their mortality.

IV

In bowls of the foamless ebb I saw the water
Rolling the home of one of its old aspects;
The skull clicked on the rocks, emptier than when
Loaded with jellies it played business or love.
And plucked from the wash, sluiced of its drink, it seemed
Too draughty a home even for the butterfly
That flitted from it to the Elysian fields.
I dropped it back, to cradle in the rocky shallow.
Once universe poured through it freely as there
The sea-gush slid or while it lay too slight

In hand the loose wind. Dead or alive,
Brimming ambiguous music like a shell,
What is it but a husk of whispers? And they?
It sighed to me: "I grieve to think how I wasted,
When I was dressed in delight, my dearth of hours
In being so careful to shun both pain and filth.
I would be glad, having the brown dung
Daubing my flesh or blood flowing from it—
Now I am a clicking system of reminders."
I answer it: Be silent. Your voice, too,
Is the sigh of a dream, irrelevance of my heart
Because I have turned away my ears from the sea.
The grieving is all my own, the cry of regret
Is mine, because I am detained by dreams:
This one, of afterdeath, and all those thousands.

Up the clogged shallows of a long inlet
Lagooned in ooze that slows the sweetening tide,
Who dreams the tidal wave, the tiger sea,
And fears the swirl of doubt around his knees?
Has he not seen dead time in heaps of shell
On any strand, or from the broken rock
The fluted stones emerge into the sun
And sure abrasive of the winds' feathering?
Beneath his terror housed on crumbling piers
I hear the music of the ceaseless shore.
And the out-tide and the in-tide of his heart.

Who dreams of Truth, of immortality,
Of forms to live forever? Nor shall he lie
Uncounted in the exchequers of dust.

Let him be comforted. I will unbind
The ringing dreams from his scared ears and he
Shall listen to the water at its work,
The washings of sleep under him, shorespeech, sloshings,
Garbling his little errors till he can hear
All blend, smooth to the diapason Sea.

V

What is the sea? The gray cartographer,
Who always loved her single blue, can tell:
The universal pool, melt of the world,
That rounds the tetter of our care with smooth.
And he who rivered all his freshet days
To irremediable salt believes he knows.
The child too, dabbling in the instant wave.
And the anemone, beaten with foam?
What is the sea, lensed to the moray brain
Whose life is hunger, whose reach is tipped with teeth?
(As ours is delicately thorned with thought.)
And to the swimmer daring the sunward blaze
Beneath unbuttressed light, the unvaulted nave,
Taking into his mouth the salt and fire
Of noon enormous as the nestling's autumn?

I will not believe only the desperate midden,
Though all its references are to the sea
I cannot disbelieve. I will not dig
In the black heap to find tomorrow, narrow
As the long flint, the bird with folded wings
That hissed in flight, the testimonial fang,
That dolphins there. I will believe the sea.
It horned the desert hills with ammonites
Before there were hands in Egypt or the moon
Shone upon Ashtoreth. Persisting whisper,
It breathes in all conspiracies of dust.
It breathed the wave that wrote, as for a sign
On the white sand, the tendrils of her hair.

Who can foretell what forms? Before us lie
Horizons empty as the heart's expectation
On the shore of morning; the sea's clear promises,
Until the end. If end. Our language questions
Mainly itself, a tangled theorem spread
Straining in the ambassadorial tide
To take the visible shoals that swarm our shores.

And all those names are lies: the gannet's bath,
The Pacific, the Dark, the User. That sea is not
What we believe, but something past belief;
And what we love most is its cry of escape
Out of our categories as it names
Forever with new names for namers' ears
Itself: itself. O word, where is thy sting?
I stood alone, hearing the sea drain down
Like memory around the established rocks
And flood enormous present up the shore,
I heard the antiphonal death and birth of waves
Covering silence like membranes lying over
Immanifest undoubted life. I thought
Of music heard in the night: beneath my head
The heart of one I love, the ways of the sea,
Epithalamion and threnody,
The music of the water and the dust,
And silence under every syllable.

Achilles and the Tortoise

Parker Tyler to Zeno the Eleatic

Divine gadder and impetuous starter:
Late, late Achilles! treading so naïvely
    Indissuadibly to win
Over the Tortoise, that glib Narcissus
Whose image unlike the deceiving earth's
    Seems actually to spin,

Why have you not ended it, not dropped out?
The lights are gone in the black arena
    Where performs the white striver
And your banal enthusiasm hears only
The perpetual echo of the Future
    Greeting the cliché Arriver.

Ah suitor laden with your flowers of sweat,
Your plexus rushes recklessly forward
    On such trim passionate feet
I am amazed that you stay rationally
Intent upon the vision of the laurel
    On the head of your Defeat:

That one whose interest is solely to exchange,
To have thrived somewhere on good good ground
    Where lush, allergic You
Have never spent an overflowing day
Or deathless, undocumented year
    That speed has thrust you through.

Adorable stretcher, immortal Second!
Those irresistible quick cities
    Whose exact mazes have been
Puzzles solved in an infinite saunter
And that country, the landscapes of leisure,
    Whose business man is Green,

Have been kind to you, stubborn Achilles . . .
They've allowed you to cultivate passions
  Though you are not a success,
And with your nude knee to knock on that doo·
At the back of All Time, to which you offer
  The heel of your Address.

In this world of immovability
And movement, what toe is Deed at the hour
  When all is coincident?
To Become is to Unbecome in this
Mêlée where the Kiss is the first and chief,
  The tactless instrument!

Yet kindness is so often worse than death
And that Victory naked in pure space
  For whose hot arms you'd die
Is a mere Venus of the Commonplace
Nor can she of the famous wings of stone
  Help you cold runner to fly.

And when life seems as fast and furious
As the improvidently precise poem
  Even you will not achieve
The sweet synonymity of the leg
Whose beautiful partner never, never
  Egotistically shall grieve

By pools which a ravishing You have passed.
My gratified desire to participate
  In your subtle deficit,
O loser! sustains me in attempting
That endless energy disreputable
  That is found germane with wit.

The poem's provoking paradise ah!
Balances on a perilous axis
  Its forever too suave
Dichotomy of movement and the Tortoise

Whose mistaken advantage is Hearsay
　　Finds his position grave.

O terrible dilemma of my own
Alert to that exotic accident
　　When the insanely humble
Machine that is Achilles shall affront
The End ahead of schedule, and logic
　　Finally shall stumble.

O feet iambic and derisive dactyls!
Assuage with your Achillean headlong
　　This sweat that rims my brow
Where the Tortoise projects the monstrous and
Indispensable sophistries of his
　　Harsh Einsteinian prow.

Is there no shape for these shapes and rhymes to fill
No single, uncompetitive Torso
　　In whose mounted, rhythmic heart-
Beats Time divests himself and naked crouches
Beneath the Future's ears and listens for
　　The fired imperative: Start?

For Art is no laggard, my Achilles,
And your spectacle of exhausted beauty
　　Drooping its spine over space
And seeing the mutually depleted
Tortoise and his tape-breaking breast
　　Like a tear-broken face

Is no joy to poet or to reader:
O magic identities! O confession!
　　This is the truant myth
That moves steadily out of the page and
Blossoms into the air the dead-heat of
　　My music's monolith.

Frank and the Vagrant Woman
Katherine Hoskins

Crossing a saddle-back in the Himalayas,
ferrying gas to Chiang Kai-shek,
Frank-Pilot looked across the brown
velours desert to where the mountains
foamed and flew like crested clouds
in winds of the world's end.
Then down to a peak that rose from the plain
below him—furze-dark at base and stripped
to rock above, too low for snow;
as if small, so alone in the desert.
Seeing it single like himself
amid tumultuous repetition,
Frank-Pilot always thought, 'Ah, here we are,'
between the cross-chops of the Himalayas.

He'd greeted the peak and slid on North
by West when he saw he'd seen a thing
in movement on it, moving up it.
And he'd reached the first low breakers
of the range before he told himself
that he, Frank-Pilot, could go back
as well as forward, or around if he chose.
'I choose,' he thought, and banked and swung
around the peak and saw and blinked
and wheeled around again and waved.
"Do you see what I see?" he called through the phone.

"You're crazy," they answered, "get on with the trip."

"I always hankered to see her again,
sassy and vagrant, gat-toothed and brown
as the saddle on her flea-bitten dan. Look—
she's riding right up to the top and down
the other side—smart like an ant.

I thought I'd forgotten—but, God, it's like now.
'Name?' says John at police headquarters.
'Virtue,' says she, and wouldn't give another
for laughs or curses. 'Virtue's enough,' says she.
'You can't write that on the blotter,' says John,
'I give you an hour to get out of town.'
I showed her the way, her talking along
about all the classier joints than ours
they'd thrown her out of; me not saying,
Lady, how did you get *into* them?
I want to see how she's made out."

"Not with us."
                        and
                    "Damn right not."

He jumped it fast before they could lay
him out for his own good as well as for theirs.
And all they could do was see that his parachute
opened all right and he'd picked himself up
and was running across the desert. They flew low
but he didn't look up. So they radioed back
his position and went on with their job for Chiang.

It was hot down here on the plain and Frank
stopped running soon and walked. It was farther
than he'd thought, the desert rougher.
But he kept on and when he reached
the peak's base, there he was—
face to face with the old woman.
"Hello," he said.
                        "Hello," said she,
"right nice of you to stop." The burro
sighed as the girth came loose and fell,
then yawped piano at the sky
and wandered off to graze. Virtue
stroked its rump and turned to Frank.
"This looks as good a place as any

for a picnic." He reached for his packet,
but, "I can't stand K-ration," she said.
"What did one governor say
to the other?" She unhooked a skin from the saddle
and drank and handed it to Frank.
It was fire-water and his eyes wept,
but once it was down he felt great.

"I wanted to ask you about the war,"
he said, though knowing that was not
the reason why he'd jumped.

> "What war,
Frank?"
> "The one I'm in—our war."

"I can't use plurals, our and their.
For me, there's you and he and you're
in several wars. One with yourself
and one with the world, to name only two."
She was stretched beside him against the saddle,
trickling fire-water down her throat.
'This old dame's not quite as funny
as I thought,' he thought. 'I'd better
mind my manners.' She was saying,
smiling kindly, smiling sadly,
('and a sight better looking,' he observed.)
"But I suppose it's the war that gave you
a nice warm uniform and taught you
guns and motors interests you.
I'll tell you, I like a fight as well
as another. And I like soldiers, especially
amateurs. *But* between you and me
and the Himalayas, I can't tell one war
from another. So there's no good asking me."

"It don't seem very important now,"
he said. "Do you want some chocolate?"

"Thanks, and you needn't go slow on the liquor.
It never gives out and you won't get too drunk."

"Your voice rings," Frank said. "It's like
a bell, a golden bell and various."

"Are you from the South?" she laughed. "You mean
my voice isn't old and cracked like me."

"It's more like what I always thought
you'd be. It's more like what I see
if I shut my eyes and listen to you talk
and say your name."

                    "You're thinking of Goodness,
maybe, or Innocence. They've stayed young—
took care of themselves. When we were girls
together, though—us and Chastity—
people couldn't tell us apart.
The holy men loved Chastity so much
they shut her up—a loss to all.
I still see Goodness and Innocence now
and again. And, as you said or I said,
they're a lot easier to look at than me.
But they stayed home and got their ten hours
every night. We're all immortal
but we work by human rules.
                    "And you see,
a woman's life depends on the kinds
of men she likes. My tastes are strong.
And it's only men with the strongest taste
like me, can stand me around at all.
And that's not just since I got old.
When I was soft and apple-breasted,
I was a hellion. But I lived in style.
O, I've known great fellows through the ages;
and once I talked correct iambics, rhymed,
though lately I've enjoyed the vulgate.
But mind you, I'm no leveling snob.

I like kings as well as pilots,
if not so often.
     "There's one thing all of you
have in common," she went on, munching chocolate,
"like the only thing you find
to say to me of a sunny morning,
'How's the war?' From Adam on
you think that when you clean your eyes
of filth you'll see me right away
all dressed in gold and standing with you.
Me—one of the back-room gang.
You all think just because you're running
fast to chop each other's heads off
that I will gallop, too,
to make things right again
and better than they were before.
I have to go my gait, the same as you."

"Couldn't you make it a little faster?
take the trouble to use a car?"

"Make more contacts, eh?" she grinned.
"I'm no salesman. Those who want
to talk to me have got to look
and use their eyes and use their ears.
As a matter of fact, I once had wings
but I went no faster than I go on the dan,
and no farther, either."

    "I'm glad I saw
you, ma'am," he said.

    "It's to your credit,"
she agreed.

    "It seems too bad,
that now you have to take a chance
of finding someone in a desert.
Old times, I guess, you lived in a palace

and had your pick of all the big shots.
I mean," he limped, as her face grew stern,
"the big shots are dead and gone
and we're small guys, small and bad."

"It doesn't take a great belief
in God to believe that the spirit of man
lives on. Can you think the spirits
of all the men I've known are *not*
alive? humanly, for this world?
And you aren't so bad—you living now.
To bear survival is to bear
the bitterest burden of them all. You're
each survivors of more wars
than you can count. Wars that happened
so far back only the blood of them
rings in your ears, and with no sense.
And there're your own wars, plural and singular.
You do all right, you survivors.

"It's not friends dying makes me sad
but thinking of the lives my friends have lived.
'Virtue is her own reward' they've said
and meant, I bring no presents.
They've sworn, good fellows, that having me
is enough to have. But I know better.
I'd have liked to heap on one at least
the riches of the world and health and gaiety."

"They don't complain, I guess," said he.

"Not they. But I complain for them
and for myself as well. I might
have had more friends if peoples' lives
had been a little easier. Your manners
and my vanity aside, my dear,
though I've been deeply loved upon occasion,
I've never been exactly popular."

He didn't so much see her younger
now as that he felt himself
increased in sight by several centuries.
As if he'd come that little nearer
through the mists that men like him
had wrapped her in. He saw her clearer.
'I wish I'd worked a little more
alone,' he thought, 'not let things drift.
She'd not have had to jape and play
the comic crone to make me listen.'
"I feel there's a lot to ask and say,"
he said, "but I'm so sleepy."

"Sleep then and ask the questions
of your dreams. They often answer.
I'll go talk with the burro here."
She laid his head in the sway of the old
McClellan and placed her blue cloak over him.
And Frank, grown big in happiness,
stretched out as if his pillow were
a mountain, his own peak close
beside his head as if his hand could rest on it.
And suave the sky that wrappered him.
Frank-Hero slept
while that great woman gossiped with her beast
and picked off berries from the twigs
between its gentle lips.

Deep deep deep Frank fell
through waves of sleep and never reached
a bottom, but floated on the black
and rhythmic surge in peace
and with no thought. Contentment liquefied
his bones and brain and made him part
in little and in large of that vast sea
that tosses up the rudely wakened
children on our shores and into which
all men wade nightly to renew their strength,

in which they drown at last.
                Then up
he rose till just himself again
and dreaming, he drove a new sedan
between the deserts down a fine straight road.
The deserts crowded him like lions
and Oklahoma City waited
at the end, a doom of towers
tied with neon cords while terror
shone from red lights and an orange sunset.
Then the stranger, known and unknowable,
lover or angel, spoke.
Hilarious courage staved off the deserts
and were they to die or lunch in the towers?
and what did it matter so long as they laughed
on the way? so long as the stranger could speak.
"O, *what* did you say?" and Frank awoke,
sweet violence in his throat and sweetest
wanting languid through his bones.
His peak was soft and rosy in the sunrise.
Invisible a great bee droned
like summer flies. And the woman's smile
admitted she had not spent all
the night conversing with her dan.
He held up his arms to catch her close
again as she approached.

                "I want
the saddle now," she said, "your friends
are near." The bee had swelled into a plane
and bumbled loud. Frank hid his face
and struggled for the saddle.

              "Don't go,"
he cried. "I've just begun, I've just
begun. How can you leave me now?"

"So well begun, you'll do alone."

"O, ma'am," he cried, "O girl, don't go."

Mounted now, the reins slack-gathered
in one hand, she leaned a little
over him and touched his cheek.
"I've stayed quite long enough to ruin
you for many practical pursuits.
We'll likely meet again, my dear."
The plane was circling lower and she tossed
her long blue cloak at it in waves.
The blue folds hid her face
and then fell from it, obscured it
and cleared once more. And Frank beheld
her beautiful and shiny, like a goddess.
And very big and also far away.

So far away, so suddenly—.
Stumbling and weeping, he pursued her.
"O girl, stay with me. Stay with me, my love."
And as he ran and yelled, her golden
voice rang against his heart.
"Come quietly, Frank-Hero.
Easy does it." He stopped
and watched her cross the plain
and mount the nearer hills beyond;
stood at attention for the mild
glow that marked her passage.
He pushed his hand across his eyes
as if to seal the sight within,
then turned and met his friends.

Science Prolonged It . . .

Mary Owings Miller

. . . so they cling like sleet, close-woven on a wall;
   not glistening in remembered glory of sun
     but simulating life as an icy vine
       with fragile tendrils grasping its host,
        end and beginning as one.

Newsprint is for criminals or heroes: not for these.
   Attic space shelters random odds and ends:
     horsehair of neglected histories.
       Daguerreotypes move stiffly into life:
        a gold canary sings in the cage of day.

Years have moved forward as a processional:
   Oh Promise Me soothed the fever of a child.
     Letters crackle with the drying sound
       of twigs on a hearth, black as hunger, and sharp
        as silence around . . .

Familiar as lines which furrow cheek and chin
   are row-tenement halls, stale as anxiety,
     where the kilowatt, repulsive as tepid tea,
       spills over the jaundiced features of the lost.
        (Perhaps a rope when the final egg is boiled.)

White as the thought of money earned and spent,
   they move on slow cobbles to the afternoon store
     where the silken past is draped on the wax of today.
       Chiclet-courtesy dims when one cannot pay:
        pride is deflated as the empty purse.

Roan racers, finished, find freedom in windy grass,
   the old stag heeds the challenge of the young
     who seeks leadership: and it will come to pass.
       Once the arc completes its fullest swing
        from nursery to tenement-hall

there is little choice: examine charity:
　grudging crumbs of acceptance in Mobile,
　　thin-soup whinings of a niece in Kankakee.
　　　If the gray-head seeks gas-oven-solace then
　　　　it's of less importance than any sport bulletin.

The Problem of Evil

Robert Daniel

Joseph on the saffron beach
  Allays the pangs of Mrs. Jones
And party of friends, by serving each
  With damp hotdogs and ice-cream cones.

Across the sands the purple hills
  Look where the purple waves are flashing.
The Joneses' daughter Betsy shrills
  To see her little dachshund splashing.

Poor Joe—her brother Herbert cheats
  Him coolly of a hard-earned quarter;
Poor Betsy too, for Herbert eats
  Her dinner while she's in the water.

Their mother lacks the granite stare
  Of Dr. Jones, to end such broils.
In town beside his dentist-chair
  He stands, and lucratively toils.

He would have served her in her need,
  For Frankie Abrams soon indulges
His love of sport by punching Sneed,
  Whose temple throbs, whose muscle bulges!

Their bodies closed in hard embrace,
  They grunt and wriggle in the sands
While Sneed smites Frankie on the face.
  The ladies shriek and wring their hands. . . .

Half-shadowed by her pink umbrella
  Nell Clark, meanwhile, hears none of this:
Too busy with her ardent fellow
  And the postponement of his kiss.

Now he has reached her sun-warmed throat,
  And should she be enticed to crawl
Beneath yonder overturned lifeboat
  She will be served before nightfall.

I saw, where teeming ocean joins
  The earth that these my kin divide,
Their hunger and increasing loins
  By thousand thousands multiplied.

From glowing sands their voices rise
  Until the ancient silence spills
Its dusk, and turns their soon-cold eyes
  To the hills, the everlasting hills.

Sentimental Aesthete

Bernard Heringman

The symmetry of pain foreshadows peace
Upon this violent room; exacts most tender
Reckoning of fears, and promises release
In the impassioned agony of surrender.

Out of this madness, unknown fingertips
Pluck living music, that the heart may yield
New harmony with the service of the lips,
New singing in a throat shattered and healed.

Pain bears the colors of its patron sorrow,
The saturated hues of flesh and blood,
The stark texture of life, which art must borrow
Of love, to achieve compassion's wisest mood.

The still earth will continue to revolve;
The infant wheels, the minute cogs, will mesh;
All sizes level when they come to solve
The final ambiguity of flesh.

Begin each stanza with some startled pain,
And make each rhyme a further mystery.
But let the maze be raveled soon again;
Let the patient rise and once more plainly see.

Let him take profit of his pain, conspire
With all the arts, and love, and they with him
Reap life from waste, as we build light in fire,
To save from burning what was dry and dim.

Negro Spiritual
Perient Trott

Sable is my throat
golden the cable
golden the column of its sound—
firm, my transplanted feet
upon this soil—
deep, my roots

I am the sounding board
the maker of songs—
mine, the folk song of America!
Sensitive, my transplanted feet
to the rhythm of the earth:
deep, my roots
in the somnambulant greatness
of the earth
in the nostalgia
of my race
in the drama
of my people
uprooted
dispossessed
transplanted—
the song of America
wells full-bodied
in my throat . . .

I am the maker of songs
the voice of colony
the folk song of empire

Oh, sable is my throat. . . .
golden, the rich cable. . . .
rich, the column of my song!
Sable, sable!
Golden, golden!

Oh, sable is my throat!

A Day by the Sea

Charles Edward Eaton

I

ATHLETE ON THE BEACH

This opulent day lids his eyes
One gold-weight nearer to a sleep;
Sun is leafing shoulder and thighs
With light-drapes diaphanous but deep.

So will the bright months gild the throat
And socket with bronze the muscled stance.
The metallic crisped hair, the remote
Haze of the head, the amber glance

Will make a statue to the sun.
And light will delta in his veins
Spreading until its rays have spun
An artifice through blood and brains.

II

CACTUS

This ochre fountain of copper root
Has struck through quartz and granite vein,
Blading the air with thorned volute
On hot bright beaches of no-rain.

No haze of heat can wilt the skin,
Weatherless, closed, glazed-stiff, and hard,
With liquid topaz lying in
The fibers of the yellow sward.

From sandy core of blistered dune,
Camel-humped to craze the burning eye,
Cool shafts through withering press of noon
Lift water prickings toward the sky.

Unsweating in the bronze of sun,
The spines toward evening lapse in light,
And coolly plume, one by one,
Slow gouts of silver in the night.

III

O SWIMMER

O swimmer, poised on a spur of rock with the fingers of the spray
Curling around your thighs, wind twisting the wave in a sparkling
    stream
Over the tan ripple of your muscled reaching—As you dive into my
    dream

Of a pure, expansive, and lucent day,
The water is struck with ecstatic opening, and the underswell
Brings from the depths of mind, where your lithe arms sway, the golden
    murmuring of an underwater bell.

IV

THE CATCH

When his brown hands tense, the rod sways and spouts a silver line,
Cast from the tight coil. Then the taut snap, the sudden churning,
The nervous throbbing, the lessening pull, the last fine

Probing of the green water-curtain of sensation. When the hands, deft
    and conclusive, give

An inward turn to the reel, the wound in the water, where the bright
    fins thrashed, closes—
The pulsing in the fingers fades, and the line moors limply a blue
    flaccid shadow floating in the wave.

V

IN LIGHT OF NOON

Now, dripping from the water rise, and let the image in you rise.
Now set the bronzed and muscled foot upon the sand,
And, closing fingers, make a strigil with the hand
To scrape the clinging water from your chest and thighs.

And where the water falls, stand tall, and of your burnished length
Make a pole for this uncertainty of space.
Division will not lacerate the sense, and in this place
Your nudity is beauty and your strength.

Crystals in the sand reflect the light of hard intent,
And noon will let no shadow free;
Between the sultry mountains and the blinding sea:
This genesis of body with its image blent.

VI

SONG OF PASSAGE

This passing love, the islands sing,
That in the streaming wave their shadows float,
Their driftage to an image fling,
An image near and then remote,

A moment pure and then diffuse
As waves spread toward the jutting towers
Of isles, beyond, where branches loose
Upon the tide a maze of flowers.

Like motion of our blood, the sea
Drowns every image in its flow;
This wash of sky and flower and tree
Gathers the forms of all we know

Into the mingle of rich wake,
Deep in an underwater fate,
And dissolution seems to take
The world until all tides abate.

When wind is still, an image clear
Burns in the calm from shore to shore,
A leaf, a flower untrembling near
The brink where islands are no more.

VII

THE DRAWING-IN

Now amethyst is evening sky
And all the palm trees shaggy-bright;
Athwart the sun, late-lucent, I
Await the inward sweep of night.

The sea gulls slanting on mauve wing
Follow the violet drawing-in;
Thickening to gray, the warm fogs bring
Dusk's phosphorus feel upon the skin.

Arm and rope in a silver twist,
The lean young men pull in the haul;
The fish pant in their horny fist
Till flashing fins, quiescent, fall.

This is an hour of landward flow,
Of light and life and thought withdrawn:
A fading from the rim, a glow
Contracting toward the source of dawn.

At last the scrolls of darkness rise,
Swooned-swift from islands of the day,
And dash, wind-flung, before my eyes
The white catharsis of the spray.

VIII

THE AWAKENING

Come in from the veranda, away from noise of the spray
Clouding the air with nirvana. All night and forever the moon will
    climb
Beyond the tenuous arms of the soul, and desire, white-stepped, must
    enter time

Once more even as now you turn into the warm horizontal of my
    hands that offer day.
I shall be tender with a slow sunrise ease of touch until the night
Of the body trembles with morning, your lips return the first full kiss
    of light.

STORIES

The Guide
Andrew Lytle

THE BIG CAR ROLLED SMOOTHLY INTO THE NIGHT. The sharp bright smudge of the headlights slid under the darkness with mathematical exactitude. Dressed in his hunting clothes, the boy sat beside his uncle and watched the road. He sat rather stiffly. His new boots, greased by his mother, prodded the boxes of shells piled carelessly onto the floor of the car. He was not comfortable. The shells gave him no easy rest for his feet, his clothes were strange in their bulk, and he could not make up his mind how to act with his Uncle Bomar. This was to him at the moment the most serious matter in the world. He tied himself into knots thinking about it. He rather felt that the childish deference to an elder was out of place now that they were going hunting together, and not merely hunting but to the Lake for ducks. The invitation was plainly Bomar's way of accepting him as a man. Bomar did not take boys duck shooting. Quail or dove hunting, but never duck. He had begged too often not to know. The boy felt that at last he was ready for a man's pleasures and responsibilities. This thought made him all the more anxious to behave as he should. This and the way his mother had seen them off.

But how was he to behave? Nobody had told him, just as nobody had told him what it meant to put on long pants. His mother had cried, his father had asked the cost, his grandfather had spouted Latin about the *toga virilis*. And his Brother Bob, all he had said was, "Keep it buttoned up, kid." "Of course I'll keep buttoned up," he had answered with shame and petulance, thinking only of the technical handling of the clothes. He knew at once he had made a mistake, even before he saw the smirk on his brother's face. Suddenly the long months of expectation, at last realized, turned bitter under his tongue and he did not know rightly why. Vaguely and with confusion it came to him how narrow had been his understanding of what he had wanted. His wish had been little more than to masquerade in grown-up clothes. But the fact was another thing. Changing clothes had changed him. He felt the same and yet he was not the same. For days it puzzled him how this could be, then he gave it up as he grew accustomed to his new condition, but for a while longer he carried about him a feeling of unease. This made him sensitive and timid, so that he would cross over to the other side of the street rather than speak to someone he had known all his life.

The car took a curve. From the darkness a large stock barn with white doors appeared, disappeared. A board fence made a slapping noise as they passed down its narrow lane. He watched the posts go down like piles. The air sucked in, the fence was gone, and he knew they were entering poorer country.

"Tommy phoned me they were coming in in big flights," Bomar said "Had been for two days."

The boy stiffened in his seat, thinking desperately hard what reply a sportsman would make to such an important statement. The moment of his indecision dragged interminably, so that he blurted out, "You reckon they'll still be there?" His cheeks burned with shame at the over-eager, inadequate words.

"If the weather holds," Bomar replied in his slow, unexcitable voice. "It's got to be cold enough for the streams and back water to freeze over before the ducks come on to the Lake in any number. It's pretty cold. I expect they'll be there."

The boy leaned back in his seat. His uncle had answered him seriously. His question no longer seemed to him childish and ineffective. He even recovered from the humiliation of the leave-taking, his mother following them to the car, pulling his scarf about his neck, telling him not to get shot, not to take cold and to promise her, if his feet got wet, to tell the man to row him in, a few ducks is not worth pneumonia. . . . Great God, Effie, the boy's going duck shooting, not to the North Pole. He had been grateful for Bomar's words then. He was more grateful now. They had not meant regret for asking him to come along. Maybe Bomar, too, knew what it was to be hindered by the solicitude of women.

The older man reached up and turned on the car's spot. He played it about the countryside, objects in the rough fields, then set it to the center of the road. The headlights swelled to a new fulness and the car took up speed. "A spot is a good thing to have in the country," Bomar said, as if his gesture needed some explanation.

"It sure is," the boy replied.

His uncle had turned as he spoke, turned easily, almost lazily, and yet all his movements showed perfect coördination. The boy felt a slight shock of surprise. His uncle was not so old a man as he had always thought, or rather he had never thought about his age at all. He had been Uncle Bomar, his mother's younger brother, sometimes whispered about in the family, but one of the opposition nevertheless who stood for authority, dullness, and obstacles to freedom. Except that he had never been so dull as the others. He had threatened older boys with Bomar's name and he would always let you go along to pick up doves. And Bomar had taken time to teach him how to shoot. He looked at the older man's eyes as if for the first time. They wore a look of furious haste which seemed out of keeping with his fleshy cheeks. As the boy looked more closely, it seemed to him that the fury had grown cold and the haste had set like the film over the racer's pupils as he is being led from the track, blinded to the shouting in the stands, to winning and losing, to all but the burning strain of the race and the gorged heart.

Bomar said, "You had better take that heavy coat off. You won't feel it in the morning. It gets cold as hell out on that Lake."

Hastily the boy took off the coat, for the second time thinking bitterly of his mother, whom he had allowed in his ignorance to dress him as she had once done for parties and Sunday school, as if the whole affair were no more than a fashion parade. His uncle wore his good clothes. Hunters changed for the Lake after they got there.

"How do you think you will like it, kid?"

"Oh, fine," he said hastily. "I've always wanted to go. Old Jake used to tell me about grandfather Laus going there. He said he went in a wagon and it took him two weeks to go, and he always stayed two or three weeks hunting and fishing. Jake said he was a little boy, and they took him along to gather up fat pine and keep the fires."

"It's quite a difference these days," the older man said.

"Oh, yes, sir. When will we get there?"

"Well, we could make it tonight, but I think we'll stop off and sleep at Center. There's a good hotel there. The quarters at Hornbec are pretty rugged. And the guides keep you up drinking your whiskey."

"Oh," the boy said. He kept silent a moment, then resumed eagerly.

"Jake said there were all kinds of hunting, and on one trip grandfather Laus brought back a live bear."

"The old boy must have been quite a sport."

"Oh, he was. Sometimes he would sleep under the trees, by a spring or creek. Jake said when he put up with people along the way, he would copy the design of a quilt he liked and have his wife make it when he got back home."

Bomar looked curiously at the boy at his side. "You seem to know a lot about that old guy. Which one was he?"

"He's the one that hangs to the right of the mantel in the living room."

"Let's see. That's the . . ."

"He hangs in the mahogany frame."

"Yeah. He was the one that was such a rounder."

"But he reformed. Mother says he received the mantle of grace when the Methodists held their great revival and built a Church for his slaves."

"When the hell was that?"

"Oh, a long time ago. I don't know rightly."

"You might know it would be a long time. The United Daughters like'm dead."

The boy regarded his uncle with a puzzled expression. "You mean the United Daughters of the Confederacy, sir?"

"I mean all united daughters. The club don't make any difference. In union is strength. That's their battle cry. But hell, boy, you don't know what I'm talking about," Bomar said with impatience. "What I mean is the only man they'll have any truck with is a dead one. After a certain age, that is. The deader the better, if he's buried deep enough so he don't stink."

The boy nodded knowingly, although his head was awhirl. He had heard his father and his father's friends occasionally refer to women in disparaging terms. One spoke of women and preachers, he discovered, in the same tone of voice. It apparently was a thing one did to relieve certain difficult situations, but there was never a particular woman, or a particular preacher, named. The reference was invariably general. And his grandfather—only with him it was religion. He never spoke impolitely of ladies, but he could fling himself into a passion about the Church, especially at the dinner table when the conversation fell off. And his grandmother gave always the same reproving speech, in the same falsely affronted manner, "Don't blaspheme before these young men, Mr. Hancock." And Mr. Hancock would reply with righteous vehemence, "The truth, Madam, cannot blaspheme." None of this banter had he taken to mean anything, but with his Uncle Bomar he felt a difference. Bomar had actual women in mind and a grievance which seemed, however mysterious, real and vaguely threatening. He could not help but be disturbed the more he thought about Bomar's remark. Did he mean his own mother? She talked a great deal about her family, living and dead. The truth heretofore hidden in things familiar confronted him: most of the people she talked about were dead.

After a while, in the silence which had fallen between the man and the boy, Bomar said, "Forget it, kid." And the boy knew it was hard for him to speak, that inadvertently he had allowed talk which he considered unseemly to pass between them.

But he could not forget so easily. Considerations too disturbing to be summarily dismissed had been set loose in his head. Was it true that ladies of his mother's years thought only of the dead, or thought of them to the disfavor of the living? He was sure it could not be so with his mother. The tales she told never called to mind the dead but only the very dearest of kin who perhaps lived too far away to visit. Above all was this true of grandfather Laus, whom she set him for example. "Hold your head up and step lightly," she would say and he knew who it was she had in mind. Or, "Always be able to look any man in the eye." And again, "Think what you please but never speak loosely and you'll have nothing to take back." These admonitions he was conscious of but never in the forepart of his mind. They underlay and gave firm texture to all he found delightful in his great-grandfather's life, and he somehow knew that had they been lacking the stories which won his heart would have seemed less true. But now that he thought of things in a way he never had thought before, all which touched him dearly lay bright and clear before his vision, the beginning, the middle, and the end clarified in a burst of illumination, where the parts were the whole and the whole defined the parts. And so it came to him that from his mother he got most of the admonitions but the stories he had from his grandfather or from Jake.

The near duel with General Jackson he liked best of all, for the two friends were parted over a horse race. This seemed to him right and fitting, for only some such great occasion was proper cause to break the bonds between two "gentlemen who held each other in the highest esteem." The story as it was told, without directly accusing the General was told to his discredit. Large sums had been placed on the race. In the last half mile the General's horse was gaining, when his grandfather Laus's horse threw his rider and crossed the finishing line several lengths ahead of his rival. Proud of himself, he turned to the stand where his master sat, and whinnied. At this point in the story his grandfather would pause dramatically. "The spectators to a man rose and cheered the gallant animal." But of course no riderless horse could win a race. Words passed, just what words he was never told, a challenge was given and taken, but the night before the morning of the duel friends intervened and the matter was disposed of to the honor of both parties. "Else," his grandfather would say, "else," he would repeat, looking significantly about him, "the history of our nation had been played out in different fashion."

Tall, gallant, and forever young, this was the man whose image he carried, not that of the picture in the mahogany frame. That never made him think of grandfather Laus. It looked like the dead or would have so looked if the straight-glancing eyes had been closed. But they narrowed too sharply out of some great reserve, above the stiff neck and stock and the black broadcloth coat. He could never imagine the man in the picture lying under the trees, wrapped in a bear skin, with the shine of the camp fire on his face and the sound of the hobbled horses grazing in the dark. The grandfather who was hunter was the man he liked to think about. Now he was going over the same road he had taken and to the Lake where he had had such great sport with all kinds of game. The road was changed, there was no more a forest, but the Lake at least would still be wild and the guides simple, noble men.

"Wake up, kid, we're here."

He opened wide his eyes, but for a moment his senses delayed. Startled, he thought the car was drawing up before the hotel in Center under its large neon sign glowing evilly red in the darkness. Here the night before they had stepped out of the frosty air into the shabby newness of the lobby, had been shown to their room by a gray-haired elevator boy. It had seemed to him that he had scarcely closed his eyes before his uncle was shaking him awake. Behind the desk the proprietor greeted them. He was dressed in hunting clothes. His eyes were bright as a bird's and he jerked about like a mechanical toy as he cocked his head to one side and talked glibly of the shooting, but what he wanted to find out was whether they would be back that night. "Bastard," Bomar said as they turned away. It was still dark as they passed a second time under the neon sign. The car was white and glistened in the dark. The exhaust made a loud noise in the deserted street. In the distance he had heard an ash can clattering. . . .

"Well, here we are," Bomar said and got out of the car with a motion which was quick for a man his size. He called into the darkness, "Anybody seen Tommy?"

A voice answered, "He stepped up to his house. He'll be on down in a little."

"Are we really here?" the boy asked. He noticed that he had lowered his voice. His uncle had spoken right out.

"This is Hornbec. There's the Lake over there."

The boy glanced toward a rough pier, but it was all dark beyond and he could see nothing of the water. They walked up the narrow street which bordered the Lake. Lights from the windows and door of a plain two-story building glared from its porch and threw a milky shadow onto the steps. But the light did not penetrate, although he could see his uncle's face and the half-solid forms of men stirring busily around him. He was wide awake now, with the cold wind from the Lake blowing his face, but he felt as if he were acting in a dream, where all was topsy-turvy yet all seemed natural. It was this very naturalness of things which made him feel as he did: people going about their business, talking in a normal voice, but all in the dead of night.

"Let's go in the hotel," Bomar said.

Inside it was warm and bright. Some dozen men dressed in their hunting clothes, several of them in hip boots, sat around a pot-bellied stove. It was red hot about its middle. He shivered and walked over to warm himself.

"How about a little breakfast, Nelly?" Bomar called out and walked into the long dining room.

The walls were plain and unfinished. Most of the tables were in disarray and he could see that the guests of the hotel had already eaten. Where he sat, there were crumbs on the cloth and somebody had spilled catsup. The woman Nelly came in with fried eggs shining white with grease, thick bacon, large thick biscuits, and coffee in heavy china cups. She flung her head and shoulders about as she walked. The boy thought he had never seen less sense in a face, but he could see the hunters liked her or at least that she thought the hunters liked her.

"Good old Nelly. She won't let us starve," Bomar called out with too loud a heartiness and grabbed playfully at her waist. She tossed her head and flung herself out of the way, but her wide bright eyes grew brighter.

"Quit, now-wah," she said.

The brazen stupidity in her dare that was not a dare chilled his spirits. The eggs were cold, but he ate the bacon and poured a lot of milk and sugar in his coffee and drank it. The coffee was steaming hot.

"Paul's wife may come up with him today," Bomar said to the girl.

"I hope she does."

"Do you now?"

"Why not, I ain't got nothing to hide."

"No. Nothing to hide. Nothing at all."

"That's right."

"Who did I see kissing you?"

"He was jest being jolly."

"Yeah. Jolly. Good old jolly Paul."

"That's right," she said. "Jolly and friendly. You all want lunches?"

"Sure. You want us to go hungry on that Lake?"

"I didn't know. I thought maybe you'd brought lunches with you."

Bomar turned to his nephew. "This hotel thinks it's got a monopoly."

"We don't care where you stay." Her head came up. A light flush at the cheek bones rushed to her eyes. For the first time the woman seemed real to the boy. His mother had told him that plain people were quick to take offense but it was her show of pride which gave her being, and he understood that it was a thing she held in common with those around her as she shared a speech which his mother called country.

"Well, will you be here tonight?" she continued.

Bomar paused. "Yeah. The kid and I'll be here."

"I jest wanted to know. I have to plan about supper."

She left the dining room, and the man and the boy ate hurriedly and in silence. From the other room they heard spurts of talk. None of it flowed easily, as happens with men who are idling. It jabbed at the silence, a silence enclosing a time of waiting upon action, when the mind grows fearful lest its edge grow dull from images. The boy was trying to catch the drift of the talk. He had not heard the soft steps ap-

proaching. He heard only the words, "Now if you ain't a pretty bastard."

He stiffened and waited for the blow which Bomar in all honor must
give. He waited a second. There was no stirring of the chair. He raised
his eyes upon his uncle's smiling, placid features.

Bomar's lips were moving. "You ain't no handsome son-of-a-bitch
yourself," they said.

"Getting in here this time of day. You drive all night?"

"Hell, no. We stopped off at Center to get a few hours sleep."

"What you think you are, a goddam tourist?"

"You got an interest in this hotel?"

"Hell, no. It's just the company you keep. When I want to sleep in
a whore house, I don't want no pimp to show me my bed. That mealy-
mouthed bastard dressing up like a hunter to catch the suckers like you,
only I didn't know you was a sucker before. And they'll steal there,
too."

"Hell, Applegate."

"Hell they don't. Last week a man from Indiana lost his purse with
ninety-seven dollars in it."

"You're just afraid he'll take away your business."

"Hell. None of the guides around here will go up there. And we
don't let him down here."

Bomar turned to his nephew. "Kid, shake hands with Tommy
Applegate."

The boy rose and gave the small heavy-set man his hand. He was
a little dazed. Bastard and son-of-a-bitch were fighting words, not
friendly greetings. He didn't understand. He knew his uncle had
fought for less, much less. And he well knew that no such greeting
would have passed between grandfather Laus and his lean, weathered
guide, when they met again at the return of the hunting season. But
of course there were no professional guides in those days. The people
who lived about the Lake at that time hunted or trapped for a living.
They might go along with a friend out of pure courtesy, or for com-
panionship, but he was sure they took no money for it. But it was not
the money either. It was the greeting which shocked and puzzled him.
For a second his hand gripped the guide's hand. He felt the inert
calloused flesh, and the strength within, near the bone, but there was
no reponse to his clasp. The man was not being unfriendly, but as he
drew away the boy felt he had been rebuffed. Later he remembered the

eyes. They were brown, which he did not expect. And there was something else, something wrong about them. They lacked the sharpness of a hunter's eyes.

"We are about ready to shove off, kid," Bomar interrupted. "We're going to the first pocket. Tommy got you a good guide. Watch him, though, or he'll shoot up too many of your shells. And you give him this at the end of the day."

The boy looked at the money. "All of this, Uncle Bomar?"

"Yeah, I know. It's too damn much, but it's what they charge."

Outside the darkness was thinning. The Lake spread out for a way like a black floor. The boy hesitated on the edge of the porch. His clothes were slick from the cold, but the blood charged through his body. It seemed a trivial thing that he had worried at not finding the place and the people what he had expected, for the surroundings are nothing. The only thing that mattered was the shoot. Hunters passed him on the steps, all with a common purpose, the same thoughts, the same sense of excitement and expectation. He could feel it as they went by. One or two looked curiously at him. He knew he must go on or they would think him strange, but still he delayed to savor the full measure of the experience before it was played out by the act. All this stir, the time of day, the learning of the guides, the rich men who hunted, who came from places where their word was law, others who came out of some urgent need they did not rightly understand—all of them now and in his great-grandfather's day, were guided, were governed by the instincts of a bird. Bomar half turned. "Where are you?" he called sharply.

"Coming," the boy answered and hurried down the steps. He noticed that Bomar's bulky clothes spreading out over his hips enlarged them. He looked from the rear like his mother.

At the water's edge two boats were drawn close into the bank. Tommy was standing in one. Bomar was handing him his gear.

"Your gun unloaded?" Tommy asked.

"You know I wouldn't hand you any loaded gun," Bomar replied.

"Be God-damned sure. I don't want you to blow my ass off."

"Don't put it where it'll get wet."

"If it gets wet, you'll get wet. Hand me that sack of charcoal."

"Your arm's not broke. Pick it up."

"What's the matter with your back? Been riding it too much?"

"My back's all right. This is Jack Daniel's number seven. Catch it."

"Three's my lucky number."

"Well, this will more than double your luck. Won't it, Goosetree?"

A man looked up from blowing the charcoal burner in the adjoining boat. The light from the charcoal showed a pair of flat eyes, with sharp points at their centers. Even in the steady red glow his features seemed pale. He said dryly, "He'll double your drinks."

"This is the kid, Goosetree, that's going with you," Bomar said.

The man nodded. "They'll make the noise, sonny," he said. "We'll bring in the meat."

"Hell," Tommy said with heavy scorn.

"I've got the gun will do it," Goosetree added. "And this boy looks like he can shoot."

"You may get a mud hen or two."

"I'm going to hole up at the point. We'll bring'm in."

"Bring in my ass," Tommy said.

"Now that ud be a right heavy load."

The boy no longer felt ill at ease with these people. At first he had been repelled by their obscenities. The words had struck him with all the force of their literal meaning. And in his disgust there had been fear, not so much of the men and the place, as of his own sensations. All things he had found different from his imaginings. Bomar's unintended remarks in the car had begun it. He had got in beside his uncle, never doubting that things could ever be otherwise than as they seemed. He had found that even a fact about which there could not be the slightest uncertainty, such as Bomar's eyes, was not a fact at all. Almost without attending it, so fast did it happen, one certainty after another had slipped away from him until he felt exposed in all his privacy. Now this in some way had changed. He had scarcely listened to the guides' talk. He watched them get the boats set for the shoot. What they did went quickly, but there was no haste to their movements, and their banter was spoken with as little attention to the meaning as the congregation repeating the doxology on Sunday.

Goosetree straightened up. His movement was unmistakable. There came a pause and Bomar turned hastily. "Now, kid," he said, "you got to lead these duck."

"Like doves?"

"Yeah. Maybe further. I can't tell you exactly. You'll have to judge. But when they come flying in at you, shoot at their bills." He stepped into the boat. "All ready, me lads?"

"We been ready," Goosetree replied.

The boy sat forward in the boat, astraddle the charcoal burner. There was barely room for his legs and he had to watch to see that his boots didn't burn. They pushed off and he thought surely the ice must chew up the bottom of the boat. The going got better after a while, but every now and then the guide had to strike the ice several times before he could set the oars to water. The darkness thinned and the cold began to bite into him. It had a different quality over water. He felt weight as well as chill. He wore two wool shirts, a heavy wool coat and next to his body close-knit woolen underwear, but it went through all these garments like air through a sack in a broken window light. He got to wondering if he could stand it all day and leaned forward to rub his hands over the open mouth of the burner.

His teeth began to chatter and he drew down his chin so it wouldn't be seen. He could hear Bomar and Tommy. Their voices had the flat clear sound of coming from a distance and yet they were not far away. And then he looked up. . . . Dawn had swamped the sky. There was no light and yet he could see. He was first conscious of a wonderful ease to his eyes. Wide open, without a thread's strain, they saw everywhere through the colorless haze. Never had he been able to see so clearly and so far. He thought it must be like this with animal eyes at night or whenever they hunt, to see and not know they are seeing, when the vision and prey are made one for the spring. A wonderfully fresh strength streamed through his body. All things seemed at a beginning. It was the world on the first day.

The boat struck a snag. He looked more closely about. Black slick tree trunks stuck up out of the water like the splintered piles of a pier which has rotted away. Occasionally they passed a stump that was still alive, but its stunted growth only made the desolate surroundings more forbidding. And the Lake, he saw, was forbidding. Miles upon miles of saw grass, more grass than water, and everywhere the illusion of solid ground. Slimy ooze, even quicksand, was its floor. His first elation drained away. He told himself the place was not meant for man. It was more foreign and distant to his experience than the most outlandish reaches of human habitation. Over him came a great and terrible loneliness.

The boats entered an open pocket of frozen water. His boat began to rock and he grasped the sides.

"Give with the boat," Goosetree commanded.

"What's the matter, Mr. Goosetree?"

"Nothing's the matter. I'm breaking the ice."

"What for?"

"To throw out the blocks." Goosetree's voice made him feel the depth of his ignorance.

The ice broke up in sheets and the boat sloshed it out of the way. Into the open water the guide began to throw his decoys. He unwound the string, glanced at the water with quick precision and then threw out the painted block. In no time the false birds rode their anchors in front of the blind. Goosetree now drove the boat into the edge of the grass. He handed the boy a pole. "When I pull, you push on that," he said and stepped into the water. His hip boots sank down and he said, "All right." At each push the boat slid further into the blind. Empty shells and cigarette butts soiled the flattened tufts of grass. One cigarette, scarcely smoked, touched the water, its damp brown insides spilling and staining the paper. A smear of lipstick gashed its upper end. Instinctively the boy averted his gaze. A blot formed in the blue-gray haze, hung for a moment to the air, desperately, noiselessly fluttering its wings, turned and disappeared. Motionless, he watched the spot where it had been, feeling he could almost have touched the duck, if duck it was, for how could its wings beat so and not make a sound?

"I reckon it's hid," Goosetree said.

"No, it just melted away," the boy replied.

Goosetree's eyes came on guard. The boy said hastily, "Oh, the boat. Yes, sir, it looks hid."

"What'd you think I meant?"

"I didn't hear you well."

He felt that his guide was studying him, trying to make up his mind whether he was responsible enough to risk in the close quarters they must keep. At last Goosetree pulled himself out of the water and began to prepare the boat for action. He set the burner between them, changed the seats so that they faced each other, set his lunch beside him, his water bottle to the rear. He took bunches of grass from both sides and tied them together over the boat. Carefully he loaded his gun and set it down pointing into the grass. He loaded the boy's and handed it to him. "Point it that way," he said, "and always keep the safety on until you get up to shoot. And don't get up until I tell you."

"Where are Uncle Bomar and Tommy gone?" he asked.

The guide was dropping charcoal into the burner. "They went to the other side of the pocket." He leaned over to blow the coals. The boy noticed that his hands were black and his face sooty from handling the coal. When the fire suited him, he dropped a tomato can over the low tin chimney, then rose in the boat. He stood with his body half bent and with a short jerk of the head looked up. A shadow passed over his eyes as he flicked them across the arc of the sky.

"See anything?" the boy asked.

"They'll be in," he replied.

Then they sat in silence, leaning toward each other over the burner. Around the boat, out of the grass, the cold boiled up through a slimy mist. Now that they were settled and waiting, the boy felt his body relax and his head grow dull. He was wondering how he could get up from his cramped quarters in time to shoot. He did not see the guide rise. He heard the shot and looked up, his heart fluttering, in time to see the red feet draw up under the white belly, see the inert body slanting to the Lake.

"When they hit the ice, they don't git up no more," Goosetree said. He added, "I seen him too late to call you."

His first feeling was chagrin and resentment. A guide should give others a chance to shoot. But in his heart he knew he had been a bad hunter. Too much excitement had worn him out. He must learn how to wait, be idle and still wound up, like a spring. That was it. Like a spring.

"There they come," Goosetree hissed.

"Where?" he breathed.

"A Susie. In front of you."

Almost overhead and to the left he saw the duck. The spring in him snapped. He heard the report of his gun, saw the bird falter, fly for a hundred yards and then go down. He shot at another passing to his front, missed, shot and missed again. He tried to aim but his eyes felt frozen and wide open. His gun and Goosetree's went off together. The bird stopped short in flight and fell straight down. For the first time Goosetree smiled.

"I missed the second shot," the boy said and his voice was trembling and his throat dry.

"You didn't lead him enough. The air from your load fanned his tail."

"We both shot at the same time. Think we both got him. I expect you got him."

"It was a teal," Goosetree said, glancing swiftly around. The sky seemed to open out of his eyes.

It seemed a long time before the next ducks flew over. At last he heard, "There!" He grabbed his gun, half rose. "Git down," the guide ordered and hastily put his hands to his mouth and called, the reedy imitation of the duck's cry rasping the air. The call seemed too urgent to the boy, faster than a bird would make. The birds dipped and turned, then flew away.

"No use aiming. Whenever they see you, it's too late."

"Did they see me?"

"Hell, yes. Never get up until you're ready to shoot."

The nasal call to death and the sound of guns traveled from different parts of the Lake, gradually drifted into silence until the whole world grew as still as the painted ducks riding their anchors in the pool of rotten ice. He and the guide were close enough to touch. The intimacy which was not intimacy began to close in on him. He felt that he ought to say something. He said, "Is your son going to follow in your footsteps, Mr. Goosetree?"

"Hell, no. There's no money in guiding. Soon's he's old enough I'm going to send him to college."

"I would think this was a wonderful life," the boy said in surprise, "being able to hunt or fish every day and get paid for it."

"It gits stale, up before day freezing your balls off sloshing around in this ice."

The guide picked up a jug of milky water and poured it into a pan and set the pan on the open mouth of the burner. "I'll make us some coffee," he said. "And we can eat. The ducks won't be back until about eleven o'clock. I've noticed that's the time they been coming in."

He measured the coffee and dumped it into the water, took a dirty rag and carefully wiped out two cups and put them beside him. Then he took a spoon and began to stir the coffee and blow the coals. "No," he said. "It's hard on you. I'm going to quit it soon. I bought me the finest summer house ever built around this Lake. Old man Simpkins built it, a rich lumber man from Mississippi. He spent eight thousand dollars on it. Built it of pine and not a knot in it, plumbing, lights, frigidaire, and good water. I heard his widow wanted to sell and I let her know by the woman who looks after it that I might, might mind you, try to buy it. So old lady Simpkins called me long distance. And I asked her what she wanted for it and she commenced telling me how much she'd put in it. I cut her off. I said I'll give you two thousand cash for it. She couldn't listen to any such figure, it was giving it away. Two thousand's my offer. Take it or leave it. She hung up on me. But a week later I got a letter from her son saying his mother couldn't bear to come up here no more since her old man had went away and that they'd close the deal." Goosetree poured a cup of coffee and handed it to the boy. "I'd a give twenty-five hundred as easy as I give two thousand." He unwrapped a sandwich. "I'm going to build two cabins, put a toilet and shower in 'em, they's eight rooms to the house, and rent by the week or month. A man and his wife can come up and fish. They come sometime with women they claim to be their wives. There'll be money in it."

"How many'd you get?" a voice from the Lake asked.

It was Bomar and Tommy. Goosetree rose. "Aw, we got'm, boys. How many'd you knock down?"

"None," Tommy said. His face was grave and averted, as though still turned from the incomprehensible workings of Fate.

"We shot twice, but they were too high," Bomar added apologetically.

Tommy began throwing out his decoys.

"Don't throw them blocks out here."

Tommy rowed about, continuing to throw them out. He asked, "Don't we work together?"

"Hell. The quarters is too close."

Bomar said in his slow, soothing voice, "Goosetree, I believe you are afraid we'll outshoot you."

"Who's got the duck?"

"Well, how many did you get?"

"Three," Goosetree said, his voice less belligerent.

"I really got one, Uncle Bomar. On the nose."

"Fine, kid."

"Yes, sir, this boy's gonna knock'm," Goosetree said. The boy felt a glow of pleasure. He was beginning to think more of his guide.

Tommy masked his boat in the grass behind the others.

"You want some coffee?" Goosetree asked.

"We got something better'n coffee," Tommy replied.

"Here, take a drink," Bomar said.

Tommy turned up the bottle. His Adam's apple worked like a piston as the bright brown liquid flowed down his throat. He wiped the mouth of the bottle on his sleeve and returned it casually. "Warms you better than any charcoal," he said matter-of-factly.

From where he reclined in the boat Bomar took a drink. The boy noticed it was much less than Tommy took. "How about it, Goosetree?"

"I got ulcers. Drinking too much in Arkansas," Goosetree replied. "Hod, but that stuff lightened you as it went down. Set your tail on fire."

"Kid?"

"No, thank you, sir." The boy knew by the way the whiskey was offered that he was supposed to refuse, but he mightily wanted to taste it. He drank his coffee instead and took a bite out of a ham sandwich. There was too much bread for the meat and he threw away the top slice.

"My daddy tole me to stay out'n Arkansas," Goosetree continued.

"Ain't nothing there," Tommy added sourly.

"I went over there to a duck-calling contest oncet. I called as purty as ever you please." Goosetree added bitterly, "They give the prize to a school boy."

"Ain't nothing for nobody in Arkansas," Tommy said.

The boy tried another sandwich, peanut butter and jelly spread together on the bread. It tasted good. At least it wasn't so dry. He finished his coffee and felt better for the food.

"Tommy, where are these duck you called me about?"

Tommy looked shocked at the question and glanced over the Lake toward the woods. "They're roosting on the reserve," he said.

"Government birds, eh?" Bomar said. "Well, they'll sit on their fat asses until we starve to death."

Tommy looked even more serious. "They'll come out after a while," he said.

"That was humor, Applegate. You wouldn't recognize it, though. It bore no reference to fornication."

Bomar drank again and passed the whiskey to his guide. Tommy took it and turned it up in one motion. He swallowed like a thirsty man drinking water. "That's seven times seven," he said. "What does it make?"

"You drunk," Bomar replied.

"It'll make you holler." He opened his mouth and his voice rang lustily over the Lake.

Bomar examined his companion's face for a moment. "Applegate," he said, "if you had rings in your ears, you'd look like a damn pirate."

Tommy shouted again, "Hi-yo!"

The boy thought he did look like a pirate, anyway like a foreigner, the way his eyes didn't suit his rough, swarthy features but looked both boldly and evasively at the same time. With Mr. Goosetree it was different. He looked like a guide ought to look, although he was a little small and didn't think much of guiding, which was a disappointment the boy didn't explore but which lay uneasily in the back of his head. But Tommy at least was human and it was somehow because of his eyes. Watching the sky, they absorbed it like a blotter. When Mr. Goosetree looked at the sky, he skinned it.

"Hi-yo!" Tommy shouted again. As if suddenly spent by the shouting, he said, "My daddy was a Jew and my mother an Indian. Now ain't that a hell of a thing?"

He had half turned away. Bomar looked at him but said nothing. Tommy continued in a conversational tone, "He used to trade up and down this country. I reckon he made a pretty good living until he took to drinking. When I was a shirt-tail boy, he'd come in on Satday nights and run all of us out of the house. I sort of liked it in summer, like a kid will. My mother would bed us down in the leaves and moss. It didn't seem to worry her much. I reckon Indians are sort of used to the woods. There was generally plenty to eat. She made a good truck patch. She'd take the littlest one and go out in the corn when it was tosseling and sing to it. Homesick kind of a singing. As I got older, I didn't like it so much. Looked like he didn't do so well trading. He'd come in during the week drunk and beat her up. She never hollered, but if he tried to take his scantling to one of us young-uns, she'd scratch and bite him like a cat.

"I was about eleven, I guess. We still had plenty to eat, well not a plenty but enough. She always managed to keep us in victuals, but we was all ragged. It takes money to buy clothes. He wasn't doing no trading at all, except he'd take her corn and swap it for licker. Well, he come a night of the worst blizzard that ever you saw, mean drunk and dirty. He looked like he'd been laying out for a week. He commenced cussin' and stumbling around and hollered, 'Clear all these half breeds outer here.' I said, 'Daddy, we ain't going out in this blizzard.' His red eyes kind of bulged at me. He picked a old table leg that was laying around and come toward me. I raised the gun. He still kept coming. I let him have it right in the belly." Tommy's voice ceased. He said after a while, "Sober, he wasn't no mean-natured kind of a man."

Without saying anything Bomar passed the whiskey over to Tommy. Nobody spoke again for a long while. Goosetree had covered himself up and gone to sleep. Bomar lay back, reclining in the boat. The day had advanced but there was no sun to relieve the cold. The frozen clouds stretched tight across the sky. After a while the boy became conscious of Bomar's soothing voice. It flowed too smoothly. It was getting confidential. He recognized the signs. Miserable from the cold and the long, trying wait, he felt the shoot would be a failure. Nobody would watch for the ducks, maybe there wouldn't be any more to come in. He felt the need to stand up. It was a little less cold up in the air. There was not a duck in the sky. He looked down and his blood danced. Three were playing in the water before a jutting strip of the grass. "Look, Tommy," he cried.

"Mud hens," Tommy said and sat back down.

Bomar had turned where he lay. His eyes were gay. "What," he asked, "would the old boy, what's his name, Menelaus, say if he knew his grandson had taken a mud hen for a duck? The pious Menelaus, our noble ancestor, unequaled in the arts of field and stream and Ovid's pupil. What would he say, kid?"

He was too surprised to say anything—Bomar wondering about grandfather Laus, too, for it was plain that he only pretended to recollect his name. . . .

"Never, oh, never, would that nonpareil, that prince among men, that cock of the walk, have mistaken a mud hen for a duck. Or so we're told. What I like, Applegate, about this revered ancestor of mine and the kid's, was his timing. Now I know that timing is everything, but damn if I can bring it off. But this guy Menelaus did. When he was young, he went the rounds. When it came time to settle down, he didn't settle, but nobody held it against him, least of all his large female connection. He hunted when he wanted to, he had plenty of money, he played the races and was a family man all at the same time. He was a genius, Applegate. And while he stepped high, wide and handsome, his Helen stayed at home making quilts and raising his young. That's the way to do it, Applegate. Be fruitful and multiply. And don't forget the quilts. He didn't. He made it a point to keep her in fresh patterns, just in case. . . . . And then when he had dropped all the grains of corn from one

jar to the other and it was time to change'm back, he saw the light. At
a camp meeting at Walnut Grove the dove, not the kind you're thinking about, Applegate, but the blessed, the miraculous dove, came bearing the twig of salvation." He paused. His voice had grown harder as
he spoke. "Don't take it hard, kid, you're not the first to take a wooden
nickel."

He couldn't make heads or tails of what his uncle was saying. What
did a wooden nickel have to do with it? It was very important. He
could tell by Bomar's voice. Before he could try to figure it out, Tommy
interrupted.

"There was a lady here fishing once named Helen," Tommy said.
"She come here with a doctor from Chicago. They claimed they were
married, but I been rowing a long time. These two didn't much care
whether they caught anything or not. She wasn't having much luck and
I said,—I wasn't thinking anything—'Diddle on this side.' I meant her
hook of course, and she said, 'What? Right there?' and giggled. You
know, it was the way she said it. And the doctor, he laughed too. They
did a sight of loose laughing." Tommy leaned over and stirred the charcoal in the burner. "When I first took up guiding people, didn't no
women come here to hunt or fish."

Bomar raised his bottle, "Here's to Argive Helen and all her kin."

The boy felt the boat move. Goosetree was awake and staring at Bomar's large, well-wrapped body. "Look at him," he said, "laying over
there like a fattening hog."

Far away, over near the island a lone gun shot once. It made no more
noise than a popgun but the men in the two boats grew very quiet.
Then all rose to their feet. Goosetree took out his watch. "Eleven
twenty," he said.

The importunate duck calls, still at a distance, now buzzed like insects. More guns went off over by the reserve. The firing was scattered.
Then somebody said, "Get down." The boy didn't see anything and he
got panicky. "Coming over you." "Where, where?" he asked in a tight
voice. And then all four of them were shooting furiously. He thought
he hit one but he wasn't sure. Two of the ducks turned and flew over a
blind across the channel. The hunters there shot up a lot of shells but
the ducks went on their way. Goosetree called out, "You want my
gun?" His voice was taunting and cheerful. "You can have my gun if
you want it."

"How about that for shooting, Applegate?" Bomar asked. His voice was even and full.

"Boy, you stopped him."

"Didn't I stop him, though?"

"Did you? A mallard, too."

"Purty good shooting," Goosetree said. "But look over here in the water."

"Here's where to look," Tommy called back. "Yours jest killed theyselves, but we had to shoot to bring'm down."

"Hell."

"We're hitting them, ain't we?" Bomar said.

"Watch it, boys," Goosetree snapped.

Down in the boat Tommy was calling. The hunters across the channel called. The boy crouched and watched the bird, the bending wings, the red feet out behind. . . . The duck dipped and dove toward the water. The world vanished. There was nothing but space, a streak in space. The moving bolt was all. His ears crashed, the thud against his shoulder, another crash, the red feet gashed the white breast. The dead body dropped and the world was.

"Not bad, kid."

"I think you got him, Uncle Bomar."

"Hard to say. We shot together."

The two of them, the boy and his uncle, were alone in the boat. They watched the guides row from place to place, gathering in the ducks. At last the long full day was over. Behind the island the darkness crouched. As if sensing the hunters could no longer shoot, the ducks now lighted everywhere around them. "God, God . . ." Bomar whispered. Then the guides turned their boat about. It sped toward the hunters. Quietly the water parted about the prow, quietly closed behind the rippling wake. No sign of passage marred its surface—it waited to receive the descending night.

"It's been a good shoot," Bomar said evenly. "But it's over."

The boy turned toward his uncle. What he saw made him raise his hand, as though for support. Bomar stood erect and waiting. His eyes were regarding the boy: they were the eyes in the mahogany frame.

A Long Fourth
Peter Taylor

For over five years Harriet Wilson had been saying, "I'd be happier, Sweetheart, if BT were not even on the place." Harriet was a pretty woman just past fifty, and Sweetheart felt that she grew prettier as the years went by. He told her so, too, whenever she mentioned the business about BT or any other business. "I declare you get prettier by the year," he was accustomed to say. That was how the BT business had been allowed to run on so. Once she had pointed out to Sweetheart that he never said she grew wiser by the year, and he had replied, laughing, that it certainly did seem she would never be a judge of niggers. It was while they were dressing for breakfast one morning that he told her that, and she had quickly turned her back to him (which was the severest rebuke she was ever known to give her husband) and began to powder her neck and shoulders before the mirror. Then he had come over and put his hands on her pretty, plump shoulders and kissed her on the cheek saying, "But you're nobody's fool, darling."

Thinking of that had oftentimes been consolation to her when Sweetheart had prettied her out of some notion she had. But really she had always considered that she was nobody's fool and that she certainly was not merely a vain little woman ruled by a husband's flattery, the type her mother had so despised in her lifetime. She even found herself sometimes addressing her dead mother when she was alone. "It's not that I've become one of that sort of women in middle-age, Mama. It's that when he is so sweet to me I realize what a blessing that is and how unimportant other things are." For Harriet was yet guided in some matters by well remembered words of her mother who had been dead for thirty years. In other matters she was guided by the words of Sweetheart. In still others she was guided by what Son said. Her two daughters guided her in nothing. Rather, she was ever inclined to instruct them by quoting Mama, Sweetheart, or Son.

Their house was eight miles from downtown Nashville on the Franklin Pike, and for many years Sweetheart, who was a doctor, had had his own automobile for work and Harriet had kept a little coupe. But after the War began the doctor accepted gas-rationing rather conscientiously and went to and from his office in the interurban bus. "We eye-ear-nose-and-throat men don't have to make so many professional calls," he said. Harriet usually walked down to the Pike to meet him on the five-thirty bus in the evening.

It was a quarter of a mile from the Pike to the house, and they would walk up the driveway hand in hand. Harriet who said she lived in perpetual fear of turning her ankle on a piece of gravel kept her eyes on the ground when they walked, and Sweetheart would usually be gazing upward into the foliage of the poplar trees and maples that crowded the lawn and overhung the drive or he would be peering straight ahead at the house which was an old fashioned single storey clapboard building with a narrow porch across the front where wisteria bloomed in June and July. Though they rarely had their eyes on each other during this walk they were always hand in hand and there was always talk. It was on one of these strolls, not a week before BT gave notice, that Harriet last uttered her old complaint: "I've always told you that I'd be happier, Sweetheart, if BT were not even on this place now that he's grown up."

"I know." He squeezed her hand and turned a smiling countenance to her.

"I don't think you do know," she said keeping her eyes on the white gravel. "He's grand on the outside, but all of them are grand on the outside. As long as we keep him I'm completely deprived of the services of a houseboy when I need one. When Son and his young lady come I don't know what I'll do. The girls are angels about things, but next week they should be entertaining Son and her, and not just picking-up after her. It seems so unreasonable, Sweetheart, to keep BT when we could have a nice, normal darkie that could do inside when I need him."

Sweetheart began swinging their joined hands merrily. "Ah, oh, now, BT's a pretty darned good darkie, just clumsy and runs around a bit."

Harriet looked up at her husband and stopped still as though she were afraid to walk with her eyes off her feet. "Sweetheart, you know very well it's not that." And making a face she held her nose and shuddered so acutely that he could feel it in the fingers of the hand he was holding.

"Well, there's nothing wrong that a little washing won't cure." He was facing her and trying now to take hold of her other hand.

"No, no, no, Sweetheart. It's constitutional with him. Last Monday I had him bathe before he came in to help old Mattie move the sideboard. Yet that room was unbearable for twenty minutes after he left. I *had* to get out, and I heard his Auntie Mattie say 'Whew!' Mattie knows it as well as I do and is just too contrary to admit it. I'm sure that's why she moved into the attic and left him the whole shack, but she's too contrary to admit it."

The doctor threw back his head and laughed aloud. Then for a time he seemed to be studying the foliage absently and he said that he reckoned poor old Mattie loved her little-nephew a good deal. "I think it's touching," he said, "and I believe Mattie would leave us in a minute if we let BT go."

"Not a bit of it!" said Harriet.

"Nevertheless, he's a good nigger," her husband said, "and we can't judge Negroes the way we do white people, Harriet."

"Well, I should say *not!*" Harriet exclaimed.

Harriet was not a light sleeper but she complained that she often awoke in the night when there was something on her mind. On the last night of June that summer she awoke with a start and saw by the illuminated dial of her watch that it was three A.M. She rolled over on her stomach with great care not to disturb Sweetheart who was snoring gently beside her. This waking, she supposed, was a result of her worries about Son's coming visit and the guest he was bringing with him. And then Son was going to the Army on the day after the Fourth. She had been worrying for weeks about Son's going into the Army and how he would fit in there. He was not like other men, more sensitive and had advanced ideas and was so intolerant of inefficiency and old fashioned things. This was what had broken her sleep, she thought; and then there was repeated the unheardof racket that had really awakened her.

Harriet grunted in her pillow, for she knew that it was her daughters quarreling again. A door slammed and she heard Kate's voice through the wall. "Oh, Goddy! Godamighty! Helena, won't you please shut up!" She knew at once the cause of the quarrel: Kate had been out this evening and had turned on the light when she came to undress. Poor thing certainly could not pin up her hair and hang up her dress in the dark. Yet it *was* an unreasonable hour. She wondered where the girls ever stayed till such a late hour. They were too old now to be quizzed about those things. But they were also too old to be quarreling so childishly. Why, when Harriet and her sister were their age they were married and had the responsibilities of their own families. What a shame it is, she thought, that my girls are not married, and it's all because of their height. Then Harriet rebuked herself for begrudging them one minute of their time with what few beaux they had.

For there really were so few tall men nowadays. In her own day there had been more tall men, and tall women were then considered graceful. Short dresses do make such a difference, she reflected, and my girls' legs are not pretty. Harriet was not tall herself, but Mama had been tall and Mama was known as one of the handsomest women that ever graced the drawing rooms of Nashville. But the girls were a little taller than even Mama had been. And they were smart like Mama. They read all the same books and magazines that Son did. Son said they were quite conversant. Nevertheless they must behave themselves while Son's friend was here. No such hours and no such quarrels! She did wish that Son had not planned to bring this girl down from New York, for he had said frankly that they were not in love, they were only friends and had the same interests. Harriet felt certain that Son would bring no one who was not a lady, but what real lady, she asked herself, would edit a birth-control magazine? Just then Sweetheart rolled over and in his sleep put his arm about her shoulders. So she began to think of all her blessings. Something reminded her that she had not said her prayers before going to bed, and so with his arm about her she said the Lord's Prayer and went off to sleep.

She forgot to speak to the girls the next day about their quarreling, but on the following day she was determined to mention it. Sweetheart had left for town in his car since he was to meet Son's and Miss Prewitt's train that afternoon. Harriet was in the front part of the house wearing a long gingham wrapper and her horn-rimmed spectacles. In one hand she clasped the morning paper and a few of the June bills which had come in that morning's mail. The house was in good order and in perfect cleanliness, for she and the girls and Mattie had spent the past three days in putting it so.

These days had been unusually cool with a little rain in the morning and again in the afternoon. Otherwise Harriet didn't know how they could have managed a general housecleaning in June. The girls had really worked like Trojans, making no complaint but indirectly. Once when it began to rain after a sultry noon hour Helena had said, "Well, thank God for small favors." Kate, when she broke her longest fingernail on the curtain rod, screamed a word that Harriet would not even repeat in her mind. But they had been perfect angels about helping. Their being so willing, so tall and so strong is really compensation, Harriet kept telling herself, for not having the services of a houseboy. They had tied their heads up in scarfs, pulled on their garden slacks and done all a-man's-work of reaching the highest ledges and light fixtures and even lifting the piano and the dining room table.

They had spent last evening on the big screened porch in back, had eaten supper and breakfast there too, so there was not a thing to be done to the front part of the house this morning. In the living room she looked about with a pleasant, company smile for the polished floor and gave an affected little nod to the clean curtains. All she did was to disarrange some of the big chairs which Mattie had fixed in too rigid a circle. Mama used to warn Harriet against being superficial in her housekeeping. "The main thing is comfort, dearest," and Harriet knew that she had a tendency to care for the cleanliness and order. So she even put the hearth rug at a slight angle. Then she went to the window and observed that a real July sun was rising today, so she pulled-to the draperies and went from window to window shutting out the light till the whole front part of the house was dark.

The girls slept late that morning. They had earned their rest, and Harriet went tiptoeing about the house listening for them to call for the breakfast that old Mattie had promised to serve them in bed. When ten o'clock came she had picked-up in her room, given a last dusting to Son's room and to the guest room, and Mattie had swept the screened porch and was through in the kitchen. It was time to go to market. Mattie had much to do that day and it was not planned for her to go marketing with Harriet. But the girls had been such angels that Harriet and Mattie agreed they should be allowed to sleep as late as their hearts desired.

Mattie put on her straw and in Harriet's presence she was on the back porch giving BT some last instructions. BT was cleaning six frying-size chickens from their own yard. Later he must peel potatoes and gather beans, lettuce, tomatoes and okra from what was known as the girls' victory garden. He was acknowledged a good hand at many services which could be rendered on the back porch, and his schedule there over the coming holiday week-end was a full one. "Have you cleaned up the freezer?" Harriet asked him. She too was standing with her hat on. She was looking critically at the naked chicken on which his black hands were operating with a small paring knife. Before he answered concerning the freezer she had turned to Mattie and said, "Don't serve the necks tonight, Mattie." Meanwhile BT had crossed the porch and brought back the big wooden bucket of the ice-cream freezer. The bucket itself had been scrubbed wonderfully clean, and with eyes directed toward her but focused for 'some object that would have been far behind her, BT exhibited the immaculate turner and metal container from within. "It does look grand, BT," Harriet admitted.

She was about to depart when she heard one of the girls' voices through their window across the way. (The rear of the house was of an U-shape with the big pantries and the kitchen in one wing and the bedrooms in the other.) Harriet went down through the yard and looked in the girls' window. She was astonished to find the room in complete order and the girls fully dressed and each seated on her own bed reading. Harriet's eyes were immediately filled with tears. She thought of how hard they had worked this week and with what unaccustomed deference they had treated her, calling her "Mama" sometimes instead of Mother, sometimes even being so playful as to call her "Mammy." And this morning they had not wanted to be a bother to anyone. Further, they were reading something new so that they would be conversant with Son and Miss Prewitt. Kate jumped from the bed and said, "Why, Mammy, you're ready to go to market. I'll be right with you." Harriet turned from the window and called to Mattie to take off her straw, for Miss Kate was going to market with her.

But she didn't begin to walk toward the garage at once. The tears had left her eyes, and she stood thinking quite clearly of this change in her daughters' behavior. She was ashamed of having thought it would be necessary to mention their quarreling and their late hours to them. Perhaps they had worried as much as she about Son's going into the Army and probably they were as eager to make him proud of his family before Miss Prewitt.

As all of her concern for the success of the visit cleared away she began to think of what a pity it was that Son and Miss Prewitt were not in love. She would have suspected that it might really be a romance except that the girls assured her otherwise. They told her that Son did not believe in marriage and that he certainly would not subject his family and the people of Nashville to the sort of thing he did believe in.

This girl was merely one of the people he knew in his publishing business. And thinking again of all Son's advanced ideas and his intolerance she could not but think of the unhappiness he was certain to know in the Army. And more than this there would be no weekly telephone calls for her and perhaps no letters and no periodic visits home. He would be going away from them all and he might just be missing and never be brought home for burial. Her imagination summoned for comfort the warmth of Sweetheart's smile and the feel of his arm about her, but there was little comfort even there.

When they returned from market they found Helena on the back porch peeling the potatoes. "What on earth is Helena doing?" Kate asked before they got out of the coupe. Harriet frowned and pressed the horn for BT to come and get the groceries. Then the tall daughter and the short little mother scrambled out of the car and hurried toward the porch. Almost as soon as the coupe appeared Helena had stood up. She took three long strides to the edge of the porch. When her mother and sister drew near, her eyes seemed ready to pop out of her head. Her mouth which was large and capable of great expansions was full open. Yet the girl was speechless.

Harriet was immediately all a tremble and she felt the blood leaving her lips. To herself she said, "Something terrible has—" Then simultaneously she saw that Helena's eyes were fixed on something behind Kate and herself and she heard old Mattie's broken voice calling to her, "Miss Harriet! Oh, Missie, Missie!" She turned about quickly, dropping her eyes to her feet to make sure of her footing, and now looking up she saw the old Negro woman running toward her with her big faded kitchen apron clasped up between her clean, buff colored hands.

The old fashioned appellative "Missie" told Harriet a great deal. She handed Kate her purse and put out her arms to receive Mattie, for she knew that her old friend was in deep trouble. The Negress was several inches taller than Harriet but she threw herself into her little mistress's arms and by bending her knees slightly and stooping her shoulders she managed to rest her face on the bosom of the white eyelet dress while she wept. Harriet held her so for a time with her arms about her and patting her gently between the shoulder blades and just above the bow knot of her apron strings. "Now, now, Mattie," she whispered, "Maybe it's not as bad as it seems. It's something about BT, isn't it? What is it, Mattie, honey?"

"Oh, oh, oh, he gwine leave."

The voice seemed so expressive of the pain in that heart that Harriet could think only of the old woman's suffering and not at all of the cause. "My poor Mattie," she said.

But her sympathy only brought forth more tears and deeper sobs. "My little nephew is gwine leave his old auntie who raised him up when nobody else'd tech him." Harriet did not even hear what Mattie was saying now, but she perceived that her own sympathy was encouraging self-pity and thus giving the pain a double edge. And so she tried to think of some consolation.

"Maybe he won't go after all, Mattie."

Saying this she realized the bearing of BT's departure upon the holiday week-end of which this was the very eve. Then she told herself that indeed Mattie's little nephew would not go after all. "He won't go," she said, "I tell you, Mattie, he won't go if I have any power of constraining him." Her blue eyes shone thoughtfully as she watched the two girls who were now making the last of several trips to bring the groceries from the back of the coupe.

"Oh, oh, oh, yes'm he will, Missie. He's gwine Tuesday. It's the war, an' y' can't stop 'm. He gwine work at th'air fact'ry 'cause the draf membuhs don't want 'm much. But ifn he don't work at th'air fact'ry they'll have to take 'im, want 'im or not." And while his auntie was speaking BT appeared from the door of the unpainted cabin from which Mattie had come. He was still wearing the white coat which he always wore on the back porch, and plainly intended to continue his work through the week-end. He ran over to the car where Kate was unloading the last of the groceries and relieved her of her armful.

Harriet's relief was great. BT would be here through Monday! She began to caress Mattie again and to speak softly in her ear. Her eyes and her thoughts, however, were upon BT. He was a big—neither muscular nor fat, merely big—black, lazy-looking Negro. As he came along the brick walk toward her he kept his eyes lowered to the bundle of groceries. He was what Harriet's Mama would have called a field nigger and had never learned any house manners at all. His face, to her, had ever seemed devoid of expression. He had grown up here on their suburban acreage and had been hardly more than twenty miles distant in his lifetime, but Harriet felt that she had held less converse with him than with any of the men who used to come for short intervals and do the work when BT was still a child. He worked hard and long and efficiently here on their small acreage, she knew, and on Saturday nights he usually got drunk down at the Negro settlement and sometimes spent the later part of that night and all day Sunday in the county jail. There had been times when he had stolen pieces of Sweetheart's and Son's clothing off the wash line, and you dare not lose any change in the porch chairs. Sometimes too they would find that he was keeping some black female thing out in the shack for a week at a time, toting food to her from the kitchen. The female things he kept were not Negro women who might have been useful about the place but were real prostitutes from Nashville (Who else would have endured the smell there must be in that shack?), and Dr. Wilson was ever and anon having to take him to Nashville for the shots. But all of that sort of thing was to be expected, admitted Harriet, and it was not that which caused her antipathy, over and above his constitutional affliction, toward him. BT was simply wanting in those qualities which she generally found appealing in Negroes. He had neither good manners nor the affectionate nature nor the appealing humor that so many niggers have.

As he passed her there at the foot of the porch steps the odor he diffused had never seemed more repugnant and never so strong when outside the house. Mattie raised her tear streaked brown face, knowing it was BT surely more from his odor than from his footstep, and as he followed the two girls to the kitchen door she called after him, "BT, don't leave old Auntie!" Then she looked at her mistress with what Harriet acknowledged to be the sweetest expression she had ever beheld in a Negro's countenance. "Miss Harriet," she said as though stunned at her own thoughts, "it's like you losin' Mr. Son. BT is gwine too."

The small white woman abruptly withdrew her arms from about her servant. The movement was made in one fearful gesture which included the sudden contraction of her lips and the widening of her bright eyes. "Mattie!" she declaimed, "how dare you? That will be just exactly enough from you!" And now her eyes moved swiftly downward and to the porch steps. Without another glance at the woman she had been holding to her bosom she went up on the porch and, avoiding the kitchen where the girls were, she went along the porch up into the U of the house and entered the dark dining room. While she walked her face grew hot and cold alternately as her indignation rose and rose again. When she reached her own room in the far wing of the house she closed the door and let the knob turn-to in her hand. She pulled off her hat and dropped it on her dressing table among her toilet articles and handkerchief box and stray ends of gray hair that were wrapped around a hairpin. And she went and sat down in a rocking chair near the foot of the bed and began to rock. "Like Son! Like Son!"

The very chair had violence in its rocking motion. Several times Harriet might have pushed herself over backward but for lacking the strength in her small legs. Not since she was a little child had such rage been known to her bosom, and throughout the half hour of her wildest passion she was rather aware of this. This evidence of a choleric temperament was so singular a thing for her that she could not but be half conscious of its very singularness and could not but be taking note of herself as her feelings rose and convulsed in their paroxysm. She wondered first that she had refrained from striking Mattie out in the yard and she remarked it humorlessly that only the approaching holiday had prevented her. The insinuation had been sufficiently plain without Mattie's putting it into words. It was her putting it into words that earned Harriet's wrath. The open comparison of Son's departure to that of the sullen, stinking, thieving, fornicating black BT was an injury for which Son could not avenge himself, and she felt it her bounden duty to in some way make that black woman feel the grossness of her wrong and ultimately to drive her off the premises. And it was in this vein, this very declamatory language, this elevated tone with which Harriet expressed herself in the solitude of her room. She was unconsciously trying to use the language and the rhetoric of her mother and of the only books with which she had ever had much acquaintance. Between the moments when she even pictured Mattie's being tied and flogged or thought of Mama's uncle who shot all of his niggers before he would free them and of the Negro governor of North Carolina and the Negro senate rolling whiskey barrels up the capitol steps, of the rape and uprisings in Memphis and the riots in Chicago, between these thoughts she would actually consider the virtue of her own wrath. And recalling her Greek classes at Miss Hood's school she thought without a flicker of humor of Achilles' indignation.

Not the least of the offence was the time that Mattie had chosen. Harriet was powerless to act until this long Fourth of July was over. She meant to endure the presence of that Ethiopian woman and that ape of a man through Sunday and Monday, till her own boy had had his holiday and gone to join the Army. His last visit must not be marred, and she resolved to tell no one—not even Sweetheart—of what had occurred. The holiday would be almost intolerable to her now, but she stopped her furious rocking and with her feet set side by side on the carpet she resolved to endure it in silence for his sake who was the best of all possible sons. Sweat was running down her forehead, and her little hands hung limp and cold.

People in Nashville had been saying for a week how Son would be missed. More than most boys, even those who had not left Nashville to work in New York or St. Louis, Son would be missed by his family when he went to the Army. People said that he had been a model son while he was growing up. And after his own talents and ability took him away to New York he had been so good about keeping in touch. He had written and telephoned and visited home regularly. That was what the older people remarked. And the young people no less admired the faithfulness and consideration he showed his parents. He had carried all the honors in his classes at school and at the University and had not grieved his parents with youthful dissipation as most Nashville boys do. What the young people thought especially fine was that, being the intellectual sort which he certainly was, he had been careful never to offend or embarrass his family with the peculiar, radical ideas which he would naturally have. After he left Nashville he had never sent home magazines in which his disturbing articles appeared, not even to his sisters who pretended to have the same kind of mind. And finally when the wild stories about his private and semi-public activities began to come back to Nashville and circulate among people, people were not so displeased with these stories as they were pleased to find on his next visit that he behaved as of old while in Nashville.

He was a tall, fair headed young man, softly spoken, and he dressed conventionally. When he came into his mother's front hall that Saturday afternoon on the second of July he was still wearing the seersucker suit in which he had traveled. Harriet was not at the door to greet him, but as she came from her room she could hear amid the flurry of greetings his polite voice asking in his formal way if she were well. She met him at the door of the parlor and as she threw her arms about him she found herself unable to restrain her tears.

She thought, of course, that her weeping would subside in a moment and she did not even hide her face in her handkerchief. She tried to speak to him and then pushing him a little aside she tried to say something to the young woman he had brought with him. But the sight of Miss Prewitt there beside Sweetheart seemed to open new valves and it seemed that she was beginning to choke. When she had first seen Son in the doorway his very appearance had confirmed the justice of her outraged feelings this afternoon. When she saw the ladylike young woman in a black traveling dress and white gloves (as an example of his taste) it occurred to her that she had even underestimated the grossness of Mattie's reflection upon him. Her weeping became so violent now and was so entirely a physical thing that it seemed not to correspond to her feelings at all. First she tried to stifle and choke down her tears physically. This failing, she tried to shame herself into composure, thinking of what a vulgar display Mama would have called this. Presently she recognized that her state was already hysteria. Sweetheart rushed forward and supported her, and Son tried to hold one hand which she was waving about.

They walked her slowly to her room speaking to her gently. All the while she was trying at moments to think of the reason for this collapse. It was not—as they would all believe—Son's going into the Army. It could not be simply the scene she had had with her cook that afternoon. Could it be that she had always hated this black, servant race and felt them a threat to her son and her family? Such ridiculous thoughts! Then she was alternately laughing and weeping, and they put her on her bed. Sweetheart attended her and then sat holding her hand till she was absolutely quiet. Later the girls took their turns at sitting with her. All she could remember about Son that afternoon was hearing him say, out in the hall it seemed, "How unlike Mother."

It was late in the evening before they would let her move from her bed or leave her room. But by ten o'clock Sweetheart was convinced that her fretting there in bed was more harmful than a little company up in the front room would be. She declared herself to' be quite recovered and after a bit of washing and powdering she presented herself to the four young people who were playing bridge in the parlor.

"Well, well, have a seat," Son said extending his left hand to her.

His manner was casual, as was that of the others—studiedly so. For they wanted to make her comfortable. Even Miss Prewitt restrained her attentions, pretending to be absorbed in the cards although she was dummy. "The girls have given us a good trimming tonight," she said.

When Miss Prewitt spoke, Harriet observed that she had extremely crooked teeth which had been brought more or less into line probably by wearing bands as a child. Her face was rather plain but her cheeks had a natural rosiness to them and her eyes though too small were bright and responsive. She wore no make-up and was redolent of no detectable perfume or powder. And before she sat down in the chair which Sweetheart drew up for her Harriet had perceived that the girl took no pains with her hair which hung in a half-long bob with some natural wave.

"We're teaching these Yankees a thing or two," Helena said winking playfully at Kate.

"Will you listen to that?" Miss Prewitt smiled and revealed to Harriet a pleasant manner and an amiable, ladylike nature. "Your daughters keep calling their own brother and myself Yankees. But of course it's partly his fault, for I learn that he didn't write you that I'm from Little Rock, myself, and that I'm on my way home for a visit."

"Isn't that man-like?" Harriet said.

Now Son dropped his last three trumps on the table and proclaimed that that was "game." He suggested that they quit playing, but Harriet insisted that they complete the rubber. Helena began to deal the cards. For a time no one spoke. Harriet pretended to gaze about the room but she could hardly keep her eyes off Miss Prewitt. For though she found her extremely agreeable she perceived that the possibility of any romantic attachment between her and Son was out of the question. The tie between them was doubtless what the girls called an intellectual friendship. In her own girlhood people would have called it Platonic, but then they would have laughed about it. Mama had always said there could be no such relationship between young men and young women. Sweetheart always showed the smutty and cynical side to his nature when such things were discussed. Yet in some matters Son surely knew more than either Mama or Sweetheart. She had of course never, herself, known such a friendship with a man and just now she was really trying to imagine the feelings that two such friends would have for one another.

Until Miss Prewitt had spoken and thus started that train of thought in her mind Harriet had been wondering how dinner came off and whether Mattie served the chicken necks. But now her thoughts had been diverted and her nerves were somewhat relieved. It was she who finally broke the silence. "For Heaven's sake," she said, "let's not be so reserved. You're all being so careful of my feelings that Miss Prewitt will think I have a nervous ailment. My dear, that's the first time in my life I've ever carried on so. You just mustn't judge me by that scene I made. I have no sympathy with women who carry on so."

Then Sweetheart and the children did begin to tease her and make light of her carrying-on. Presently the conversation became animated and she was soon calling Miss Prewitt "Ann" as the girls did. Helena and Kate, she had never seen more cordial to a stranger than to Ann. She had never, indeed, seen them sweeter with one another. It was not until they had played their last card and had shaken hands across the table in acknowledgment of their complete victory that the strangeness of their behavior occurred to Harriet. It had been many a day since they had sat down at the same bridge table, for if they were partners they usually ended by calling each other "stupid" and if they were not partners they not infrequently accused each other of cheating.

Now Harriet felt herself trembling again and she was unable to follow the conversation. After a few minutes she said, "I think what we all need is a good night's sleep." The girls agreed at once, and so did Sweetheart. But Son suggested that he and Ann would like to sit up and talk for a while. Nobody seemed to take exception to this but Sweetheart who gave a little frown and shrugged his shoulders. Then he led Harriet off to their room, and the girls followed inquiring if there was anything they could do for Mother. As Harriet left the parlor she glanced back and observed that Ann's legs were as large and graceless as two fire plugs.

Sweetheart was in bed before her and lay there watching her own preparations at the dressing table. She felt that she was barely able to conceal from him the difficulty she had in rolling her hair and pulling on the net. But when she turned to put off the light she found him fast asleep.

She was standing in the dark for a moment and she heard the voices of Son and Ann out on the porch. Without even considering her action she stepped to the window and listened to their lowered voices.

"She's a very pretty and attractive little woman," Ann was saying, "but from things you had said I was not quite prepared to find her such a nervous woman."

"That's true. But I don't think she really is a nervous woman," Son said slowly. "I believe nobody was more surprised than herself at what happened this afternoon."

"It's not just what happened this afternoon. She was trembling most of the time in the living room tonight."

"I can't imagine what it is. Something seems to have come over her. But there's no visible change. She hasn't aged any. I looked for it in her hair and in the skin about her neck and in her figure." It hardly seemed possible to Harriet that this was Son talking about herself.

"She's certainly past her menopause, isn't she?"

"Oh, certainly. Several years ago when I was still in school."

"That's rather early."

"Yes. . . . Yes."

"The girls are much more conventional than I imagined, much less independent, more feminine.—"

"Something," Son emphasized, "seems to have come over them, too."

"They're too young for any sort of frustration, I suppose."

This whispered but clearly audible conversation caused Harriet to feel herself alienated from all around her. It was Son's disinterested tone and objectiveness. Her mind returned to Mattie. She wondered how she and BT would behave through the week-end. And now looking out into the back yard where the moon was shining on the shingled roof of the cabin and through the trees to the porch steps she considered again the words she had used to Mattie out there this afternoon.

The girls had planned a small party for Monday night which was July Fourth. It was not to be at the Country Club, where they had always before preferred to entertain, but at the house. But on Sunday night one of Son's old friends named Harry Buchanan had invited the group to supper at the club. Harry was married and had two small children.

At the breakfast table Sunday morning Helena said to Ann, "We didn't plan anything for last night because we knew you two would be tired from traveling. But we're having a few friends to the house tomorrow night, and tonight the Buchanans"—she hesitated and closed her eyes significantly—"have asked us to supper at the Club. I don't know why some people must entertain at clubs and hotels."

"It all sounds quite festive," Ann said.

"Yes, I'm afraid 'festive' is the word," said Kate. "When people ask you to a hotel or a club, instead of to their home, if the occasion's not 'festive' or 'gala' what can it be? I don't take such an invitation as a great compliment."

Ann said nothing. Son looked over his pink grapefruit, perplexed. Harriet was completely mystified now by the things her daughters were saying. It sounded like pure nonsense to her although she was pleased to see them in such accord. She could not say that she disagreed with them, but it did sound like nonsense because it was the very reverse of ideas they usually expressed. Perhaps it was because they were growing older and more like herself. "One never realizes when one's children are growing up," she thought. But whether or not she agreed with them in principle she did think it ungracious and unkind of them to speak that way about Son's friend who was entertaining them tonight.

"Kate," she said, "the Buchanans have two small children and their house is so small."

The two daughters laughed. "Dear, dear Mama," Helena said, "you're such a Christian. You wouldn't say anything against *any*body on Sunday, would you?"

"Let me ask you this, Mama," said Kate. "Would your Mother have liked entertaining visitors at a Golf Club?"

Harriet shook her head. "That was long ago when Mama entertained, and it was not the custom then."

"There you are. We're only thinking as you've taught us to think, Mama, when we think that many of the customs and ways that used to pertain in Nashville were better than what is replacing them."

Harriet asked herself if that was what she had taught them to think. She didn't know she had taught them to think anything. But her only real interest in the matter was the defense of Harry Buchanan whose wife's mother, she presently said, was a dear friend of hers and was from one of Nashville's loveliest families and certainly knew how to "do." Then Helena asked with apparent artlessness what her dear friend's maiden name had been. And the question led to a prolonged discussion between the girls and their mother and even their father of the kinship of various Nashville families. Nothing yet had amazed Harriet more than the knowledge of those kinships and connections which Helena and Kate proceeded to display.

"Why, you two girls," Sweetheart said in his innocence, "are getting to rival your mother in matters of who's kin to who." But Harriet was observing Son and Ann who remained silent and kept their eyes on their food. She herewith resolved that she would make it her special task during the remainder of the visit to avoid such talk since it seemed to cause a mysterious antagonism between the young people.

After breakfast Son and Ann left for a walk about the premises in the company of Sweetheart who wanted to show them his orchards and his four acres of oats and the old cotton patch where he had had BT put in lespedeza this year. They were also to see his poultry and the Jersey cow whose milk at breakfast had tasted of wild onions. He urged Helena and Kate to come along and show off the vegetable garden where they had worked and directed BT's labor. But the girls declined, saying that they were through with outdoor life until the weather was cool again. Harriet said to herself, "They're perfect angels and don't want to leave the housework to me this morning."

Later Sweetheart came back to the house and settled himself on the porch with the Sunday morning paper while Son and Ann walked down the Pike toward the Confederate Monument. Harriet debated the question of going to church. Sweetheart advised against it in view of her nervous agitation. Then she dismissed the idea, for she dared not reject Sweetheart's advice in such matters, though for a while there did linger the thought of how restful church service would seem. When the straightening up was done the girls went to their reading again and Harriet made a visit to the kitchen that she had been postponing all morning.

"Mattie," she said, "do you have everything?" Mattie was seated at a kitchen table with her back to the swinging door through which Harriet had entered, and she did not turn around. The table was in the center of the huge, shadowy kitchen. Directly beyond the table was the doorway to the back porch, through which opening Harriet could see BT also working at a table.

"I reckon," Mattie answered after a moment. There was no movement of her head when she spoke. And her head was not bent over the table. She seemed to be staring through the doorway at BT. She was seated there on a high, unpainted wooden stool which she had long ago had BT make for her (though she had complained at the time of having to pay him for it out of her own stocking), and since BT had selfishly made the stool to accommodate his own long legs Mattie's stockinged feet drooped, rather than dangled, above her old slippers that had fallen one upon the other on the linoleum.

She was not wearing her white cap or white serving apron, so there was absolutely no relief to her black dress and her head of black hair. She was the darkest object in the whole of the dark old fashioned kitchen—blacker even than the giant range stove whereon the vegetables were boiling and in which a fire roared that kept the kitchen so hot that Harriet had hesitated to step beyond the door sill. Harriet looked about to see if the windows were open and found them all open but that window where the winter icebox was built on, and she knew Mattie would not open that window while there were so many tomatoes and heads of cabbage and lettuce to keep fresh.

In the kitchen there was only the sound of water boiling. Through the back door she could see BT in the bright sunlight on the porch and hear the regular thumping of his knife on the table as he chopped a cocoanut for the ambrosia. He seemed to be unaware of or totally indifferent to Mattie's gaze upon him. Harriet stepped back into the pantry and let the door swing shut drawing a hot breeze across her face. The two Negroes doubtless had been sitting like that for hours without a word between them. It was a picture she was not able to forget.

Among the family friends the Wilson girls were admired no less than Son though they were considered to have more temperament. (By this it was meant that they occasionally displayed bad temper in public.) They were spoken of as devoted daughters and thoroughly capable and energetic young women. Helena who was known generally as the blonde Wilson girl, though her brown hair was only a shade lighter than Kate's, sometimes taught classes at Miss Hood's school during the winter. She usually substituted, and could teach mathematics, art appreciation or modern literature to the seniors. During the winter when there were more colds and throat trouble, Kate helped with the receiving and secretarial work at Sweetheart's office.

They had large, round pleasant faces which often seemed identical to strangers. Their voices were considered identical by everyone outside the family, even by close family friends who often remarked that they didn't speak with the vulgar drawl that so many Nashville girls have adopted. Their vocabulary and their accents were more like those of their mother. They pronounced girl as "gull" as all Nashville ladies once used to do. And so it was often shocking to a stranger after hearing their slightly metallic but very feminine and old fashioned voices to turn and discover that both girls were over six feet tall. Their ages were "in the vicinity of thirty," as was Son's, and they too never seemed to have considered matrimony.

As Harriet was returning from the kitchen her ear recognized Kate's familiar touch at the piano. It was by the bass that she could always distinguish the girls' playing; Kate's was a little the heavier but with more variations. She was playing accompaniment to the ballad *Barbara Allen,* and presently Helena's straining falsetto could be heard. Then as Harriet passed through the hall she saw through the open front door Son and Ann walking up the straight driveway from the Pike. Son wore white linen trousers and a white shirt open at the collar. Ann looked very fresh and youthful in a peasant-like shirtwaist and skirt, though the flare of the skirt did accentuate the heaviness of her legs. They walked over the white gravel beneath the green canopy of the trees and the picture was framed in the semi-circle of lavender wisteria that blossomed round the entrance to the porch. The prettiness of it made Harriet sigh. It seemed that her sorrow over Son's going into the Army would not be so great if she could believe that he and Ann were in love. This old house and the surrounding woods and pastures had always seemed to her the very setting for romance. From the time when her girls had first begun to have a few beaux she had considered what a felicitous setting the swing on the front porch or the old iron bench down by the fence stile would be for the final proposal; and during her walks with Sweetheart in the evenings she would sometimes look about the lawn trying to fix upon the best spot for a garden wedding. Now the sight of Son and Ann in this pretty frame only reminded her of their unnatural and strange relationship. They were walking far apart and Ann was speaking with deliberation and gesturing as she spoke. But apparently at the first glimpse of Harriet, Ann broke off speaking. And Harriet perceived in an instant that there was at least a trouble of some kind in their relationship. She recollected now that though Son had not been talking he had been shaking his head from side to side as though in exasperation.

Kate was still playing and Helena singing (after her fashion) when they entered the parlor. Son was not long able to restrain his laughter although he had actually pressed his hand over his mouth. When his laughter finally did explode the two girls sprang up from the piano bench. Their mother stood paralyzed, expecting a greater explosion of temper from them. But they only smiled with a shamefaced expression that was utterly artificial. Ann had turned to Son and was remonstrating with him. "I really should think you'd be ashamed," she said.

"Why, he's completely shameless and unchivalrous," Helena said with the same false expression of tolerance and good nature on her face. It was this expression which the faces of both girls were affecting that stunned and mystified Harriet beyond all bounds. She knew now that they were in league to accomplish some purpose. She could see that they were fully prepared for Son's reaction and that it was even desired.

"Hush, Son, you idiot," Kate smiled. Then turning to Ann: "That old ballad is one Mama taught us when we were children. Of course none of us have Mama's music, but we weren't expecting an audience." And finally she addressed her sister, "The only trouble is, Helena, you were not singing the right words—not the words Mama taught us."

"No," Son derided, "you were singing from the Oxford Book of Verse."

"I know," Helena admitted with her feigned modesty and frankness. "But, Mama," she said to Harriet, "sing us your version—the real Tennessee version."

And they all began to insist that Harriet play and sing. At first she would not, for she felt that she was being a dupe to her two daughters. It was for this that the whole scene had been arranged! If she could avoid it she would not assist them in any of their schemings. If there was to be antagonism between her children she was not going to take sides. At breakfast the girls had led her to support their criticism of country club life and modern ways by bringing in Mama's opinions. Now her singing of an old ballad would somehow support their cause.

But Son and Ann were insisting as well. She looked at Son and he said, "Please do sing." So if her singing was what they all wanted, how could she refuse? Perhaps it would make them forget whatever was the trouble. Besides, Harriet loved so to be at the piano singing the old songs that were fixed so well in her ear and in her heart.

As she sat down before the piano Helena ran to get Sweetheart, for he would never forgive them if Mother sang without his hearing it. She would also get Mattie who loved hearing her mistress sing above all else. Then Helena returned with her father saying that Mattie would listen from the pantry.

So as Sweetheart took his stand by the upright piano and watched her with that rare expression of alertness in his eyes and as the young people grouped themselves behind her Harriet began to play and sing. Her soprano voice came as clear and fresh as when she was nineteen.

When she had finished *Barbara Allen* she followed with other ballads almost without being asked. Anyone listening could tell how well she enjoyed singing the old songs that her Grandpa had taught her long ago and how well she remembered the lyrics and the melody, never faltering in the words or hesitating on the keyboard. But her lovely, natural talent was not merely of the music. She seemed actually to experience the mood of each song. And her memory and ear for the soft vowels and sharp consonants of the mountain dialect were such that what was really a precise rendition seemed effortless. All her family and their guest stood round remarking on the sweet, true quality of her voice.

At the dinner table the girls began to talk again of who was kin to whom in Nashville. "Mama," Kate said, "I didn't know till the other day that Miss Liza Parks is Mrs. Frazier Dalton's aunt. She's one of that Parks family who used to live at Cedar Hill."

Harriet could hardly resist saying that Miss Liza was also second cousin to Mr. Bob Ragsdale. But without even looking at Kate she said, "Now, what interest could that be to Ann? Tell us, Ann, how you liked Sweetheart's little farm."

"Oh, it's a beauty," Ann said. "And his methods are quite modern. He even rotates his crops and paints his barn. Dr. Wilson is certainly no backward Southern farmer. BT showed us the garden, and I think BT is a wonder."

"He's grand on outside work," Harriet said.

The two girls began to laugh, and Harriet frowned at them.

"Son has told me," Ann whispered to Harriet, for Mattie was passing in and out of the room, "about the poor fellow's peculiarity. He's going away for the duration, I understand, but when he comes back why doesn't he try to get a farm of his own and make a real business of it? You can tell he has a genuine love of farming, and he's quite intelligent, isn't he? He ought to——"

"Now, Ann," Son interrupted, "how on earth is a poor Negro just going to reach out and get himself a farm? How can you ask such a question with all your knowledge of conditions?"

"I was thinking that Dr. Wilson would help him. Wouldn't you, Doctor?"

"Yes, of course, if he wanted——"

. The girls were laughing together again. "That's just it," Helena said, *"if* BT wanted to. But he's a gentleman's nigger, Ann. He worships Daddy, and Daddy couldn't live without him. It's a very old fashioned relationship, you know what I mean? It's the same with Mother and Mattie." At this point Mattie came in. She was serving the last of the four vegetable dishes. Nobody spoke while she was in the room. The picture of Mattie and BT in the kitchen this morning returned to Harriet, and she found herself thinking again of what she had said to Mattie yesterday in the yard. The brooding expression in Mattie's eyes and her repeated glances at Son as she passed round the table suggested anew the hateful comparison she had drawn. But Harriet could not feel such strong resentment now. She told herself that it was because she saw now how great was the real difference between her Son and Mattie's little-nephew. It was too absurd even to consider. She must have been out of her head yesterday! Her nerves had been on edge. That was the answer. And Mattie had spoken to her about that foul-scented BT just when she was grieving most about Son's going into the Army. Today the real pain of that grief had left her. It would doubtless return. But why, she considered, had it left her now? It seemed that his putting on a uniform was as unreal and indifferent a matter to her as the mysterious life he led in New York and his intellectual friendship with Ann Prewitt and this conversation they were having at her table. Last night she had overheard Son and Ann discussing herself as objectively as they were now discussing BT and Negro "conditions." Then she rebuked herself and allowed that Son simply lived on a higher plane. She felt that she should be ashamed to understand so little about her son and about her daughters and the antagonism there was between the young people.

When Mattie had left the room Kate said, "Yes, it's quite the same with Mattie and Mama. Yesterday Mattie was upset by some bad news and she came and threw herself into Mama's arms and wept like a child. It seems to me that's what they really are: a race of children, a medieval peasantry. They're completely irresponsible and totally dependent upon us. I really feel that Southern white people have a great responsibility——"

"We are responsible," Ann Prewitt said, "for their being irresponsible and dependent, if that's what you mean, Kate."

"Oh, that's *not* what she means," said Helena. "Their whole race is in its childhood, Ann, with all the wonders and charm of childhood. And it needs the protection, supervision, discipline and affection that can be given only by Southern white people who have a vital relationship and traditional ties with them. The poor nigs who I feel for are those in Chicago and New York who have no white families to turn to."

Ann was looking at Son to see if he were going to make an argument of this. But Son said only, "What do you think of that, Ann?"

With an aggrieved, shy glance at Son she said, "I think it's a lot of nonsense. But that's only my opinion."

"Well, it's my opinion too," said Son. "The people in the South cannot expect to progress with the rest of the nation until they've forgotten their color line. The whole system has got to be changed. In some strange way it hinders the whites more than the blacks. When BT was in the garden with us this morning I felt that this was his home more than mine and that it was because of him that I feel no real tie to this place. Even when we were children it was so. . . . The whole system has got to be changed . . . somehow . . . some way."

"Somehow!" Ann exclaimed. Then she lowered her eyes and seemed to regret having spoken.

"You have a definite idea of how, then?" Helena asked.

"Equality: economic and social."

"You can't be serious," the girls said in one voice.

"Of course, she's serious," Son rejoined. Ann was silent. She appeared to have resolved not to speak again.

"You two are speaking as New Yorkers now," Helena began, "not as Southerners. Didn't it ever occur to you that the South has its own destiny? It has an entirely different tradition from the rest of the country. It has its own social institutions and must be allowed to work out its own salvation without interference."

"Sister," Son laughed, "you're beginning to sound not merely old fashioned but unreconstructed."

"Then unreconstructed it is," defied Kate with a gallant smile. "Who can say that the Southern States were wrong to fight for their way of life?"

"For slavery, Kate?"

"The Southern master was morally responsible which is more than can be said for the industrial sweat-shopper."

Now Son slapped his hand over his mouth and presently his vehement laughter burst forth. He pushed his chair a little way from the table and said, "Now the cat's out of the bag! I know what you girls have been reading and who you've probably been seeing—those fellows at the University in Nashville. You know who I mean, Ann! Why, Ann, I've brought you into a hotbed of Southern reactionaries. How rich! How really rich this is! Now I know what you girls have been trying to put across. You and all Southern gentlemen and gentlewomen are the heirs and protectors of the great European traditions—the agrarian tradition, I should say. That's what all of this family pride and *noblesse oblige* means. And Ann here, my comrade, believes that come the Revolution it will all be changed over night. How rich!"

His laughter was curiously contagious and there did seem to be a general relief among all. "And now, my wise brother," asked Kate, "what do you believe?"

Ann and the two sisters were managing to smile at one another, for Son's derision had united them temporarily. While Son was trying to get his breath Ann leaned across the table and said, "He believes nothing that's any credit to him. He's been reading *The Decline of The West!* A man his age!"

Harriet was utterly dismayed, though she did sense that the incomprehensible antagonism had reached its crisis and that the worst was over. At least the young people understood each other now. But as they were leaving the table she wished, for the first time in many years, that she could be alone for a while this afternoon. She wanted to remember how Son and Helena and Kate had been when they were children—the girls quarreling over scraps from her sewing or playing dolls on the porch and Son begging to go off swimming with BT when the creek was still cold in May.

Everybody slept late on the morning of the Fourth of July. Sweetheart was still snoring gently at nine-thirty. He awoke when Harriet started the electric fan. "I'm so sorry, Sweetheart," she said, "but you looked so hot there I thought the fan might help." She was already half dressed, but before she had snapped the last snap in the placket of her dress Sweetheart had put on his clothes and shaved and gone out onto the porch. She smiled as she thought of it; and then she began to hurry, for Son's voice could now be heard on the porch. Besides there was a lot to be done in preparation for the supper party tonight. Probably the girls were already helping in the kitchen. They were being such angels this week-end!

She was smoothing the last corner of the counterpane when Kate came in.

"I feel like the devil," Kate said. She was wearing her silk negligee and her hair was uncombed and even matted in places. She was bare-footed; and the girls always looked taller to Harriet when in their bare feet.

"And you look like the very devil," Harriet said.

"Thanks, dear." She sat down on the bed which Harriet had just now made. She struck a match on the bottom of the bedside table and lit the cigarette which she had brought with her. She patted the bed beside her indicating for Harriet to sit down. Harriet could always tell when the girls had been drinking a good deal the night before by the sour expression which the heavy sleep left on their features. She was long since accustomed to their drinking "socially," and to their smoking, but she still did not like to smell the whiskey on them next morning. She pulled up her rocking chair and sat down.

"Mother, I do wish that Helena wouldn't drink so much. She just doesn't know how."

Harriet only shook her head, saying nothing, for Helena would have a similar report about Kate later in the morning. The truce between them was evidently over. "How was the Buchanans' party?" she asked.

"It was pretty nice." Then she shrugged her shoulders. "I want to tell you about Ann."

"What is there to tell?"

"I thought you wanted to hear about the party!" Kate said sharply.

"I do."

"Well, listen, that's what I mean—how Ann behaved last night."

"She didn't misbehave?"

"I should say not. She's a perfect little lady, you know. A perfect parlor pink, as we suspected—Helena and I."

Parlor-pink meant nothing to Harriet. She turned her face away toward the window to indicate that if Kate persisted in talking the kind of nonsense they talked at the table yesterday she didn't care to listen.

"She holds her liquor well, all right," Kate continued, "but after a few drinks she's not the quiet little mouse she is around here. She talks incessantly and rather brilliantly, I admit. And what I'm getting at is that when she talks Son seems to hang on her every word. He plainly thinks she's the cleverest woman alive."

"What does she talk about?"

"For one thing, she talked about birth control and its implications to Lucy Price who is a Catholic. She was really very funny about the Pope as the great papa who *doesn't* pay." Harriet had no full understanding of birth control itself, much less of its implications. And she knew that she was unreasonably prejudiced against Catholics. Why couldn't Kate talk about Ann without dragging in those things?

"She quotes Marx and Huxley and lots of young British poets. And all the while Son sits beaming with admiration as though she were Sappho or Margaret Sanger, herself."

"Is he in love with her then, Kate, if he does all that?"

"Not at all."

"And Ann, herself?"

"Hardly! She's not the type. She never looks at him."

Harriet sighed.

"But there's something between them," Kate said speculatively.

"I suppose intellectual friendships can have very deep feelings."

"Pooh," said Kate.

"Then the girl is in love with him, and he——"

"No, Mother. I don't believe it." But Harriet looked at her daughter with the matted hair and the sleep-creased face and the cigarette with its smoke drifting straight upward into the breathless air. *Her* girls had never been in love. And it isn't their height, she thought, and it isn't their legs. They're like Son, she thought, and it isn't in them. She got up from her chair and as she left Kate behind she met Helena at the door. Helena's face and hair and general attire were about the same as Kate's. "Kate's in there," Harriet said and brushed past the daughter who towered above her in the doorway. She went into the parlor to draw the draperies before the sun got too warm.

The day grew warm. You could almost hear the temperature rising if you stood still a minute. Harriet was so busy about the house that she thought it her activity that made her perspire. But now and then she would step out to the porch and slip on her spectacles to look at the thermometer. "What an awful day," she would say to Sweetheart who was sleeping in his chair.

The girls remained in their room until afternoon. Once or twice Harriet heard them speaking irritably to one another. When they finally appeared Helena turned on the radio in the parlor and Kate sat on the porch. They would show no interest in the coming party. They sulked about as though they had been disappointed or defeated in something.

"Quit buzzing around, Mother," Kate said. "There are only a dozen or so people coming and it's supposed to be informal."

"Oh, Goddy, I never saw so much commotion over a cold supper," Helena said.

Ann tried to help, but Harriet said, "There's nothing left to do. I just have to cut the melon balls and everything will be ready."

Later Sweetheart and Son went off to Nashville to pick up the whiskey at the hotel. Ann went along to make her Pullman reservations, for she was taking a train at one A.M. She said she had to be in Little Rock the next day.

Most of the guests parked their cars in the back yard alongside BT's shack or in front of the garage. As they arrived Son went out into the yard to greet them or welcomed them on the screened porch. Supper was served buffet style, and Sweetheart brought everybody two or three drinks before they began to eat. "We want you to have an appetite," he would say.

The guests were, for the most part, Son's old school friends and their wives. There were two young men of sufficient height to escort the girls from room to room. And there was a young professor from the University and his wife who had taught at Miss Hood's School with Helena. Son was most cordial to this couple, introducing himself to them in the yard since Helena was not present when they arrived. The young professor (he explained that he was really only a teaching-fellow), wore a small mustache and a dark bow tie with his linen suit. He was very timid and spoke only a few words in the course of the whole evening.

While dressing for the party Harriet observed in the mirror that her face showed the strain she had been under. She spread extra powder under her eyes and applied more rouge than was usual with her. When she had finished her toilet she removed all her personal things from the dressing table, opened a new box of powder, and brought from the closet shelf an ivory handmirror and comb and brush. The ladies were going to use this as a powder room. From the closet shelf she also brought four small pillows with lacy slipovers which she arranged on the bed.

She was arranging the pillows when Son knocked at her door. He entered with his own large glass in one hand and a small tumbler for her in the other. "It's mostly gingerale," he said, "and I thought it would cool you off. It's right hot tonight."

It is this moment, she thought, that I've been waiting for through the whole week-end. And in this moment she banished all the despair that had been growing in her feelings toward Son and the girls. The insufferable insolence with which Mattie had treated her today also seemed as nothing. He has come to tell me what is in his heart. Or at least he has come so that we may have a few minutes alone before he leaves for the Army tomorrow. She glanced up at the childhood pictures of him which with pictures of the girls and a few of Mama and Papa and of Sweetheart covered one wall of her room. She pointed to a picture taken when he was thirteen wearing a skull cap on the back of his head and a sleeveless sweater. "That's my favorite," she said. "I began to notice a new look in your eyes when you were that age."

Son looked at the picture. Then his eyes roved indifferently over the other pictures there. "Well," he said, "I'd better go out and see that the girls are not sticking hat pins in Ann just to see how she reacts. Or at least not miss seeing it, myself, if they do."

The guests were beginning to leave by eleven-thirty. Harriet was sitting in a straight chair on the front porch. She had been sitting there in the dark for an hour with her hands folded in her lap. Sweetheart was slumped down among the pillows on the swing near by, asleep. The party had all been vague, like a dream of some event she dreaded, to Harriet. After Son left her standing alone before the gallery of pictures in her room she was hardly able to go into the house and meet the guests. There were no tears and no signs of nervous agitation. Rather, she felt herself completely without human emotion of any sort as she lingered there in her room for a long while. When finally she did go forward and take her place by the buffet in the dining room she pretended to be preoccupied with the food so that the guests would not notice how little concern she had for them. There were things she had planned to watch for this evening; but those things had become trivial and remote.

Early in the evening most of the party was gathered in the parlor and much of the conversation referred to things that had been said and done last night. Harry Buchanan urged Ann to express her views on something, but Ann declined. Several times Son was asking Ann what she thought about this or that, and always it seemed that Ann spoke two or three monosyllables which were followed by silence. Conversation between Son and the young professor did not materialize, and the girls did not try to draw him out as Harriet had expected. Ann and the professor were once heard talking about the "fragrance" of the wisteria. Helena took her tall, stooped young man to sit on the screened porch. Kate took hers to the chairs on the lawn. Now and then the two beaux appeared in the house on their way to the pantry with tall, empty glasses. Nothing could stir Harriet from her torpor, not even the information that in the middle of the evening BT had put on his hat and gone off to the settlement or to Nashville.

When she realized that the guests were beginning to go she placed her hand on Sweetheart's knee and said, "People are leaving, Sweetheart." He followed her into the hall and the two of them stood smiling and nodding and shaking hands of guests amid a hubbub of giddy and even drunken talk about Son's going into the Army. As the last of the automobiles pulled away, backing and turning in the gravel before the garage with its headlamps flashing on BT's shack and on the house and then on the trees and the white gravel of the driveway, someone called back, "Goodbye, Private Wilson!"

Harriet stood on the screened porch after the headlamps had gone round the house leaving the yard in darkness. While she was there she saw the light go off in the kitchen. The back door closed, and presently Mattie's dark figure moved sluggishly across the yard to the shack. There was no window on the near side of the little cabin, but when Mattie had put on the light inside, Harriet could see a square of light which a small window threw on the thick, green mint bed over by the fence. "She's going to wait up for BT," Harriet said. And now she went through the house and into the warm kitchen to see in what state Mattie had left things.

The dishes were not washed but they were stacked neatly on the table and in the sink. The back door was locked, and Harriet unlocked it so that Mattie could come in that way to go to her bed in the attic room above the kitchen. "Poor thing is so distracted she locked herself out," she said. She stood with her hand on the knob for a minute, for she wanted to go out and see Mattie. She could not bring herself to go.

When she came into the parlor she found that Ann had changed to her traveling dress. Helena and Kate were sprawled in two of the large chairs. Sweetheart was standing by the fireplace talking about train schedules to Little Rock. Ann was seated on the piano bench with her feet close together and her small delicate hands folded in her lap. Harriet had crossed the room and was taking her seat beside Ann when Son entered with the luggage.

"It's not quite time to go," Son said. He set the two bags by the hall door and drew up an odd chair. Harriet had taken one of Ann's hands between her own and was about to make a little farewell speech when Ann spoke.

She was looking into Harriet's face but as she spoke she turned her eyes to Son. "He thinks I have not behaved well tonight."

"Oh, for Heaven's sake, Ann," Son said turning in his chair and crossing his legs. Kate and Helena visibly collected their sprawled persons and looked attentively from Ann to Son.

"He does, indeed," said Ann. She stood up and walked to the mantel and stood at the other end from Sweetheart. "Very badly. He always thinks a person behaves badly who doesn't amuse him. He cares nothing for anything I say except when I'm talking theory of some kind. He was very willing to bring me here before your friends to express all manner of opinion which they and you find disagreeable while he behaves with conventional good taste. He even discouraged my bringing the proper clothes to make any sort of agreeable appearance. Yet see how smartly he's turned-out."

Son had now ceased to show any discomfort. He was watching Ann with the same interest that the girls showed. He was smiling when he interrupted her, "You are really drunk, Ann. But go on. You're priceless. You're rich. What else about me?"

"Nothing else about you," she said, undismayed. "But about me now. . . . We have had a very beautiful and very Platonic friendship. He has shown a marvelous respect for my intelligence and my virtue. And I, alas, have been so vulgar as to fall in love with him." She turned to Sweetheart who stood with his hands hanging limp at his sides and his mouth literally wide open. "It's a sad story, is it not, Doctor?" The doctor tried to smile.

Son rose from his chair saying, "Now it *is* time we go." And he and Ann left the room in such a hurry that Harriet was still seated when she heard them step out onto the porch. Then she jumped from her place on the piano bench and began to follow them.

But she had only reached the doorway to the hall when one of the girls said, "Mother, can't you see how drunk that gal really is?" As she stopped there in the hall her eyes fell on the mahogany umbrella rack where Sweetheart kept his seven walking sticks. She counted the sticks and it seemed that there were only six of them. Then she counted them again and found that all seven were in their places. She counted them several times over, and each time there were still seven sticks in the rack.

Harriet was on her knees at her bedside. She had already repeated the Lord's Prayer twice but still was unable to think of the meaning of the words as she began it the third time. Her elbows were pressing into the soft mattress, and though the room was in darkness her eyes were closed. She was repeating the prayer slowly, moving her lips as she pronounced each word, when the fierce shout of a Negro woman seemed to break not only the silence but even the darkness. Sweetheart had sprung from the bed and put on the light. Harriet remained on her knees and watched him go to the closet shelf to get his pistol. "It's Mattie," he said. "It's Mattie screaming!"

"No, it's not Mattie," she said. "I don't think it was a scream either." Sweetheart turned his eyes to her with a suddenness that struck her dumb for a moment. When she was able to speak she said, "It's one of those women BT has." But the doctor had understood her before she spoke again and in his white pyjamas had already disappeared into the darkness of the hallway.

His hearing had been keen enough to detect that it was a Negro's voice. But his ear was not so sensitive as Harriet's. She was the only one in the house who knew that Mattie was waiting in the shack, and the shout had come distinctly from that quarter; but her ear was not deceived for an instant. She raised herself from her knees and faced her two daughters who had come to her door. She knew as well now as they would know when they were told a few minutes later what scene was taking place in the low doorway of that cabin. In her mind she saw the very shadows that were then being thrown on the green mint bed.

The first shout was followed by other distinct oaths. Now Mattie's and BT's voices could be heard mixing with that of the third Negro.

So Harriet knew too that there had not yet been a cutting. "Hurry, Sweetheart," she called in a voice that hardly seemed her own. The girls stood watching her, and she stood motionless listening for every sound. Presently there came amid the voices the crunching sound of gravel under the wheels of her own coupe. Son was returning from the depot. She pushed herself between the girls and went to the window in their room. From there she could see that the incident was over. Sweetheart and Son stood in the bright lights from the headlamps of the automobile. They stood talking there for several minutes, and then Son came toward the house and Sweetheart went into the shack.

Son came into her room where she and the girls were waiting. His face was pale, but he was smiling. "It's not really anything," he said. "BT had brought one of his lady friends home, and his auntie would not receive her. I think his auntie even struck her. The lights of the car scared her off into the woods, and BT followed. Dad's bringing Mattie into the house."

Harriet put on her robe and went through the house to the kitchen. She waited there a long while watching the lights in the shack. Finally Sweetheart appeared on the stoop. He stood there in his white pyjamas for an endless time speaking into the doorway in such a quiet voice that she could not hear him. When he did turn and see her at the kitchen he left the shack and came to her at once.

"You'll have to talk to Mattie," he said. "She doesn't want to come in the house, but of course she'll have to. That pair just might come back tonight."

Harriet gazed at him blankly for a moment and then closed her eyes. "I can't go," she said.

"Harriet? You'll have to go, Love. I'll go with you and wait at the door. The poor creature needs you."

"Did she ask for me?"

"No. She didn't think to. She's in a terrible state. She doesn't talk."

"Did you tell her I was coming?"

"Yes," he said, "and that's the only thing that made her even look at me."

Harriet turned away and moved toward the dining room. When he called to her she was at the swinging door and she said, "I'm going to dress."

"You've no need to dress," he said. He came round the kitchen table and stopped a few feet from her. She had never known him to speak

to her in private from such a distance. "Harriet, why should this be so
hard for you?"

There was no sympathy in the question, and actually he did not seem
to want an answer to this precise question. He seemed to be making a
larger and more general inquiry into her character than he had ever
done before. She dropped her eyes to the floor and walked hurriedly by
him to the back door. She paused there and said, "Wait here."

Mattie was seated on a squat, ladder back chair whose short legs had
the look of being worn away through long usage. Her brown hands
were resting on the black dress over each knee. A dim bulb hung on a
cord almost at waist level, and the gray moths that flitted around it
were lighting on Mattie's head. Harriet came in and stood directly before her. When she first tried to speak she felt that she was going to be
nauseated by the awful smell of BT, a stench that seemed to be compounded of the smell of soiled and moldy clothing and the smell of
condensed and concentrated human sweat. She even glanced about the
room half expecting to find BT standing in one of the dark corners.
"Mattie," she said at last, "I was unkind to you Saturday. You must not
hold it against me."

Mattie raised her eyes to her mistress, and there was neither forgiveness nor resentment in them. In her protruding lower lip and in her
wide nostrils there was defiance, but it was a defiance of the general
nature of this world where she must pass her days, not of Harriet in
particular. In her eyes there was grief and there was something beyond
grief. After a moment she did speak, and she told Harriet that she was
going to sit here all night and that they had all better go on to bed in
the house. Later when Harriet tried to recall the exact tone and words
Mattie had used—as her acute ear would normally have allowed her to
do—she could not reconstruct the speech at all. It seemed as though
Mattie had used a special language common to both of them but one
they had never before discovered and could now never recover. Afterward they faced each other in uncommunicative silence for an indefinite
time. Finally Harriet moved to the door again, but she looked back
once more and she saw that besides the grief and hostility in Mattie's
eyes there was an unspeakable loneliness for which she could offer no
consolation.

When she told Sweetheart that Mattie still refused to leave the shack
he sat down on the porch steps and said that he was going to keep

watch for a while. She didn't try to dissuade him, and he said nothing more to her as she put her robe about his shoulders and went inside.

In her room she tried to resume her broken prayers. Then she lay on the bed with the light still burning and she longed to weep as she had done when she first saw Son in the doorway. Not a tear would come to her eyes. She thought of all the talking that Son and the girls had done and she felt that she was even beginning to understand what it had meant. But she sadly reflected that her children believed neither what Ann Prewitt or the professors at the University were offering them. To Harriet it seemed that her children no longer existed; it was as though they had all died in childhood as people's children used to do. All the while she kept remembering that Mattie was sitting out in that shack for the sole purpose of inhaling the odor in the stifling air of BT's room.

When Sweetheart finally came she was on her knees again at her bedside. She heard him put out the light and let himself down easily on the other side of the bed. When she opened her eyes it was dark and there was the chill of autumn night about the room.

A Man of Doubtful Character

James Ross

THEY BURIED MAJOR WILKINSON one Sunday afternoon in October, forty years ago. The funeral was held at the Cottonville Methodist Church. The day, I understand, was clear and mild and people attended from as far away as Cheraw, South Carolina. Since then the congregation of Cottonville Methodist Church has dwindled away and the building itself no longer stands on its original site. Some years back a farmer in the neighborhood bought it, put rollers under it, and hauled it home with a tractor. He uses it now for a hay barn.

But nobody wanted to buy the graveyard. If you go there in the dead of winter you can still see perhaps two hundred tombstones of various sizes. They range in color from the reddish sandrock the settlers used to take from the bluffs along Rocky River to the blue granite from the tombstone factories of Mount Airy. The dates on the headstones begin at 1802 and end a hundred and thirty years later. There is a stake fence on the West side of the graveyard that separates it from the vegetable garden of a Negro named Joe Dunlap. Along this wall there is a gray slate rock about three feet high that says James Monroe Wilkinson was born April 6, 1830 and died October 7, 1905. Underneath the bare statistics are these words, hollowed out in the rock: "Blessed Assurance, Jesus Is Mine."

But if you go there in the summertime to see for yourself, then you might as well take a brushhook along.

The Major was my father's great uncle and in our family they always spoke of him as Uncle Jim. But everybody else called him Major Wilkinson. As far back as I could remember I'd heard his name used as a kind of measure. "He's got eyes kind and blue as Major Wilkinson had. Wouldn't trust him too far." "Trouble with Will, his tongue and im-

agination keeps running a race. Big a liar as Major Wilkinson was."
"Fully as lazy as Uncle Jim. Wouldn't strike at a snake that had bit his
Ma."

And once when I was visiting an elderly, vinegary relation who was
named Aunt Bett, I noticed a stately Rhode Island Red rooster that kept
walking slowly back and forth across the front yard. "Yes," Aunt Bett
said in a rueful voice, "I have poor luck with fowls. That rooster's not
much good. Just struts around the yard all day and crows. I call him
Uncle Jim."

But when I asked her about him she just said she guessed he was a
harmless old hypocrite. "Well, what did he look like?" I asked. "Why
he was tall and kind of stout in his old age. I can't really call a good picture of him to mind, it's been so long ago," she said.

My Grandmother told me he always wore gray homespun trousers
and a white shirt. "He never wore overalls. But then he didn't need to.
He never did any work that was dirty. Nor much that was clean," she
said, adding: "He *looked* like a very sensible man."

"He deserted from the Confederate Army in 1864," Pa said. "That
was the reason he turned Republican. Before the War he voted Democratic."

"What did he look like?" I asked.

"I don't know," Pa said. "I never saw him until after he was dead.
We were living over in Anson when we got word of it. Your Grandpa
and myself hitched up to the surrey and attended his funeral. There
were droves of people went."

"He must have been a popular man," I said.

"Why, he certainly wasn't unpopular," Pa said. "Still he wasn't The
People's Choice for anything in particular that I know of."

"Maybe it was because he was so notorious," I said.

"Well, no. He wasn't to say a notorious man," Pa said.

"Then how come so many people went to his funeral?"

"I don't know," Pa said. "But it was a pretty day when they buried
him. It was a Sunday too and maybe folks just wanted to go somewhere."

For a long time they shook me off like that. But one afternoon in
August when I was about sixteen years old I think that for a short time
I saw the faint shadow of his earthly form pass before my eyes.

I had a chance to make three dollars that afternoon, pitching for the
Corinth baseball team, provided the two regular pitchers were sick, and

if I won when I pitched. But as I was passing the row of peach trees in front of the unpainted frame house where Mr. George Hill lived, somebody spoke to me in a dry, nasal voice: "What's your hurry, Son?"

It was old Mr. George himself. He was sitting there in the latticed shade of a stumpy peach tree, his head resting against the lower part of the trunk. He was a small, dehydrated man, with skin the color of a ten-cent cigar. His little eyes were black and piercing. He was said to be ninety-four years old, but got around better than most men of seventy.

"I'm going to Corinth," I said. "What time is it, Mister George?"

"Early," he said, without looking at his watch or the sun. "You got all the time in the world. Sit down here in the shade with me. Pretty soon a car's apt to come along and give you a ride to town."

He turned his face to the right and looked back down the road. "Here comes something now," he said.

"It's somebody driving two mules to a buggy," I said.

"Durant Burris, no doubt," he said. "Generally passes here every Friday about this time of day. Goes to see the doctor down town."

The two red mules brought the buggy closer. Its top glistened black like patent leather. The paint on the wheels and spokes gleamed yellow even through the foggy dust. Old Mr. Burris wore blue glasses to keep the glare of the sun from his eyes. He sat on the left of the seat, hunched forward, resting his weight on a curved walking stick that he'd propped against the dashboard. He wore a blue serge coat, in spite of the weather. Sitting beside him, holding the lines, was a small, freckle faced boy, whose right cheek was swollen with a chew of tobacco.

"Howdy, Durant! Stop and chat with me a minute!" Mr. George shouted.

"Whoa!" Mr. Burris said to the boy, who relayed the message to the mules, "Whoa!"

"How you feeling, Durant? You look hearty," Mister George said. "But it's mighty hot and dry today. I want you to drive by the house and have a glass of cider with me."

"Much obliged, George. But your cider's hard and I've done quit drinking," Mr. Burris said in his old, rumbling voice. Then he grinned in a sheepish, patient way like a man remembering some ridiculous thing he has done in the past.

"Well, come to see me, George. We got to be going now, I guess," he said. "Drive on, Bud."

The wind was beginning to blow a little. The dust rose up after the buggy wheels and began to gain on them. Mr. George Hill nodded to himself.

"Always drives on when I mention cider."

A fretful look came over his face.

"Except for him I'm the oldest living voter in Pee Dee County," he said. "But he's two months older than me. When he goes to town and idles down the street, tapping along on that walking stick, folks point him out and say, 'There's the oldest man hereabouts. And the most righteous.'"

Mr. George paused here and smiled to himself. It was a sly, patient smile.

"So Durant has got to be mighty careful on account of the reputation they have made up for him. Now I drink a little hard cider for a kind of tonic. I can do that and still be just as good a Christian as I could on water. But the time was when Durant Burris drank like a hog. Once he got started he didn't have no gauge. He was a profane man in his language too. But he repented one night at protracted meeting and was saved right there on the spot. Just turned his back on sin and walked off in the other direction. He's trod a chalk line ever since. Everybody speaks well of him. Even his own folks. Now I don't like to talk about people, but somehow, Son, I got very little confidence in Durant's religion. I just don't believe it'll last and endure."

"What makes you say that?" I asked.

"Because he was converted by a worldly man. The power of the preaching that changed his course came from a man who was in a way, at the time, under the influence of the Devil Himself."

"Who did the preaching that converted him?"

"Major Jim Wilkinson," Mr. George said.

"Did you know him?" I asked.

"Like I know my own name," the old man said.

"What did he look like?" I asked.

"Like most anything he wanted to. Folks had the idea he was a big man. He *was* kind of chunky through the chest and shoulders. But he wasn't specially tall. He just stood up straight and looked everybody solid in the eye like he figured he was tall as they were. Maybe a fraction taller. When the Spirit was on him he would put on his black swallowtail coat and a wide, black necktie, set his face with a Godly look, get the pitch of his voice just right, and look more like a Bishop

of the Church than old Doctor Rowe himself. He just had a little country store out there in Cottonville and Gaston Yonce furnished him the
goods like he would furnish a nigger on one of his farms. But you let
Major Jim go to Corinth and sit down in Gaston's office and take off his
derby—he had a black derby that he always wore to Corinth—and look
at that fine head of pepper colored hair, and watch him put on his specs
and lower his gaze to the top of Gaston's bald head, then on down to
Gaston's little goatee beard that was always wiggling and dyed with
tobacco juice until it looked like the tail of a nervous red fox, and you
would reach a false conclusion. You could be standing outside the glass
there, hearing Gaston talk shrill as a cricket, then Major Jim's voice
coming out deep and patient and satisfied like he was a man well provided for here on earth, and a big stockholder in the Kingdom to Come,
and you'd feel kind of sorry for Gaston Yonce, but know in your mind
that Major Jim wasn't going to be too hard on him. And all that time
they'd probably be arguing about a case of snuff the Major claimed he
didn't remember getting on the credit.

"He was a Justice of the Peace for thirty years. He used to hold Court
in his store about twice a month. You go in there on a Saturday morning when Court was in session and he would be sitting in an armchair
that had higher legs than any other chair in the store, his arms folded
across the bosom of the black coat he wore—he never held Court in his
shirt sleeves. And when the Major had heard the evidence, he'd sit there
for a while, weighing it. His eyes would be leveled off like the two ends
of a set of cotton scales when they hang free. Then one eye would go up
a little, or one would go down. He'd reach back to the shelf above him
where he kept his law book. 'I'll have to consult Blackstone, Gentlemen,' he'd say. Then the fellow that was up for stealing cotton in the
seed, or for whatever it was, would groan and commence shaking his
head. For Blackstone always gave Major Wilkinson the same advice:
'Fine that man ten dollars and the costs.'

"Times were hard back in those days. But Durant Burris always
made money. For one thing he had more and richer land than anybody
else. Then he seemed to be born with the knack of farming. Whatever
he planted growed off well and fruited up. But he was bad to get
drunk. Him and his oldest boy, Spurgeon, would stay drunk a week at
a time. They had a big roan horse named Dan that they used to drive
to a two-wheeled cart. Many a time on Sunday morning I've looked out
the church window and seen them go splitting down the road, a stone

jug bobbing up and down in the foot of the cart. Their beards would be dusty or splotched up with mud, depending on how the weather was. For two or three years they were Major Wilkinson's steady income. I remember one time they drove through Plez Thompson's prize cotton patch. It was the shortest cut Durant knowed to where Rich Lingerfelt had his still. Plez lawed them in Major Wilkinson's Court. They was fined ten dollars apiece and the costs. Another time Spurge bet his Pa he could hit Will Dumas's cow with his rifle at three hundred yards, which was about the distance from the road to where she was staked out in a meadow. Spurge won. Anyway, had the satisfaction of knowing he had hit the target. But it was Major Wilkinson that collected ten dollars and the costs. The same thing happened time and again. Nobody ever found out if it was completely legal or not. Nobody had the gall to put such a question to the Major. He might have fined them ten dollars and the costs.

"He was brought up to be a Presbyterian. When he was a young man he told his folks that he felt a call to the ministry. So they sent him to Davidson College. He stayed there from one September till Christmas. But when he got back home he commenced teaching school at the Fork Academy. He did a little local preaching when the regular pastor couldn't be there. I don't know if he was ordained or not. But he used to marry couples for a dollar, and baptize babies for nothing.

"Then war broke out with the Yankees. The Major joined up. He was just a lance corporal though when he deserted the Confederacy in 1864. There was a lot of men deserted that year. They said it was a rich man's war and a poor man's fight. Nobody around here had any niggers to speak of."

"What made them call him Major if he was just a lance corporal?" I asked.

"Because about five years after the war was over he saw the value of military training. Him and George Jeans who come home toting a sword he claimed somebody gave him when they made a lieutenant out of him down in Mississippi, they got together and organized the Tyson Township Militia. They and a small company of plowhands used to drill half a day at a time on the campmeeting grounds back of Silver Springs Church. George was the commanding officer when they first started out. He appointed himself captain and made Jim his lieutenant. But George shot a fellow one night in Corinth when he was drinking. He had to leave the county for four or five months. That left Jim in charge. When George got back Jim had done promoted himself to Major. So he outranked George and made him his adjutant. The Militia finally busted up anyhow. The plowhands got grown and commenced courting the ladies in what spare time they had.

"But I was going to tell you how it come about that the Major converted Durant Burris to his own regret—he doubtless made more from the fines Durant paid him than he did from his store. Well, when he was sure the war was over and it was safe to show his face, he commenced going to the Presbyterian Church again. The Yankees had pretty well thinned out the stand of men around here, so for lack of anybody better Jim was made Sunday School Superintendent. He held the job for eight or ten years. Then folks got tired of seeing his face in front of them every Sunday and they voted him out and Squire Bill Crump in. It like to killed the Major. It was a shock to him. He shut up his store and hung out a sign: 'Business Suspended Until Further Notice.' Then he went home and stayed drunk two weeks.

"When he sobered up he was mighty crestfallen. But I will say that he didn't try to excuse himself. He just sent out word that Court would convene in his store the following Saturday morning at ten o'clock. Everybody was on hand that could wedge himself in. Then the Major rapped on the counter with that little mallet he'd carved out of ash wood and the Court was in session. Following that the Major stood up and read the charges against James Monroe Wilkinson: 'Willful intoxication from the use and drinking of spirituous liquors.'

"Then for the only time in the history of that Court, the Major took off his coat. He folded it and put it on top of the glass showcase where he kept the stick candy and the gum drops. He unbuttoned his collar and set the lines of his face in hard, righteous lines. His chin stuck out and his eyes got cold. Some of the less Godly in the crowd commenced edging back toward the door.

"First he accused sin of causing things to stay in the mess they did. Then he condemned sinners. He went on and narrowed it down to sinners that drank liquor. Then he turned loose on James Monroe Wilkinson. There was a long mirror back there at the dry goods' shelves. He cleared a path to the mirror and paced up to it and pointed his finger at it. 'Thou art the man,' he said. Then he turned around and marched back and got ready to act as counsel for the defense. He pulled in his chin. His face looked round like it generally did. You couldn't help but

believe he was the most patient, kindhearted man in the State of North
Carolina. He looked straight out at the crowd and smiled kind of slow.
It was a mighty pleasant smile, but sad too in a way. 'Gentlemen,' he
said, 'I come before you today not to try and whitewash the defendant,
but to explain how come him to act the way he did.'

"But he didn't go on. He looked down at the floor. The smile left his
face and the hard, rigorous lines formed there again. He shook his head.
Then he turned around and faced the empty chair with the high legs.
'Your Honor,' he said, 'the defendant pleads guilty.'

"He put on his coat again and buttoned his collar. He sat down in the
Judge's chair. He sat there a long time. Then he said, 'Gentlemen, I'll
have to consult Blackstone on this matter,' and reached up for that
dusty old book.

"It took him longer than it generally did. He thumbed through
plenty of pages before he found what he was looking for. Then he shut
the book and handed it to a little black, gaptoothed nigger named Jean
LeGrand who always served as a kind of page to the Major at a session
of the Court. Jean put Blackstone on the shelf again. The Major rose up.
He stood straight as a post. His eyes was the clearest and bluest I ever
noticed in my life. They were eyes to weigh things with. Looking at
him there you would have been obliged to say: 'That's a just man. That
man is fair.'

" 'The verdict is guilty,' the Major said. 'The defendant is sentenced
to pay a fine of twenty dollars and the costs. He is also put on probation
for a period of twelve months.'

"Nobody ever found out who he paid the fine to. If he just shifted the
money from one pocket to another, or if he made out a due bill to himself.

"He didn't get much business from anybody for a couple of months
after that. It was like Jean LeGrand said to me one day: 'Old Blackstone's done jumped his price to twenty dollars. But wages and cotton
ain't gone up none. Guess the government ain't yet got wind of how
prices is taken to rising around Cottonville.' Jean winked at me when
he said that. He was a nigger with a long neck and a face that would
have been blank as a sheet of paper if paper was colored black.

"But the lawless element of the community breathed easier when the
Major tried Durant Burris again for being drunk and unruly in public. The fine was ten dollars and the costs like it had been before."

"How did he catch all those people?" I asked.

Mr. George turned around, put his hands against the trunk of the tree and gave it a shake. But no peaches came down.

"Well, he was a Justice of the Peace," he said. "If he saw or heard of somebody disturbing, or fixing to disturb, the peace, why the case was cut and dried. He just sat down and wrote out a summons for the man to appear before the Court at such and such a time. As a general rule it would be Jean LeGrand that served the summons. That nigger could read either printed matter or script.

"Major Wilkinson never went back to the Presbyterian Church. Said he didn't feel worthy to be a Presbyterian after staying drunk that long. So he kind of slunk off to the Baptist Church and found him a seat on one of the back benches. But when the organ started playing and the choir commenced to sing I guess he just couldn't keep from joining in with that deep bass voice of his'n. Pretty soon they had him sitting up there in the choir. One Sunday they called on him to pray. Now the Major was a fluent man at prayer. Specially when his conscience was a little guilty.

"They had preaching at the Baptist Church once a month. The preacher was a man named Harward. He was a circuit rider from Blytheville and had eight churches. He was a good man that didn't care about anything much except converting people to the Baptist faith. He once stated in the pulpit that it was his honest belief that a camel might easier pass through the eye of a needle than for a man to enter the Kingdom of Heaven without he'd been baptized by immersion. He was a short, chunky man and had a gimlet eye when he felt the least bit stubborn about anything. Well, one Sunday when he was due to preach at Cottonville, he didn't show up. His wife was sick, I think, or maybe it was his horse. Anyway, somebody made the suggestion that Major Wilkinson go ahead and preach them a sermon, which he did. It was well taken. After that he did it every Sunday except when it was the regular day for Preacher Harward to preach.

"That went on for two or three months. Then Preacher Harward got wind of it. 'Why that man ain't even a member of the church,' he told his deacons. 'His status right now is just a kind of visitor that nobody ever specially invited to start with. Furthermore, he was baptized in the Presbyterian fashion—if you want to call sprinkling a little water over the head baptism. If he's going to be even a substitute preacher in the

Baptist Church he'll have to be baptized and join up with us according to our rules.'

"Major Jim was willing to go part of the way. He owned it didn't look quite right for a man that was still being carried on the Presbyterian books to preach from a Baptist pulpit. 'But all that's needed to transfer me over is just to make an entry in the Church Book,' he said. 'It ain't necessary for me to be re-converted all over and baptized again. Such harrowing experiences are for ordinary sinners.'

"So things were tied up there until the Saturday night before the Sunday when Preacher Harward was due to give a sermon at Cottonville again. He rode in on his saddle horse that night and hitched in Major Wilkinson's back yard. But he never spent the night there. The next morning the Major wasn't at church either. First thing the Preacher said when he got in the pulpit was that he'd wrestled half the night with Major Jim Wilkinson, trying to get him to agree to be baptized in Rocky River. But finally the Major told him no, he'd see him in hell before he would be baptized in that muddy water.

" 'But he won't ever see me there,' Preacher Harward said in his most stubborn voice.

"That was in the fall—September or October. The Major never set foot inside a church all winter. He seemed to take a renewed interest in his business though. Right after he fell out with the Baptists he shut up his store and hung out a sign: 'Closed For The Time Being. Taking Stock.'

"He took stock all that week. Nobody saw hair nor hide of him. Not even his wife. She said he must be reorganizing even the mice to stay down there in the store like that and eat his meals out of tin cans and the cracker barrel. At the end of the week he opened up again and things looked about like they always had. But the Major said his books had been in a terrible mess. 'Didn't know if I was coming or going,' he said. 'You find out which?' somebody asked him. 'Yes, I did,' he said. But that was all.

"He took stock again the next month. That time he started on a Tuesday. It took him all the week. Several customers knocked on his door. But the only man that got it open was Jean LeGrand. He come into town one night toting a jug made out of some kind of yellow crockery. He went around to the back and frammed on the door three or four times, then hollered out, 'Open up, Major. It's Jean. I fetched your stuff.' Then the door eased out maybe an inch and the Major spoke: 'That you, Jean?' 'Yessuh.' 'Who are you?' 'Nobody but me, Major. Jean LeGrand. I got the jug.' Then I guess Jean must have smelled a distant rat, knew folks were watching and listening. 'I done and fetched the lamp oil jug, Major. You know. I was talking with you Saturday and say I come off and forgot my lamp oil jug and you say to bring it next time I come in to trade. I got it now.' Then we saw the door open and heard the Major say: 'Come in, Jean. I had to make sure.'

"In about five or ten minutes Jean left again. He was toting a jug too. Which didn't exactly prove he'd brought it empty, nor left with it full. That was the way things went all winter long. The Major would put up his sign, lock the door and take stock for a whole week. His wife got so she wouldn't even talk about it. The Major kind of shied away from the subject too. And it always happened during stock taking week that Jean LeGrand would run slam out of lamp oil and have to make a trip to the store, bringing his jug of course to take the oil back in. Mister One-Armed Bill Mack run a store back then in Cottonville too, but he never stayed open past sundown. And Jean never come in for his lamp oil till it was good and dark. When we questioned him about it he claimed he had so much work during the day that he couldn't get off. Then we asked him how it was he could get in the store and nobody else could, was he a privileged character? Not privileged, Jean told us, just a neutralized character. We asked him what he meant, neutralized. 'When he takes that ere stock the Major don't want nobody bothering him,' Jean said. 'And him and I is done and neutralized our character against one another. We passes and repasses time and again and ne'er one of us bothers the other no more than a stray spark or two striking his cheek would upset the Old Scratch.'

"Nobody ever had the brass to question the Major. When he closed up, folks went over and traded with Mister One-Armed Bill Mack, who was an independent kind of fellow and hardly ever bothered to ask his customers if they felt good or not. When the Major reopened, his customers come back and traded with him and told him their troubles. He had a sympathetic ear and tongue.

"The last stock he took was in the month of May. The following Sunday after he got through, he went to the Methodist Church and sat down on one of the back benches. The Methodists was hard put to it back then. They didn't have no regular preacher. Once every three months the Presiding Elder, Doctor Slack, used to ride a horse down

from Salisbury and hold Quarterly Meeting to make collections. They
got a sermon then, but betweentimes they had to depend on Will
Dumas that stuttered so bad it took him about five minutes to get the
word 'Amen' out of his mouth, or on Charley Braxton who was a good,
humble fellow, soft hearted as they come, and kind of soft in the head
too, or on some young fellow who had enough brains and eyesight to
see that he was liable to harvest more and sweat less following in the
footsteps of Jesus than the tracks of a Southbound cotton mule and who
wanted to get in a little practice behind a real pulpit. So the field was
wide open for a man with the talents Major Jim Wilkinson was known
to possess. I think it was the third Sunday he attended the Methodist
Church that the Major finished working his way from the back benches
up to the pulpit itself. Soon as he stepped up on the rostrum it looked
like a natural part of him, his foundation, you might say. The brand of
preaching sure did improve fast. Taking all that stock hadn't rusted his
voice any; he could still make it roll majestic as thunder heard of a
summer night, away off in the distance. And he could use his limbs and
motions to make the right flourish to go with his words. When he
preached on the text of Christ driving the bankers out of the Temple he
frammed and whacked so much with his arms and fists till pretty nigh
the whole congregation was leaning away from him and toward the
door. But if he was trying to persuade the cold and indifferent, he could
plead with the very ends of his fingers.

"Before long the question come up again about the Major joining the
church he preached for. But this time the Major just got Charley Braxton to ask him the vows one Sunday, and there he was a Methodist.

"I guess Durant Burris hit his peak that summer. There was some
talk of declaring him an outlaw, a man suitable to be shot at on sight.
He would have made a poor target though. Objects that move rapid
generally are. By then he'd traded off his buggy-horse, Dan, and rode
a pot-bellied mule named Frone. She was the swiftest animal in Tyson
Township. When Durant got drunk he would climb in the saddle and
away they'd go, up and down the big road all the livelong day. Durant
hollering and singing the one song he knew part of the words to: 'I'm
The Man That Rode The Mule Around The World.' He pitched it
various ways and sung it to most any old tune. He just about kept up
the Major and Rich Lingerfelt, a little possum-faced fellow that made
liquor all the time down there where Crib's Creek eases into the river.
It got so the Major jacked Durant up in Court every Saturday morning.

Once Durant swore on the Major's Bible and proved by eyewitnesses that he'd been cold sober all the previous week. 'However,' Durant said and got out his pocketbook, 'I'm fixing to commence a slight drunk just as soon as this here Court is adjourned. I'll give you the ten dollars now so you won't go summonsing me again till Saturday after next.' The Major studied a bit, then took the money. 'All right, Durant,' he said, 'provided you don't commit no more than your customary depredations against the peace and real estate of Tyson Township.'

"I reckon the Major reached his peak too that summer. Along about the beginning of Dog Days when the protracted meetings started, he was highly in demand at churches all over this county and Anson too where his reputation as a preacher and Justice of the Peace had already preceded him. He kept his store closed most of July and August. 'The Lord's business comes first,' the Major said. 'Mine can wait.' Specially since it was the slack season for merchandising anyhow.

"He was primed by the time he finally got around to holding protracted meeting in Cottonville. It was September then. The season of repentance was going fast and cotton-picking time was at hand. Still the services were well attended. They lasted a week, two sermons a day. One started at ten o'clock in the morning; and the other was eight o'clock at night. Every sermon was against a different type of sin, such as Backbiting, Tale-Bearing, the Pride That Goeth Before a Fall, Enviousness, Vulgar and Profane Language, the Worship of Mammon, and Resistance to Temptation. The meeting was to close Saturday night. Saturday morning the Major announced from the pulpit that his sermon for the night would be against liquor.

"I recall that Saturday like it was last week. It was a still, blistering day. Folks mostly stayed inside the house or in the shade that afternoon and tried to sleep or just fanned themselves. There was a little racket about three o'clock when Durant Burris rode up to the place where there was a few pitching horseshoes in the shade of the oaks back of the blacksmith shop. When Durant caught sight of Rich Lingerfelt he dismounted his mule and started running toward Rich. Rich just said, 'God, have mercy!,' threw down his horseshoes, and struck out for the woods beyond Squire Bill Crump's pasture. Durant was gaining on him when they went out of sight. Somebody hitched the mule to the rack there at the blacksmith shop, making sure they had her in the shade. Then they went on with the game. Rich and Durant was always falling out over politics and cards. Durant would dive at Rich and generally miss, then he'd run him a mile or two, cussing and snarling through his nose. When he got tired, he'd go home and forget it.

"The Major got to church kind of late that night. He stumbled and like to fell as he stepped up to the rostrum. When he got behind the pulpit and faced that crowd—every bench was full and some stood in the back of the church—I could see he was mighty tired. His eyes were bloodshot as if he hadn't got no sleep in several nights. And when the choir sung the opening hymn, I took notice he didn't join in. He sat down there behind the pulpit, bent over like he was tying his shoe laces. Then he raised up and cast his eyes toward the dark that was outside the window. Meanwhile the choir sung, 'Jesus Savior, Pilot Me.'

"When they finished the hymn the Major got up slow and preoccupied. His voice carried to the back of the church when he spoke. But it was like he was talking and thinking to himself:

> Jesus Savior, pilot me
> Over Life's tempestuous sea;
> Unknown waves before me roll,
> Hiding chart and treach'rous shoal.

"Then he looked up and knew we were there. 'Good Friends,' he said, 'I had aimed to preach tonight on a text from the Book of Proverbs, namely: 'Wine is a mocker; Strong drink is raging, and whosoever is deceived thereby is not wise.' But walking down here from the house tonight something told me not to raise that doubtful issue. I'm going to start out talking and let the Lord direct my words whichever way he sees fit. That song you just finished singing puts me in mind of a man's life. We start out from a land that's actually but dimly known to us. For every man begins from time and happenings and things and men gone by. And we set out, whether we want to or not, on life's perilous sea towards the shore of another unknown land.'

"The Major stopped then and went into a fit of coughing. There was a shelf right behind the pulpit where he kept his Bible and a big-bowled lamp that had a sawed off chimney. I guess his coughing shook the shelf, for you could see the light wavering a little.

" 'And well might the man who wrote that hymn rise up and ask for a Pilot, for some Wondrous Sovereign of the Sea, to take charge of his foundering bateau and steer him past the treach'rous shoals,' the Major said. 'There will be shoals, reefs that are hid, storms and disasters—you can count on that. For I want to stand here humble as I can tonight and take issue with that statement in the Bible which says the way to salvation is marked so clear that the wayfaring man, though he be a fool, cannot lose his way. I beg to state that he can mis-read the signs.'"

Mr. George turned sharply toward me. His eyes glowed like sooty coals away back in their dark sockets.

"That was getting mighty close to blasphemy! I turned and looked around at the congregation (I was in the middle aisle that night, second bench from the front one that was reserved for whatever mourners might turn up later.) But some of the folks was even nodding like they agreed.

"Still I was about to rise up and call the Major to account when I heard something outside. There was two separate sets of sounds, a fast, thumping one like a goat's hoofs would make, followed by a heavy mule loping hard. Next was an overlapping sound like the church steps being knocked loose at one blow of the goat's hoofs, then kicked out of sight by the mule. But all at once things got quiet except for two sets of common footsteps.

"The leading ones was made by Rich Lingerfelt. He was coming down the aisle on the left hand side, blowing hard. He was only a bantam-size fellow to start with and now he was pretty near dragging the floor with his chin, walking all limp and bent over like the next step would be the one that throwed him. Durant Burris was right in his wake. He was long and loose-jointed back in those days. When he walked he swayed like a sapling in a ruffling breeze. Durant's face needed a haircut. His beard was red and kind of speckled where dust had struck it, then turned to mud when he sweated. Neither one of them was dressed very stylish. They both had on overalls and shirts that had better a been in a washpot than church. Durant had on a straw hat that was high crowned and wide brimmed like a cowboy would wear. Rich had on a little hunting hat that was faded white. He come on up to the mourners' bench and set down. He kind of cringed away when Durant eased in beside him. But even Durant recognized the rules enough to admit that Rich had done gained a sanctuary for the time being. He composed himself and faced toward the Major, who had come out in front of the pulpit and was scrutinizing the two of them like they were some kind of strange varmints cast up from the sea.

" 'Bretheren,' the Major said, 'this here bench is generally reserved for them who come up to mourn for the sins they've committed in the past, both of omission and of commission. They generally come forward toward the close of a sermon when the message has struck home and pierced their hearts like an arrow. But I scarcely started my sermon tonight. Can I take it you're truly repentant, having done and converted yourselves in solitude beforehand?'

" 'Well, I know I ain't always acted like a good Christian,' Rich was saying when Durant broke in. 'It's kind of crowded in here tonight, Your Honor,' he said. 'Just thought I'd sit here and listen to the sermon. I'm awful tired and tuckered out. Till the time when this here bench is needed by the mourners, I'd be obliged if you'd let me set.'

" 'Help yourself, Brother Durant,' the Major told him. 'I'm mighty glad to see you here tonight. Brother Lingerfelt too. But your hats give you a kind of transient look. I wish you'd take them off and stay a while.'

"They snapped off their hats. The Major moved behind the pulpit again. All at once he was struck with a fit of coughing. It didn't sound like the coughing that comes from the grippe, or smoking, or dust. It had a puffing, manufactured sound. While he was coughing, the Major got too near the lamp and blew it out. I could hear him fumbling around up there and thought I heard him take a drink of water. But when he struck a match and re-lit the lamp, I didn't see a pitcher nor glass anywhere.

" 'You'll have to bear with me tonight. I've got a hacking cough that won't let me rest,' he said, and went from that into the sermon. 'So man's life is a journey across a poorly mapped sea. I hate to tell you, but you have got to navigate it mostly alone. Excusing only the help you can give and get from your fellow travelers that are just as much in the dark as you are.'

"I noticed his voice was getting more modulated. It took on a vibrous tone. His face was still drawn, but livelier too some way. I kept watching him and Durant Burris, who was keeping one eye on the Major and the other on Rich. The Major went ahead and drawed a picture of how poor life was if men didn't have compassion and use it. Folks that was present kept referring back to that sermon for years to come. But I can't remember it being anything extra. In fact, it was a sinful sermon. He preached like a man didn't even have Christ to save him, nor Heaven to look forward to. What he said was, 'And all men finally come to the shore of that last, veiled land. The Territory of Death. I can't undertake to say, and no man can, what's waiting for you there.'

"About then he had another fit of coughing. This time he coughed right over the lamp. I was ready to swear I heard water flowing before he got around to striking a light.

" 'Bear with me tonight, Good People,' he said. 'For I'm sore afflicted.' It sounded like he had a chew in his mouth. But he never chewed. When he went back to preaching I noticed Durant Burris was paying attention only to him now. The Major must have forgot that he'd just finished saying life was a trip on the sea. He started talking of it as a road, uphill mostly, mountainous even, with now and then a short downhill stretch. Or if it was level, still there was dark woods, thorny thickets, deep rivers to ford, and mud bogs to contend with. Once when he got to a high mountain in his talk, the Major hushed for a minute. Just stood there with his hands clasped behind him, looking up toward the ceiling. Then he shook his head, fell to coughing, and blew out the lamp.

"After the fifth or sixth time he'd coughed out the light, I remember he said (by then his face was getting flushed. His voice was tolling clear as the very churchbell), 'Good People, don't do like I do myself. I just hope you'll do *like I tell you to do.'*

"And he went on with what to me was a mighty negative sermon. Not once during the whole course of it did he promise anybody a seat in Heaven, nor punishment in Torment. From what I remember, the gist of it was just a simple rule that anybody could have stated in less than a minute: Before you lash out at your fellow man try to stand in his shoes a while and see how things may look from there. Then he kept referring back to our pilgrim journey, sometimes on land, sometimes out on the dark blue sea, that to hear him tell it knowed nothing but storms. He seemed mixed up that night about which way folks was traveling. It struck me as a mighty quiet and poor sermon to wind up a protracted meeting with. When he finally got through, all the Major did was just open the doors of the church like any other preacher. He said, 'If there's anybody here who wants to join the church, the vows to be taken at a later date, let him come forward now and give me his hand. Meanwhile, the choir can render a hymn.'

"Before they could even start singing, Durant Burris rose up from the mourners' bench and said, 'I want to join the church.'

"You could tell he was dead serious about the matter.

"Major Wilkinson's mouth fell open at that. He picked his way from behind the pulpit and come on out and stood in front of Durant. He searched his face.

" 'You sure about this thing, Durant?' he asked.

" 'Yes Sir, I am, Your Honor,' Durant said. 'You set me to studying deep tonight. When I first dashed in here I was trying to get hold of Brother Rich Lingerfelt so I could knock him black and blue. I wanted to jar his frame with my fists like that tongue of his'n had jarred my pride. So it's like the Lord's Own Hand led me inside this church, with Brother Rich for the bait. And it come to me, resting here accidentally on the mourners' bench, that maybe it ain't accidental at all. Because I believe the Lord's trying to tell me that I have reached the forks of the road. I got a family of children growing up at home. I've took less pains with them than I have my livestock. I got as good and true a wife as any man has got. But it's been years since I took any notice of her unless dinner was late. I didn't think of nothing but my own selfish pleasure. Now my pleasure's getting kind of threadless and worn. I'm going to leave my sinful path. My mind's made up.'

" 'I believe you, Durant,' the Major said and shook his hand. The Major seemed to sort of wilt then though. His frame went slack and I thought for a minute he would surely fall. But he didn't. Just stood there looking down at the floor. There was thoughts and feelings all over his face. It was like he was mortally ashamed of himself, but kind of sneaking proud about something too.

"Soon as they got over being stunned by his words, it looked like everybody in the house wanted to shake Durant's hand at the same time. The women commenced to cry over him like he was the Prodigal Son and a flock of Lost Sheep combined. 'I just wish Susan (his wife's name was Susan) could be here,' somebody said. 'Going to be a happy time when she hears about this.' 'Her prayers have been answered,' another one said, 'and mine too. I have prayed for Durant Burris's soul ever since I can remember.' Then everybody was taking credit for helping save him from a life of sin. Durant just stood there quiet and thoughtful. He shook their hands. But he didn't shout and take on like freshly converted folks used to. (Which is another reason I'm afraid his religion won't stay with him. It didn't tear him up enough at the start.)

"Then Old Aunt Minerva Barbee commenced to shout. I don't know if you ever saw anybody shout. It's about gone out of style now. These new-fangled preachers from Duke University don't encourage it. But back then they called us the Shouting Methodists. At protracted meeting, and specially toward the height of a sermon, some folks always got so full of glory and thanksgiving that their feelings got out of control and flowed over the banks. Then they would cry tears that come from happiness, they'd shout and sing, and praise our Great Redeemer's Name. Aunt Minerva's feelings was always easy to touch and when she started that night her voice was the charge that set off the rest. Some shouted, some cried, some slapped one another on the back and shook hands. Debts were paid, or marked paid, forgiveness was asked and freely give, vows and promises was made by the dozen, and so many folks were converted that the mourners' bench didn't begin to hold them all. And while the Major's always got credit for saving twenty-eight souls that night, it's a credit he don't deserve. It was a case of the Spirit entering the congregation and they converting themselves. Even to Rich Lingerfelt. When he finally quit shouting and calmed down enough to talk, he said, 'I been blockading whiskey all my life. But when I get home tonight I will bust up my still before I go to bed.' He did it too and joined the church the following Sunday. But while Rich was fast of foot and a mighty clever fellow, he was afflicted with a weak character. Before the end of the year he was out stealing copper anywhere he could, to make him another still. Some have always fell by the wayside.

"I guess the quietest ones during it all was Major Jim Wilkinson, Durant Burris, and myself. Durant and the Major both just stood there, looking like their thoughts was on some distant scene. And somehow I doubted the value of everything that had happened that night.

"Then the Major—his face was beginning to get pale again—raised his hands and his voice, hoping maybe to finish the meeting. He made the suggestion we sing another hymn. So somebody struck up 'Revive Us Again' just simultaneous with somebody else starting 'I Am Bound for The Promised Land.' That didn't quieten things down any to speak of. Because by then everybody was so full of brotherly love that they tried to sing both hymns at one time, so as not to show any partiality and maybe hurt somebody's feelings.

"Major Wilkinson appeared to be awful tired. But he still had that sheepish, pleased look. He caught Durant's eye and smiled. As much as to say, 'Well, Durant, I tried to get you loose, so you could go home. But you see how it is.'

"Then the Major narrowed his eyes. He was watching his chance. Pretty soon he started easing around behind the pulpit again. I reckon he figured nobody was paying him any mind. But I was. I edged out from the crowd that was congregated around the mourners' bench. When I saw the Major duck down out of sight behind the pulpit, I mounted the rostrum fast as I could, bending a little, keeping the front of the pulpit between me and him. Then I jumped. I pounced down on him like a cat on a mouse. He pried the bottle loose from his mouth. He was a little too surprised though to swallow.

"But I'd left the lamp out of my calculations. Anyhow, that shelf ought to been made wider than it was. The lamp exploded when it fell in the Major's lap. When he blew at it, his spit caught afire. You see this line on my thumb where it shows up white? Come from a burning piece of glass.

"That's about all there was to meeting. They stomped out the fire before it spread. Nobody'd noticed me going up there. They took the Major's word that he'd upset the lamp when he put his big Bible down on the shelf. The pieces of glass from the bottle looked like the ones from the lamp. Specially in the poor light of folks striking matches and the moon shining in the window. And I found out then how kerosene smells louder than liquor.

"The Major wasn't hurt so bad after all, though his lips was blistered. When Will Dumas told him he ought to be thankful he was still alive, the Major agreed. 'But the Lord's always took mighty good care of me,' he said. 'Has guided me through war and pestilence and preserved my soul from evil. I rest on His Unchanging Grace.'"

Mr. George Hill paused then. The sudden quiet that came seemed to intensify the heat of the sun that was well on its downward way toward the treetops now. Mr. George shook the tree again. No peaches came down.

"How come us to be sitting here under this barren tree anyhow?" he asked. "No peaches here. And I'm hungry as a dog."

"Did they ever find out about him being drunk that night?" I asked. He shook his head.

"I guess not. He wasn't to say drunk. I kept it to myself. The Major had his following. Such folks wouldn't a believed me. They would have said, 'Yes, he's been a drinking man in his time. But he was always open about what he did. Ain't anything sneaking about Major Jim Wilkinson.' The ones that wasn't specially his followers would have.

laughed and passed it off with some sort of excuse for him. It was like everybody had got together and issued him a special license to be and act different from anybody else.

"But he never preached again as long as he lived. His excuse was that he'd breathed a draught of fire that night and it left his throat in a tender condition. But I think it was a case of locking the barn door after he had done and been tricked into aiding and abetting the stealing of the horse. He missed that money Durant used to pay him in fines. He had to cut out his drinking too. I think he felt like he was obliged from that day on to set a good example for Durant Burris to follow. For I believe the Major worried a little to the end of his days about the good chance of Durant backsliding into sin.

"Durant's not done it yet. But I tell you, Son, he has got to be mighty careful and watch himself close. Right now he's afraid to drive in and have a glass of hard cider with me. One drink might call for another and there he would be, wallowing in drunkenness again. An old man like him. That's the trouble with getting saved by a man of doubtful character. Durant don't know. He can't ever know for sure he's saved until he's dead. I hope for the best. But still and all, Son, I misdoubt his religion. I'm afraid it's a thing of short duration."

"How long has it been?" I asked.

He seemed to think for a minute.

"Eighteen Eighty and this is Nineteen Thirty-five. Why, it's fifty-five years!" he said. "Seems more recent. Like it was maybe summer before last. But I long ago quit figuring time by months and years. The set way is wrong because some periods are longer than others, measuring the same. 'For a thousand years in Thy sight are but as yesterday when it is past, and as a watch in the night.'"

He stood up lightly and looked toward the sun.

"Soon be suppertime again," he said. "And here I am gossiping like the day was before me and endless to boot. Was there something, Son, you wanted to see me about?"

The Trigger

George Marion O'Donnell

I

AGNES GEORGE ROLLED OVER ON HER SIDE and looked closely at the clock, square and green, with a brass binding around the face and a gilt square in the middle of it and, between the brass and the gilt, the black numbers on white. The short hand was nearly on *3* now, and the long hand had just passed the *9*. A quarter of three. It seemed insensitive, somehow, dense and insensitive of her that so many times she had watched the hand climb like this from the *9* on to the *10*, on to the *11*, rising toward the perpendicular, yet had never realized that she would be watching it on this particular Saturday. And that denseness of hers was now doing its harm, which could not be evaded. In ten minutes he would be at the front door, knocking.

She noticed how the sun flashed beyond the tree-shade outside her window. As the leaves moved in the wind a little, the shade itself was sparked with sun. The katydids had started the humming that seemed endless and actually stopped only in late September or October. Even the wind, when she felt it occasionally, was warm, a May wind. To-day, she thought, it should be the walk along the river bank, even though, or perhaps because, days were not necessarily good when the sun was shining or bad when rain was falling. For when Larry knocked, fifteen, ten, five minutes from now, and she went to the door and spoke, smiling—from that minute she would have to begin to tell him. By the river, the telling might be easier. . . .

The first day, she had seen him. When she opened the classroom door, heard the too-quick silence in the room, saw them all turn to watch her as she walked toward the desk, she knew that they were speculating about her, expecting her to be perhaps like the other teacher, who had quit at mid-term. She meant to surprise them. So she started by reading them *The Highwayman*.

Beginning, she realized almost at once that the attention of curiosity was relaxing. Two of the girls had started writing to each other in a notebook held on the tablet arm between them. In the middle of the room, a dark girl who shot up one eyebrow without moving the other was alternately glancing at her and drawing. "To illustrate the obituary," Agnes George thought. When she read the line about the Highwayman wearing a "cocked hat," she heard a snigger and looked at the back row in time to see a boy with greased, hay-colored hair elbowing the sweatered boy who lounged against him. They looked at each other, their eyes blinking fast in parody of the twinkle she was reading about, the bandit's moonlit weapons. And as she recited how the Highwayman whistled his tune, she heard, more breathed than whistled, a three-note call that she could not stop to silence. The girls were keeping up their note writing. Deliberately, she looked at the front row.

His blue eyes stared straight into hers, and she could feel her own eyes misting as she saw the barest glaze over his. Then his face moved a little, in unconscious imitation, and she knew that she was assuming the expression of the character she was reading about. And suddenly, without her knowing the moment it happened, she was still in the classroom, with the smell of the too-hot radiator and the pervasive chalk dust, yet she was leaning out a casement, not in a classroom at all; it was her hair falling down, loosened, in the black cascade, and his blond hair had become the dark red that she had plaited into hers; then she was waiting for dark to become dawn and dawn to become noon.

She heard her own voice saying, matter-of-factly, "Part Two." But once more she watched out of the casement window, and it was dawn, and noon, and the marching redcoats came instead of the dark red hair. She heard their heels on the cobbles of the court-yard; on the stair, the broken, hollow sound of their tread; then they were in the room. The redcoats were there, yet the blue eyes watched and mirrored hers. Now they had tied her up and she could feel the hard, washer-like circle of the gun barrel pressing into her breast. She began to twist her arms against the cords, and the mirroring face twisted a little around the mouth. It would have been a sensual mouth if it had not been afraid. Her little finger began to feel metal. The trigger was hers. The road waited. And the hoofbeats came.

The cluck-cluck from the back of the room sounded somewhere at the edge of her mind. The boy with moldy-hay hair was laying his arm along his friend's thick leg, imitating the hoofbeats as he squeezed the leg in rhythm. Eyes moved in the room before her, feet touched subtly, sidewise glances crossed each other, heads nodded knowingly.

But the road waited and her finger was waiting against the steel. As she forced her finger down, her eyes grew wide for a moment, and the blue, echoing eyes grew wide also. Then the eyes and the mouth were afraid together, and she knew that he had heard the shot. . . .

That Saturday she was looking out over the vacant lot next door, where sage was desolate under a January sky, and she only half heard through her reverie a knock and talk at the front of the house, as though someone were collecting for a newspaper. Then there was a sharp rap and at her "come in," Mrs. Lyon stuck her head past the barely opened door.

"Dressed, Miss George?" She was half-whispering. "Larry Gordon is here." Then, coyly, she flexed the corners of her mouth, stretching them painful-tight like her hair, and her head withdrew.

Agnes George stood up. In the instant of putting Larry Gordon and the blue-eyed boy together in her mind, fusing them both with the Highwayman, she glanced toward the mirror and smoothed her skirt at the hips. Then she went down the hall and into the dim parlor.

He was sitting upright in one of the leather chairs with broken springs. Above his blue eyes, the hair seemed to rise a long way straight up from the forehead before it began to wave gently back. As he got up, she noticed that he was holding a notebook in his hands.

"Hello!" she said, putting out her hand to him. "Let's sit over here." She walked quickly toward the high leather sofa near the window. "There's a little light over here, anyway."

He was crossing the room, fingering the notebook he held. She sat down.

"I'm so glad you came. It's a lonesome sort of day, isn't it?" She looked at the notebook. "I hope you've brought me some of your poetry to read. I thought the other day maybe you liked it; then your theme—"

"—Yes'm," he said. He was sitting on the sofa now, stiffly, facing her with the notebook held upright on his knees, his back against the carved wooden endpiece.

"You like it, don't you? I mean—," his face was very serious, "—you don't mind reading it?"

"Of course not; I love to read it." She smiled. "I'd love to see what you've done." The smile seemed to make him more at ease; he opened the notebook and began glancing at it, turning the pages. Then he looked up, and she saw that the blue eyes were a little misted over, as they had been the first day.

"Won't you read it to me?" Again she covered his fear. He looked down at the page once more, and she drew her right leg up under her and leaned back into the corner as he began reading.

His voice had entirely changed; it was a soft baritone. But as he read, nervousness made it almost a contralto. The poem was about flowers in a drab room, and she could not help glancing up at the china-painting-on-canvas roses here in Mrs. Lyon's parlor. He had been brought up on the wrong poets. Then, just as she knew that he had finished, she realized what his last line had been.

She leaned toward the center of the sofa, reaching out toward the notebook.

"Let me look at it too, this time," she said.

They sat side by side, watching together the handwriting that was almost like print, while he read the poem again. As she watched and heard too, the poem seemed worse. It was full of clichés, twisted in syntax. But this time she saw and heard not just the last line but also the one that came before it:

> But roses die within an airless room
> And, lest the corpse should smell, are thrown away.

As his voice stopped again, she realized that the contralto quality had disappeared from it. She looked up to find the blue eyes facing hers.

"The last two lines—" she said.

"They're bad?"

"No," she said. "They're good. They're the best lines in the poem." And she closed her eyes and repeated them aloud:

> But roses die within an airless room
> And, lest the corpse should smell, are thrown away.

"They sound wonderful the way you say them," he said, staring out the front window into the gray afternoon. Then he looked at her directly:

"They're the ones I really wanted to write."

"I thought that." She studied the manuscript again. "—Of course, *smell* should be *stink*."

"But that's an ugly-sounding word."

"Of course it is. Of course. But death is ugly, too, and the odor of decay is ugly." She had her knee on the couch again and was half-turned toward him. "Besides, you want a startling word there, and you want an exact word. Remember the story about Dr. Johnson?"

He blushed. "No'm," he said. And she suddenly realized that she had been talking to him as though he were one of her fellow students at Columbia; with pleasure, too, she understood that he had been arguing with her without knowing that he was doing it.

"Oh, it's just the one about Dr. Johnson at the dinner party. You know, he never was strong on bathing. Well, the woman next to him was a little shocked. Finally she turned to him: 'Why, Dr. Johnson!'—" (she imitated the gesture of the raised lorgnette and sniffed like Edna Mae Oliver) "—'you smell!'" Larry grinned broadly. She pointed her finger at him, smiling. "But Dr. Johnson was always the dictionary maker. He drew himself up. 'Madam,' he proclaimed, 'you smell. I *stink*.'"

As he laughed, she saw that the mist was gone from his eyes, and in the blue there were hazel flecks that she had not seen before. He took out his fountain pen, crossed out the word, and printed the other above the blot.

"There," he said.

"I'm wondering too," she said, "about *within*. Maybe it ought to be *inside*. Wouldn't that be more natural?"

They tried it over together, sitting side by side, heads bent above the page.

"No," she said. "It won't do. It looks too much like a rhyme for *die*."

Then he began to turn to other poems, to ask questions, even to argue, though still, she knew, without realizing that he was doing it. And soon she had forgotten to be sympathetic, for she was in the work itself, and in the mind that had written it. Already she had started convincing him that he must develop his observations, the details, forget all he'd learned before and remember only what he had wanted to put in but feared would not do for poetry.

They were bent over the poetry notebook. His hair had fallen loose over his left eye, like a girl's, and he had forgotten to push it back. Suddenly he looked up at her, past the blinder of hair. "I've never talked to anyone before," he said. Then they turned around, simultaneously, and saw that the winter dark had settled against the window behind them. . . .

After that, he came every Saturday. In the notebook that they held between them as they sat on Mrs. Lyon's uncomfortable, hard-leather sofa, the poems grew, tortuously at first, then more easily, naturally as spring grew through the soggy ground outside. And when spring came, and sunny days, they began to walk together across the steel bridge south of town, then along the river bank or through the flat woods, on one of the packed dirt roads that lumber-haulers used. The spring warmed; oak and sweetgum and broken-topped cypress came to life about them; and, almost overnight, undergrowth clogged up the spaces between the trees. The sky was the blue she had always imagined for the Mediterranean, and they would have to take off their coats and carry them in their hands.

The sky was like that this afternoon, Agnes George knew, though when she looked up she could not see it for the water oak just outside her window. She looked at the clock again. Between the gilt center-square and the brass-banded edge of the dial, the tip of the long hand stood between *11* and *12*. She breathed heavily; then she realized that the sound was the one she had heard old women make after climbing a long flight of stairs.

She sat on the edge of the bed, looked a moment toward the blinding sunlight beyond the oak-shade, and stood up. As she raised her hands, adjusting her hair, she heard the knock at the front door.

Taking the knob in her hand, she thought: "How does a smile feel on my face?" But she could not remember. The muscles above the corners of her mouth felt tight now, strained. And they would not relax, she discovered as she opened the door.

"Hello!" she said, trying to make the last syllable rise and hang cheerfully in the air, wondering if he noticed that it did not. He was wearing a blue polo shirt, the exact shade of his eyes, and the loose waves of his hair were freshly combed.

Inside, he pulled out a parcel that he had been holding behind him and extended it toward her.

"For next fall," he said.

She took hold of the package. She thought she could hear herself breathe again like an old woman.

"Why Larry, how thoughtful! May I open it now?"

She had carried the package to the window and was standing beside the stark leather couch.

"Of course," he said. He was crossing the room, following her. "But there's something inside that you're not to open till later."

Her hand did not tremble as she undid the tissue paper around the oblong box, and she was surprised. He was standing beside her, watching, she knew without looking up. She took off the lid of the box and lifted the inside folds of tissue. There lay a woolen scarf, rough enough to fight the autumn wind, the very gray of her tweed coat, Indian-patterned in dark red and black and white. It was the most beautiful scarf that she had ever seen.

"I ordered it," he said. "I hope it goes with the coat. . . . It's for the Saturday walks. . . ."

For this moment, she thought, I must forget yesterday and what I must tell him to-day. I must. And as though she watched a motion-picture she saw herself walking, wearing the red and gray and black scarf, her coat gray against a lighter gray sky; Larry was walking beside her in his dark-green overcoat; his hair was bright; the leaves, yellow and red, fell around them; and air seemed to suck the leaves under their feet. She could hear the snap of the leaf as she stepped on it.

"It's beautiful, Larry," she said.

She began to unfold the scarf and saw the white oblong of an envelope.

"That's for later," he said, "for next week—when you're at home."

She made herself laugh and made her eyes laugh as she looked at him. "I can't open it now?"

He raised his right hand, palm outward. He was grinning. "God forfend, Madam!" he said.

She grabbed the uplifted hand in hers and pulled it down, laughing. She looked straight into his eyes and saw through the mist in her own that they were misted too. "Thank you, Larry," she said, squeezing his hand. She was surprised how fragile it felt. "Thank you," she said again.

She released his hand and turned toward the hall door, folding the scarf as she went. "I'll put these up," she said, "and then we'll go for our walk."

II

They had walked a long way, and at every landmark she had thought, now I must tell him. But he had been so gay that she had almost made herself believe there was nothing to tell him after all. Yesterday afternoon had not occurred. They were walking the packed dirt roads for the last time this spring; but they would walk again in September, when the leaves would still be thick as now, though dusty, limp, half-wilted with summer; and later they would walk the same way, stepping aside for the lumber-haulers with the damp, fresh-cut wood on their wagons, under a gray November sky, and she would wear the scarf—gray, with red and black and white.

Now it was nearly supper time and they were sitting together on the levee up beyond Pat Pool's place, across the river from town. Turning, they could have seen the steel bridge across which they had come; but they faced west where the river made a long bend and all they could see was the water, high for May, red with hill mud, and beyond it a wall of green already darkening at the base. They had been talking about the sounds the river made, sometimes like the sucked breath of a drowning man, sometimes almost a chortle, as though the river were laughing at the men who put up levees to hold it in its banks. Now they were very quiet, listening.

He was looking at the water closely, squinting against the reflection of the sun, and he did not seem to notice when she turned and stared at him. The straight line of his nose, the high forehead were cut out sharp against the almost black base of the river wall.

Quickly she gazed straight up, where the sky was still so blue it almost hurt her eyes; then she looked lower, toward the reddening haze above the trees. She had seen that same red haze yesterday afternoon, when she had looked out the schoolroom window and said, "Of course, Mrs. Gordon. Of course, you're right. . . ."

". . . It's because we're so anxious for him to be a rounded, normal boy," Larry's mother said.

She started to speak, breathed in. From the lungs down, her body had disappeared. She looked out the window, where the sun was reddening a haze that was not quite clouds.

"Of course, Mrs. Gordon," she said. Then she discovered, astonished, that the four words had emptied her lungs again. Deliberately she filled them, above vacancy. "Of course, you're right."

She turned quickly, saw Mrs. Gordon's face before the white hat-brim could conceal it. She almost jumped. She could smell the laboratory at the university. She saw again the dog's head, the white-furred horror that lay on the table, the neck ending in sticky twists of hair,

tubes stringing off where body should have been, and the doctor pushing the meat along the table toward the head, watching; then his eyes
would set as the dog's purpling lips twitched and a thread of saliva
began to slip out. It was his look that she had just seen on Mrs.
Gordon's face.

Larry's mother turned her head a little to one side; the hat-brim still
shaded her eyes. "Now I do want you to understand one thing."

"Yes, Mrs. Gordon?"

"This has nothing to do with the talk."

She did not have time to fill her lungs again, but Mrs. Gordon went
on as though she had heard the thought answer.

"It's just small-town talk. I don't listen to it."

She imagined that she could see the doctor's look in the other
woman's eyes again, even in the shadow under the hat-brim.

"The whole thing's just ridiculous."

Agnes George smiled, gently. "Of course, Mrs. Gordon. Of course."

She looked out the window again. She could feel that Mrs. Gordon
was watching her; the eyes were the doctor's again; and she knew now
what she must say.

"I won't be able to help you much with Larry, though. I won't be
back next fall."

"But I thought you—." The voice showed real surprise, almost frustration.

"No," she said. "I won't be back next fall. . . ."

Mrs. Gordon's heels were loud in the empty hallway, echoing. She
knew that she had heard the sound before, but not here, and she could
not think where. She had thought about it a long time. Now, sitting by
the river, under the reddening dusk, while Larry looked sharply across
the water, listening, she could hear the loud heels again, echoing, coming closer. And she knew now what the sound was: it was the redcoats
marching in the sunset—on the cobbles of the inn-yard, on the stair,
in the room.

"Listen at it now," Larry said, not moving, staring at the river.
"Which sound do you hear now?"

She looked once more toward the squinted eyes, the rising line of
throat and chin and hair against the blackening green. She knew that
he meant to ask what sound the river was making, whether the noise
of death or laughter or both. But she could hear only one sound, that
of marching feet, echoing, sure and passionless.

"I don't know," she said. "Which do you think it is?"

He turned toward her, and she saw the mist of pleasure in the blue eyes, unsquinted now but still with little wrinkles around them that would disappear in a moment.

"I think it's laughing," he said. "I think it's always laughing. Only sometimes it nearly chokes and has to catch its breath."

He was leaning back on his elbows, his chin up. "It's laughing at those people over there—" jerking his head in the direction of town— "because they don't know how to listen to it."

The last sunlight struck his hair, reddening it. She started. She could hear the marching feet, louder now. Then they were in the room. She felt the quick hands, then the rope against her wrists and the sudden jerk as the cord tautened. She knew that she was tied upright, straighter than she had ever stood before, and there was something hard and round under her left breast, a pushing against the lower ribs.

They were laughing. Then she heard fragments of their talk.

"Of course we don't believe——"

"No, of course he's not coming."

"No. He's a normal highwayman."

"Don't you want him to be a normal highwayman, Bess? Don't you want him not to ride up the road in the moonlight, Bess?"

"You don't want him to be a good target, do you, Bess?"

"Of course not."

"Of course she doesn't."

"Of course we don't believe. . . ."

Then she was hearing them laugh again, and hearing above the laughter the horse's hoofbeats and out of the past the baritone voice: "Look for me by moonlight. For the fall. Watch for me by moonlight. For the fall. For the fall. For the fall."

She knew that the thing under her breast was a gun and she ought to try to reach the trigger. She ought to warn him, to let him know the redcoats were there and they'd still be there in the fall or whenever he came. She felt the cut in her wrist as she twisted her hands. But she could see the redcoats kneeling at the window, taking aim. She realized that it was too late. And the cords were tight around her wrists.

The Passing-Away
LeRoy Leatherman

"Corley, here's Jim Daigre."

The little flame of Mrs. Wagner's lamp wavered in the wind and made the room rock. The walls came alive with shadows . . . up from the deer antler hat rack over the washstand jumped a maze of black twisting lines, through them, one black solid pole made by Corley's casting rod suspended on the antlers. The whorls and curls and curves of the iron bedstead became black flowers on the walls. In the bed Corley, nothing but a hill under the yellow-blue-green quilt, did not move.

"Corley!"

Mrs. Wagner went over to the bed. Her headless jittery shadow lengthened toward the roof. She held the lamp out to one side, her shadow leapt from one wall to the other, and as she bent over to wake up Corley, her shadow curved over the window. She shook him, the shadow jumped. Corley still did not move.

"He ain't goin' to wake up. You go on and go to bed. I'll leave the lamp for you."

She put the lamp down on the washstand; the shadows, the room, settled, and she went out.

Instantly the wind closed around the room, isolating it. It was like a closet, just big enough for the bed jammed into one corner under the window, and the washstand, and now it was like a closet cut off, sealed up, blowing away in the storm. It had no ceiling; on the rafters over his head were balanced stacks of old newspapers and magazines. Beyond, the dark space up to the roof . . . where spiders lived, probably. He looked down quickly. On the door there was tacked a cover off the Children's Bible Weekly with a picture of the Shepherd on it . . . He was wearing purple robes, carrying a yellow lamb, he had a yellow circle around his head and above it the sky was blue and gold and green. Jim looked at it; the wind whistled in the corner eave. He thought how warm the lamb must be, contented and safe. Quickly he undressed, dropping his clothes on the floor, and crawled over Corley and got under the covers on the inside of the bed. A moment later Mrs. Wagner came and got the lamp. The room was then totally dark.

The old house cracked and snapped and whispered as if the wind were a ten-ton load careening around on the roof. He could see nothing, hear, besides the wind, nothing but Corley's distant breathing. He was cold all over except for one thin line of warmth on his right side from Corley's body. He lay for a long time thinking about being cold, then about being alone because Corley did not even know he was there in the bed with him. And he hated his mother and father for leaving him in this strange house . . . you'll just be in the way, son, up there, your poor old grandmother is real sick . . . He closed his eyes and tried to go to sleep but then he saw the highway whirling past under the car window and scene after scene of their strange journey came up, towns and trees and barns and houses and hills constantly shifting, speeding, leaving home behind, his seat at school vacant. And he could hear Miss Ada's voice calling the roll, calling his name, some little girl saying "He's absent!" Just as he thought how pitiful it was, there were, all at once, arms and legs all around him, he was pulled down under the covers, and was kicking and tossing over the bed, fighting with Corley. Everything was darkness and warmth and motion. The bed rocked, the covers flew off, the cold air closed in around them, and then, as quickly as it had started it was over, and Corley was lying on top of him, moaning "Oh . . . Oh . . . Oh . . ." as if he had been hurt. Jim turned slowly and let him roll off. He moaned louder.

"Did I hurt you?"

Corley sobbed. Jim found his shoulder and patted it. Then Corley's arm came across his chest and Corley's breath sputtered into his ear. He was laughing.

"Fooled you! Ain't it funny you being here? I watched out for you all day."

"I thought you were asleep. We drove fast."

"Before the old lady took sick I didn't figure you'd be here until the summertime. Old Man Ed told me you was comin'. She dead yet?"

Vaguely, on the far edge of the warm world he was in now, he saw an old woman lying white, dying, and all her children around her and her one grandchild, him, her old dried-up hand wiggling in the air, trying to catch his.

"No."

"Let's go see tomorrow."

"Mother told me to stay away from over there."

"God damn!"

"Why do you want to go over there?"

"I ain't never seen an old dead woman . . . besides . . ."

The last word was a long breath blown into his ear . . .

". . . I know somethin'."

And these words were the wind itself blowing into his head, moaning and whistling there in an echoing darkness, and instantly he was back in that moment of the summer past, hearing Corley say, "Want to see somethin'?", the magnolia leaves whirling and tapping in the dark over their heads, and he saw in one chaotic scene all the scenes of the summer adventure with the bull. And he knew that something was starting, or had already started, that he was in it, and he gritted his teeth at the thought.

"What?"

Corley's arm tightened around his chest.

"Your Aunt Annie and your Uncle Virgil done stole all your grandma's property except'n the old house out here and they're goin' to git that if your pa ain't careful and he won't git nothin' but a one dollar bill."

"How do you know?"

"Ed says so and he knows. There ain't nothin' he don't know."

"Is that why you want to go over there?"

"Jesus, no! I know somethin' else."

"What?"

"You seen that old cot out in the hall over there?"

"No. My mother wouldn't let me go in."

"Your Uncle Virgil sleeps on that cot every night, right out in the open."

"Why?"

"Your Aunt Annie makes him."

"Why?"

Corley giggled.

"So that man of your Aunt Nellie's can't git to her."

"You mean Uncle Ray?"

"Christ! He ain't your uncle any more'n I am."

"He is!"

"Damn it all, he ain't. They're just engaged. Ed says they been engaged for fourteen years because she had to take care of your grandma and now she's gone flat on him and maybe he won't ever marry her . . . but your Aunt Annie caught him in bed with her the other night and . . ."

He himself in bed now with Corley, Corley's arm around him . . . Ray in bed with his Aunt Nellie, fat, warm in the dark, whispering . . .

". . . and she tried to make your Uncle Virgil shoot him but he wouldn't, I reckon he was scared, and now she makes him sleep out there right in front of your Aunt Nellie's door and that Ray is hangin' around like a bull out to pasture."

Corley whooped in his ear, but he heard it distantly. He was far below in some mysterious dark outer place, held there by a warm cloying odor and the faint sound of his own voice whispering words seen on sidewalks, on the wall in the school basement, heard faintly from a small group of boys leaning against the schoolhouse, secretly grinning.

". . . Come on, let's go over there tomorrow."

The boys against the schoolhouse looking at him, grinning, saying, come on over.

"All right."

The storm broke; rain roared down onto the roof, bringing a further isolation. But now he was warm and not alone, and as he went to sleep he saw the woods and the houses blowing away in the wind, his mother and father, aunts and uncles and his dying grandmother flying through the air, furniture whirling around them, and he and Corley somewhere far below, safe, standing on the edge of a secret.

In the morning the wind and the rain were gone. The sky was clear, faintly blue, blank except for one white cloud far to the south. The back of the house was built high; the level of the kitchen window cut the close trees just across the middle, so that there was a solid border of green across the bottom of it and higher up a broad varying gleam . . . the sun on the top pine needles. Down in the yard, on the dull red rain-beaten ground, five gray-white hens and a bright little bantam rooster stepped around, made noises, pecked, their feathers still rumpled from the storm. Beyond them, down on the edge of the trees, the outhouse stood wet and clean-looking, but around the bottom of it there was a new mud-stain.

They were eating breakfast, he was just taking a mouthful of oatmeal when Corley grabbed his arm, spilling the oatmeal, and said,

"We got to git a move on. Look!"

He pointed into the corner by the cookstove. There was an axe.

"She want me to chop kindlin'."

"I'll help you."

He wondered if he could lift the axe.

"Well, God damn, I ain't goin' to do it. That's why we got to hurry."

They were out of the house into the woods when he heard Mrs. Wagner calling "Cooorrrrrlllllleeeeeyyyyy . . ." and Corley ran away from him down the path.

The Spring sunshine came down like a gold mist through the pine needles and the leaves of the cottonwood, sweetgum, oak and dogwood trees. Everything was shiny new green, washed by the rain. The air was soft. He felt his hair blow gently in a breeze that came whishing through the woods, shifting the shadows and the sunlight, setting everything into a fine light motion. He smiled, let the breeze catch him too, and started to trot, half-dancing along the path, making the colors of Spring run together like paints on a bright green palette.

He found Corley standing on the creek bank, skidding rocks out across the surface of the water.

"Them black ones are best . . . the flat ones . . . bet you can't do it!" His arm snapped back, snapped forward, and the little black pebble flew straight out, dropping, hit the water, skidded, bounced, hit, skidded, bounced, four times before it sunk.

"A good one'll do it six times. Let's git goin'."

They went east for a while along the flooded creek, past jams of driftwood, across soggy places where the ground clung to their shoes, where the young plants had been flattened down against the mud and were just then drying out in the sun. At a place where the creek divided, Corley turned abruptly left and took a path that angled back off into the woods. Here the sunlight came down in rectangles through the trees, like shining rods rammed down into the path. Jim held out his hand and let it go through them . . . they were solid; it was his own hand that was intangible. Ahead of him the sunlight and shadows of leaves moved over Corley's head and down his back. Off both sides of the path, under the trees, down close to the ground, among the bushes and Spring seedlings, there was a dim gray light, the last pale shadow of the night before.

Corley took a strange winding route. Sometimes he left the path and struck out through the woods, trompling down the new plants. They jumped a flooded branch, later jumped it again, and then they were back on the path, going straight ahead. Sometimes he stopped, listened. Slowly his walk changed. He became stealthy. He tiptoed. He gave signals to stop, to whisper, to creep. In every movement there was a suggestion of danger nearer, as if they were walking on the very edge of something. He became older; his whispers, the quick jerks of his arm, the cautious touch of his toes on the path, were a man's, a soldier's . . . he was a captain of infantry. Jim aped him exactly; he crouched, crept, crawled, listened, whispered . . . they were soldiers spying out a doomed fortress. They would race back this way, later, bringing the crucial knowledge.

The path led up to a blackberry briar and ended. Corley gave a snappy signal, jumped to the right over a low bush, became nothing but a brushing and rattling of leaves. Jim stood rigid, looking straight ahead into the briars, seeing most clearly one sprig on which there were five dull green berries, perfect miniatures of the big black ones Corley would make wine out of in the summertime. There was a dead stillness. Then one of the leaves twitched, a car sounded far away on the road, a dog barked, and under all these there was a constant uneven sound, as if there were a house close by. He looked up and saw vague chimney smoke high over the trees. Corley came thrashing back.

He worked through the bushes and followed Corley around the blackberry patch, through a thicket of stubby trees, slid down a little sandy bank and finally stood beside him under the dropping branches of the magnolia tree, looking up the steep hill toward his grandmother's house.

"Now we really got to go careful."

Captain Corley prepared his man for the worst.

"By now they're all in front. I spied 'em out yesterday. Come on. Keep low."

They jumped the branch. Jim landed on a twig. It snapped.

"God A'Mighty. Be quiet."

They dodged out of the shadows of the magnolia tree, across, into a stand of trees on the left side of the hill.

"Crawl!"

Up through the soggy leaves he crawled, the soles of Corley's shoes just in front of his face, kicking, going away. Somewhere a door slammed . . . the first rifle shot. At the edge of the trees they stopped.

"We got to run for it. Head to the corner of the house and keep up against it. Git down under the steps as quick as you can. Watch them goddamned chickens."

Corley crouched, flexed his knees, ready to sprint, then darted out into the sunlight, ran along the wall and under the steps. The chickens spewed out, squawking, wild, flying down the hill. Corley shook his fist at them and signaled to Jim to wait. He started getting scared when he saw the distance he had to run alone in the open, in the glaring sunlight . . . Corley signaled to come on . . . his clothes were wet, cold, his body was stiff. He got up slowly and before he knew it he was in the sunlight, running, brushing the side of the house . . . under the steps at last . . . happy, pleased with himself. Corley took his hand.

"Good . . . it's goin' to be worst when we get to the door. We're gone goslins if there's anybody in the hall. Come on . . . quiet."

The long flight of steps rose up ahead of him, the screened-in back porch. In the slanting light the screen was opaque. Step by step they went up. Halfway, there were footsteps in the hall, more rifle shots. Jim flattened down against Corley's legs. Whoever it was went toward the front of the house. He could hear now the mournful suppressed drone of the people on the front porch. Corley's legs moved; they went on up.

"Quick now!"

The screen door spring whined, Corley grabbed his shoulder, and he was at once inside, through the final barrier, on, across the back porch, flat against the wall.

"Jesus!"

He could hardly hear the sound.

"Your grandma is right on the other side of this wall."

Jim stepped away instantly.

"Git back!"

Just then an ugly bubbling sound came from inside the room. Corley gasped, clutched Jim's hand and edged slowly along the wall. Jim's ears roared. He stared at Corley's head, at a little tuft of hair sticking up on top that waved whenever he moved. He saw it stop waving, saw

Corley's head at the window frame gradually turn. At the second when he knew Corley was looking into the room, he felt him dig his finger-nails into his wrist and begin to twist it.

"Jesus . . . Jesus . . . look!"

And he was again yanked forward and then he was standing directly in front of the window looking in.

"Git back . . . git back . . . oooohhhh, git back . . ."

But the Captain's voice died away and he could do nothing but look.

His Uncle Virgil was less than a foot away from him, half-turned, in profile to the window. His skin was yellowish. He was standing at the foot of a big old tester bed. On the far side of the bed was his Aunt Annie. She had on a black and yellow flowered dress. There was a brilliant yellow lacy handkerchief bunched, dangling, at her bosom. Suddenly his uncle backed up against the window, the whole scene vanished, then as quickly reappeared. His uncle had edged in on the near side of the bed. His aunt bent over. His uncle's arm and shoulder appeared out over the bed, went down, came up, his aunt straightened up, and he saw between them in the bed a shape, gray and gangly. They were trying to make it sit up, but it kept slumping back.

"Nellie, get the tablet!"

A military order, instantly to be obeyed.

He looked away over the foot of the bed and saw on the far side of the room by the door a fat woman standing. He could only see her back. She was facing the door, slumped up against it.

"Nellie!"

His Aunt Nellie, fat, in bed in the dark with Ray, whispering . . . Her arms jerked. Then he thought that when she turned around he would learn at last the secret knowledge. The mission would be completed. His breath blew back hot, like a Summer wind, from the window pane. She turned away from the door and walked to a table on the right side of the room, then came over to the bed. Her eyes bulged as if something invisible were being tightened around her throat. She handed a tablet to his uncle . . . it was a Cardinal tablet, a big crowned red bird on the cover . . . school . . . his vacant seat . . .

"Get back there now and watch the door!"

She went back and slumped against the door and he had learned nothing. She could tell him, Corley could, but he would never ask . . . he was again isolated, far from the vital knowledge.

His uncle's head bent down close to the shape. He lifted its arm and put a long yellow pencil between its fingers . . .

"Sign your name . . . your name . . . Mama! . . . Sign!"

Mama? Mother? Slowly onto the indescribable shape on the bed he saw his grandmother's familiar features come, one by one. Then she was all there, like his father a little, and his Uncle Virgil, Aunt Annie, Aunt Nellie, the foundation bones all the same, out of the same old worn-out mold, seen through his own reflection in the window pane. He screamed.

Corley caught him and ran toward the door. His Aunt Annie got there first.

The world spun. There was a chaos of color, of sounds . . . screaming, cursing, his own name, yelling, printed colored flowers, yellow silk, Corley yelling, leave him alone, leave him alone . . . his Aunt Annie's face spinning in front of him, her hand coming at him, and then a series of distinct rapid shocks as she hit him and hit him again and hit him again.

He woke up in Corley's little room. It was nearly dark. Corley was sitting on the side of the bed, running a ram-rod back and forth through the barrel of his .22. The smell of oil was in the air of the room. He closed his eyes and felt the skin of his face pulsing, burning.

"It's hot in here."

"Jesus, that pill the nurse gave you sure did make you sleep. How you feel?"

"Where's my mother?"

"She's up at your grandma's. They carried you down here when that pill put you to sleep, then . . . God A'Mighty, you didn't see!"

Corley dumped the gun on the floor and got up beside him on the bed. He put his hand on Jim's head. Jim watched, as if through a hot fog, his little old-looking face come closer, closer, until all he could see was his eyes.

"Your grandma passed away while they was all fightin'. I seen her through a crack. Her mouth was hangin' wide open and your mother was standing over her and I could just see your mother's hands come down slow with something white in them, a strap maybe, or a handkerchief, or something, and it went around her chin and all of a sudden it tightened up and snapped her old mouth shut!"

Mr. Milkman
Eleanor Ross

LUKE PRENTICE APPROACHED DOC's service station at X-Way walking erectly and lightly as a boy forty years younger than himself, carrying only the still blue-edged oil can, its spout plugged with a raw spring Irish potato, plugged without need because the last of its contents had gone to fill his lamp last night, but plugged by habit lest some future light be lost on the dirt road home.

A young man in a corduroy hunting cap sat in a cane-bottomed chair by the door. He cleared the integuments from his esophagus and spat them cleverly behind his chair.

"Gimme another one," he said, "fore Mr. Luke here gits in ahead of me and buys you out."

"That's what I got 'em for, Lexter," Doc said. "I got 'em to sell."

"And long as I got the cash, wher you like it or not." Lexter scratched his chest beneath his overalls bib. "And long as the government keeps on arunning us three shifts a day making piecet goods."

Luke Prentice set the oil can on the short counter that resembled the altar-table in the church several yards down the road. He removed and held at his side his tall-crowned straw hat, but did not raise his hand to the moist ring of hair around his high, receding forehead.

"Well, Lexter," he said somewhat formally, "I couldn't afford it if I used it."

"Lookahere," Lexter said to Doc. "A man that can pay fifty dollars on the new parsonage, not to say a nickel when they pass the hat every Sunday." He turned to Prentice. "You living by yourself, got no wife, no chillun, no ortamobile, don't use tobacco nor whiskey—man, you're bound to have money!"

Prentice laughed heartily, in his thin, restrained manner, his eyes almost closing, his gums shining.

"Well, I'll say this for Prentice," Doc said. "If he's got it he's got it

buried somewheres in a hole in the ground, as I've never seen him here
with more'n two or three dollars at the time since he's been trading
with me."

Prentice set out in the direction he had come, carrying the oil can
and a paper package of crackers and ginger snaps with the same tennis-
shoe tread with which he had approached.

Bound to have money, he repeated, grinning graciously to himself.
It was natural that loud coarse fellow whose mother was a distant
cousin of his, and who spent his earnings on drinking beer and carous-
ing should also worry himself about The Dollar Mark.

Well, it's a good thing I never worry myself much about money, he
thought. Could worry up a big doctor bill to no purpose.

Probably even Lexter resented, as the women in his family certainly
seemed to, his not "undertaking the responsibility of marriage and a
family" as Mary referred to it, praising at the same time and as a rebuke to his trepidity the saintliness of the various unmarried women
in the community.

What was it he had found himself telling Mart's child? . . .

*I have always felt that a cat is a suitable companion for an unmarried
man living alone. When, as a young man, I first left home to try working in the hardware store in Raleigh, I used to feel positive beyond a
doubt, when the letters from your Grandma and aunts failed to mention anything relative to the welfare of Ring, my 'coon dog, that Ring
had died and they wished to spare me this new grief in the agony of
my homesickness. . . .*

But Ring lived to accelerate somewhat the pendulum motion of his
tail upon his return home a few months later, and to disturb them,
baying through the night till morning at something he had treed down
by the branch, for many years while he lived with Ma and Pa after the
rest of the children had married and settled down to raise families of
their own.

After Pa died in 1926 ("There's no doubt," Mart's wife had said, "his
religion as much as his ungovernable temper shortened his days") he
farmed the place, and Ma cooked and—as the neighbors said—"did for"
him and had a little garden, until in 1932 she fell on the back doorsteps
and broke her hip. He waited on her the two years she lay in bed, the
bone unset, her legs swollen in a strut—doing the farming when he
could get the time, on days when she seemed to be resting easy, and
when he could spare another hour or two of sleep.

"Well," Harley had said, "I know I speak for all of us well as myself when I say there's nothing we wouldn't do if we were able. But now—the depression like it is—it looks like it's much as we can put on one another to pay the doctor bill—much less undertake a hospital bill—when we all know—at her age—it's reasonable to face it—she isn't likely to get over this." The children had met and tried to make some financial arrangement, but that was the outcome of it.

The doctor said he became rather expert at nursing; he learned to lift her—a heavy woman, being big-boned, though her flesh wasted away as eventually she was unable to keep any quantity of food on her stomach because of the drug in her system (the big handsome country woman who had become outspoken and blunt from the Dutch girl she had been, gay, ignorant, light-headed and delighting to sing and dance among her brothers and sisters—Aunt Maria and Aunt Hilda and old Aunt Annie, frivolous sisters she never saw after her marriage unless she set out and walked the five miles to spend the night at Annie's, leaving her own oldest girl Mary at ten or eleven even to do the cooking at home and look after the others, leaving her children to the temper and the cold selfishness which her own mind, comprehensive because it was of discerning age beheld uncomprehending because it had always been guided by that indefinite core not heart because that was physical, not soul in one so empty; but that which must have been feeling such as a child would have because she had had it since she was the smallest she could remember)—and he would lift her carefully, gently, with as little jar as possible to the poisoned member.

It worried her to have company, but you couldn't keep her own children away. Sallie and Mary came every week, and the others as they could. On Sundays there would be a great gathering there. They would all sit up around the fire and shut off the heat from Ma's bed. They came to see Ma, he supposed, but they never talked to her beyond asking her how she felt, and then they paid no attention to what she said. She had got to be hard of hearing and it was, he knew, something of a strain to carry on a conversation with her. She never was much of a talker. Mart's wife said once that came of living with Pa, but Priscilla never had much use for Pa.

During that last winter she complained of a draft about her head and took to keeping her head covered when she sat up; mostly she wore a black hat, broad-brimmed, of a sort of plush material. It had been her Sunday hat before she fell. She would sit up in bed over in the dark corner of the room, wearing her hat and talking to God about Flint Prentice's soul.

He remembered one Sunday; with most of the family present, she began talking about Pa, bringing up old grievances she had never mentioned in the six years he had been buried, much less before.

"And I said to myself," she said with tearful defiance, " 'You'll never whip him again.' But he died soon after. . . .

"He always told me I wouldn't go to heaven, and I just want to know he's not there. . . ."

Then she would shift her teeth about so that the younger of the grandchildren looked half scared to death, and her eyes would rove along the ceiling. Presently she would begin to talk coldly, in a low voice, about something else.

"And Mary had that growth on her shoulder for the longest time, and he never would have the doctor. . . ."

It looked as if it hurt Mart's wife. She would look at her hands in her lap, then look at Ma, and swallow hard.

"I don't remember a thing about that," Mary whispered suggestively to her. "Ma's out of her head. It's the morphine."

If it were pretty weather Mart's wife would say to her girls, "Children, wouldn't you like to see the old ciderpress?" and take them off to the branch and the old lane, beyond the new one, where Mart had once in his youth shot at a wildcat and to the old smokehouse which had been visited by Yankee raiders (long before the place came into Prentice hands—who ever had heard of a Prentice Negro?) or to crack black walnuts on the big rock under the edge of the woodshed. But it was a raw day that day. All of a sudden, as she would do, Ma seemed to come to herself and see who was in the room. She looked at everybody and seemed to be listening to what was being said. Then her eyes fell on Mart's youngest girl, Sue, who was sitting beside her mother. She was a child of about eight or nine, just started to school—a quiet, timid child who had had a long body as a baby and had Ma's light hair and eyes.

"Stand up, Suke! and let's see how tall you are," Ma said.

The child stood up timidly, while the other grandchildren looked even more terrified at this request. She was, indeed, quite large for her age and too young yet to realize what her beauty would be. She tried to smile at her grandmother, but there was no response to this childish appeal. The talk soon started up again. Ma seemed hardly to see the little girl; she only stared in her direction in a daze (and wearing the imposing hat as if she understood her position as a guest and a traveler) till her half-shut eyes fixed on the window behind her granddaughter; she said nothing more for the rest of the afternoon. After a while Priscilla reached forward touching softly the child's outgrown coat, "You can sit down now, Babe."

During the week, when there was no company, she would be better at intervals, and tell Luke how to fix the milk to churn and ask him to see that the hen nests had fresh straw. But she was too deaf to enjoy talking, and she had never been one to read. He couldn't be with her all the time. He knew it was wearisome for her, to lie there day after day, would have been wearisome to a person not suffering as she was.

"I don't know why the Lord don't take me," she would say. "I pray to die. Every day I pray to die." She died in August of 1934, shortly after her eighty-second birthday; it was a blessing and he thanked the Lord for it as a blessing when her sufferings ended.

After she died he stayed on to gather that fall's crops. There was some talk of having one of the family move into the house with him, but "I got along all right without anybody to help me when Ma was sick," he said calmly. "I think I can shift for myself now." Furthermore, he didn't relish the thought of having a gang of children around the house—something a bachelor like himself did not easily become accustomed to—so he did not press the matter.

"You ought to sell the farm and go live with some of the rest," Harley said. . . . *You have no home of your own to invite anybody to live in.* . . . (And when he saw that I did not intend to leave the place he insisted on my having a dog—a watchdog, as he said—there with me, and when he saw that I did not intend to have one, he got a half-grown shepherd puppy from one of his members—"a saintly woman" he said —and brought it down at scuppernong time.) *Why, it was a nuisance from the beginning, whining all night to be let in the house, and under my feet and the mules' feet, and nipping at the cows' legs all day, and of course I had nothing to feed a dog. It's all I can do to keep the payments going on the farm and keep enough tools to work with and something in the safe for myself, and, Harley, you know a dog like that can't live on bread and milk. When I started to town or to church I had to tie him to keep him from following me and being a nuisance. It was a good thing the Bowman boys were carried away with him.* . . .

Nothing had been forgotten. The bread, the oil, the pants Priscilla pressed. He had hitched the team at the barn, and sat, his hands and his tall-crowned straw hat flat on his knees, watching her wrists and her interest bent on her work, the regular small rise of steam and the moldy smell. He answered speaking of his health, the crops, the neighbors:

Bowman is going to farm the land right next to me this year. Seems to be a pretty good sort, and his wife is a good woman too, I think. She has to work pretty hard, I reckon. She always seems eager to divide with me—sends me something of whatever they have. One day she sent one of the boys over with a stew pot of cucumbers. There were thirty-four cucumbers in there. I'm not a great hand for cucumbers myself. I can eat one or two, but there were thirty-four in that pot. The next day she sent eighteen. I did eat a few of the first ones, so I could thank her for them. I had to give the rest to the chickens. A woman could have canned two or three jars. But you take those boys of hers, they can eat a raw cucumber, without any bread or salt whatever, like it might be a banana. As for myself, I'd have to be pretty hungry to do that.

(One day when he was there, to ride with Bowman into Harmon City in order to return some books to the library, Mrs. Bowman came out and handed her husband some money. "I found this fifty cents at the well," she said. "Providence will work in my favor, spite of all I can do, as Uncle Jimmy used to say. Now, Herman, I want you to get me some silk stockings to wear to church, size ten and a half, and not too dark of a color, just about the color of that chicken there."

On the way back he had asked Bowman if he had any trouble finding his wife's stockings. "No," he said, "I got two pairs. Cotton, though. They ain't got no silk stockings for fifty cent. Cheapest they had was eighty-seven cent."

He reckoned Mrs. Bowman thought she'd have to get Providence to work a little harder in her favor.)

That oldest boy—Treece, they call him—came over collecting money for the Red Cross to turn in to his teacher. I gave him five dollars. "Oh, I wouldn't give that much," he said. "We just give fifty cents." I reckon they have it pretty hard. There are—six, I reckon—children, two not in school.

The boys were carried away with Harley's pup, and I encouraged them to pet him, till he took to following them home, and finally got to staying over there more than with me.

I reckon their daddy and mammy had no objections. One more mouth to feed is not as much of a burden where there are eight already as where it doubles the family. Of course I didn't mind the food; it was the trouble of the thing that got me. To make the boys feel right I said I would take one of the kittens in exchange for the dog. They always had a yardful of cats, though Bowman would take a bunch off every few months. I had got interested in this set, from going over in the evenings, a couple of times a week, after my hens stopped laying, to get eggs, and getting there just around milking time. The cat had her kittens in the stable, and Treece would give them warm milk, squirting it from the teat into their mouths. It was right entertaining to watch them. . . .

There had been three to begin with, but they found one dead one morning, whether the cow had stepped on it, or the tomcat or Shep killed it, they never knew. Of the two left, one was white- and tabby-spotted, and the other was all white. He remarked that it was rather unusual to see a cat without a colored spot on it anywhere, but this kitten was completely white, a male, and promised to be a big cat.

He enjoyed watching them frolic at twilight, when he was over at the Bowmans'. As they got bigger they left the stable and drank milk from a white pan at the wood-pile. One night as he was watching the white kitten lap up his milk he suddenly lost the outline of his head against the milk and the pan. His eyes shut, he was completely white and without form. If it had not been for his tongue and the linings of his ears with their dull glow of animal blood it would have been useless to try to tell where the cat ended and the pan of milk began.

He had just learned to dig in the soft dirt of the wood-pile around the milk saucer. After sitting for some time over his excavation without the anticipated results, he grew exasperated, attributed his lack of success to the structure beneath him, and with some vexed mewing to himself, impatiently clawed out a few more showers of loose earth, sat again. He sat for a long time. His tail, wrinkled and straightened spasmodically, his eyes closed. Mewing again, he turned hastily about, and in real resentment retired to another spot to dig afresh. When finally his diligence was completely rewarded, he became so involved in refilling the excavation that with his forepaws he buried his hind legs to the joint in chip-manure and chips.

The Sunday he went over to get his cat the two kittens were frolicking in the pecan tree in the Bowmans' yard. Suddenly, at a distant roar of machinery, both stretched out like arrows. They supplied themselves with pairs of retreating feet and advancing feet—hind feet retreating from the territory occupied, the fore ones advancing to better fortified positions.

"They shore is giving that airplane plenty room," Treece said.

Treece fixed his pallid eyes on Mr. Luke with the respect of a tall, poor, studious boy for a tall, poor man who when he came across a Greek or Latin word in his Sunday School lesson would lift the old muslin cloth, its flowers now recessed irrevocably into the muslin from the sunlight and dust, and crawl under the table in the side-porch-room, lifting the thin, heavy textbooks, opening the stiff covers, turning the novel substance of the pages, wondering presently how he found himself here:

I took him home in that shoebox. He didn't like it much, but it wasn't far, and he soon made himself at home. I've fixed him a box under the woodshed, but he likes to sleep on the woodshed roof in the daytime, and carouse around at night. He gets bigger and bigger. Already an object of curiosity to strangers, and especially to every buck nigger that passes. "That am a big white cat," they say with reverence. Because of his size they suppose him to be a good mouser, as he is, and something of a retriever, as he may be too, though I never actually take him hunting, never having been much of a man to hunt, Treece.

The relatives insisted on his having a name, and supplied me with a number of suggestions, somebody I believe suggested Panderosa, but I finally called him Milkman, because Mart's youngest girl called him that. He was drinking milk one night when they were there at the house, and I reckon he looked about the way he had to me that evening over here.

I'll bring you a chair on the porch, Sue. I won't invite you in.

Living by yourself, you know, you're liable to get into irregular habits, and habits that strike other people as peculiar. I long ago stopped admitting women to my house. You know it's the hardest thing in the world to keep them out. But just let Mary or Sallie or any of them come, and they want to inspect my housekeeping. They want to see how a man keeps house. They walk through every room, looking under the beds and in the closets and on top of the shelves, even in the safe. One day I happened to be at work on the pasture fence when Mary and Lum and their girl drove in. When I got to the house the women folks had already made the rounds. "Uncle Luke," Millie Rose said, "haven't you got too much milk in that churn?" She wasn't a bit embarrassed at having taken the lid off my churn. Not as embarrassed as you are at hearing about it. Since that, I stop women at the door in the summertime, and try to be away from the house, with the doors latched, on Sundays during the winter. I don't mind seeing them—you're mighty welcome—but I don't want them nosing in my churn.

Mr. Milkman never has been any trouble to me, from the first. You know, a civilized animal like that can be at the mercy of the fellow he happens to belong to, and I take care to see he gets enough to eat. But he never has asked for much. He could do without anything I furnish him. He goes off for days at a time and comes back one morning plump as you please, but standing against the porch screen, ready for a little civilized cow's milk. At such times he seems to want to rub against my breeches-leg and purr a while, and it seems that out of pure charity I ought to rub his back.

Occasionally he brings up a chipmunk or a big rat and plays with it, tossing it into the air and pretending to fear it will get away until he has wrested my attention and approval in the form of "Smart cat," or even "Good Milkman."

I have even got to talking to him. He looks at me and blinks and mews, purring all the while. I don't believe I have ever seen a cat that appreciates more the provident adjustment of life with man. When he gets back scratched and torn up from a scuffle with some brassy little wild animal he will stretch and roll on the kitchen floor and give forth —in expression of the luxury of tame life, I call it—a string of queerly-humanly arranged mewings. In such moods it is actually possible to make a remark to him and get an answer. Sometimes I ask him the very natural question, "Where have you been, Milkman?" But my communication with Milkman does not go so far as to comprehend his reply. . . .

He remembered the first time he had caught himself speaking aloud alone.

His eyes had searched warily about the room for the strange sound. This was followed by the feeling he had had the first time colored Virginia asked him (something Lexter might have said to him but did not because white people never said it to him directly, only wore themselves out talking around it) the feeling that he had just laughed at something perhaps not laughable, with the simultaneous feeling that he might be the object of a humor too ponderous for laughing-at. From then on he reminded himself humbly that it was not to his kitchen to accord the silence seemly in the church or in the churchyard. . . .

"Ain't you feared you'll die off down there by yourself?" . . .

Days on end by himself, the Bowmans as he himself absorbed in the ridging into combed rows and the planting of fields set off and edged on all sides by unthinned woods and approached only by a track through and under the trees where he would nettle alternately with the plowlines and with words the skittish red mule who would lift her ears and feet gingerly, shy at being run so close to the still, slick-bottomed puddles and the unworn branches; night after night alone, in summer the little bugs drawn through the darkness through the screen, their wings and their legs making no sound, the only sound the tapping of their bodies against the lamp-chimney, and the light tap as another curious insect, too inconsequential even to be identified and relegated to his species, fell into the ring of charred insects on the table, then a larger night creature hitting with a sudden impact against the lighted screen, its arrival expected and astonishing, and over his book he would be aware of the nightly silence and the silence to come.

In winter the darkness was longer, and, unable at his age to read for long by the poor light, he would sit by the fire, the lamp unlighted, knowing well, being alone, the artificiality of his pine walls (the pines his father could not wait to allow to dry before having them dressed and nailed green onto the pillars—these walls with the three great knots in a row beginning with the third plank above the hall door which his mother had watched from her deathbed for two years; they had had plenty of time to dry in the years since they went up) yet not willing to dispense with them entirely any more than Milkman would willingly relinquish his regular portion of civilized cow's milk, any more than he himself would have lived, now that his filial duty was done, with a family within these or any other walls.

The days of rain without were less intolerable because less free; shut in discomfort by discomfort watching the long strings of water hour after hour spinning themselves into the ditches, the shorter strings striking themselves into the hills, the earth combed and carded; the wood burning with deliberation and with more smoke in the room dark as lamplight; then he could feel himself attracted to the pull of human voices in human communication, the magic that could cast up so splendid an edifice in the silence.

At hog-killing time Harley had come down. He was a great eater of spare-ribs and sweet potatoes, and of course it was true that Luke would not have kept a hog just for himself if he had not been able to divide it with somebody. He had plenty of company at hog-killing time, and scuppernong time, and apple time, and at Christmas, when they all wanted Christmas trees and holly, but he had no trouble recognizing Harley's car as soon as it balked at the drive. He drove it, Luke said, as no mule deserved to be driven, and rode as nobody ought to be made to ride. He always knew who it was, though Harley traded cars every year, and always gave the dealer the better end of the trade. He had a car always as much as six years old and with an individual knock, to be on the safe side of his board of stewards. When he traveled he put a couple of coats, one a raincoat (he called it a "slicker") on hangers in the back of his car, his "grip" open on the front seat beside him with necktie, sunglasses, handkerchiefs, a bottle of digestive-aid tablets, a flashlight, two extra flashlight batteries, and his wife's concentric-striped umbrella handy. In the back were various presents from his wife to the female relatives he might visit on an inconvenient day: apples, bags of peppermint candy, and back numbers of women's magazines. There was also a large box which had the appearance of containing food, but whether this was for an emergency, to be opened in case the hog had not yet been strung up, or merely a tool box, he had never had the opportunity to establish.

Harley had been moved to a better charge, a church in a small town. He brought Luke a mother cat and two kittens. These animals had accrued at his last charge; there would be no place "in town" for country cats. How he had brought them a hundred miles in a wooden box in the car was as unanswerable to Luke as the good reason he must have had for bringing them. They were half wild when they got out.

However, they tamed. In less than a week they lined along the back porch screen half the day, mewing for food and dashing under one's feet in all directions.

Milkman, after he had smelt them thoroughly cat-fashion, kept his distance from this new crew, outside the fact that one day he brought up and deposited in the yard a de-entrailized rabbit which relieved the congestion at the door considerably for a short time.

Harley visited around with the rest of the brothers and sisters for another week, then came back, to pick up the sausage which had been made up by Virginia now, and possibly to give the cats a final blessing.

Early the morning of his departure the cats were clustered about the doorstep. Luke had strained the milk into the buckets on the floor, and he called as Harley started out, "Don't let the cats in yet, before the milk's cooled."

One of the kittens slipped between his legs, and in his effort to keep the others out he stuck his foot forward, hitting a smart crack with the toe of his shoe directly in Milkman's face. Milkman's eyes shut; his tail flew into the air. He tumbled onto the ground, then sprang up and sailed across the yard toward the barn.

Harley looked after him surprised. "Well," he said, "I didn't mean to hurt the cat"; then he looked around.

He supposed his feelings were written all over his face.

"Well, ha! ha!" Harley said, "I suppose he's just mad. Got his feelings hurt. Gone off to lick his pride. He's not hurt. A mad cat if ever I saw one." He went on out, and Luke fried some sausage and made coffee.

After breakfast, Harley said he thought he'd walk about the old place a bit. Luke mixed the milk in the can, and washed and scalded the buckets. Then he got a biscuit and put on his hat and went out to see if he could locate Milkman. He didn't know whether he might be hurt, or was hiding somewhere. He went up toward the barn, and when he got around back of it he heard Harley poking in the bushes at the edge of the lot calling, "Kitty? Come here, kitty? Kitty?"

"Have you found him?" he asked.

Harley straightened up and came back toward him.

"No, he's gone off, ha! ha! An indignant cat, that's what he was! He'll get over it!" He chuckled again. "An indignant cat!" He went briskly off toward the house.

He looked in the stables and the hen nests and under the grape vines, all the places he had liked to sleep. Well, he thought, he's had no breakfast, I reckon he's gone off to catch a field rat.

Harley was to leave around eleven o'clock; when Luke got back he had already put his grip into the car and hung his clothes in the back and put the sausage and a sack of black walnuts on the seat beside him. He shook hands with Luke. "Well, Luke," he said, "if I don't see you again soon, write to us, take care of yourself." He said he would. Harley got in and started the car. As it began to roll off he put up his hand and said with the same merriment, "Hope your cat turns up all right!"

For a week or so he looked for him back, and sometimes he would call him when he fed the others at nightfall remembering: he could have got along without anything I furnished, and wondering: why didn't he kick me in the face instead?

No More War
Mary N. S. Whiteley

FRÄULEIN HOHLER WAS SERVING TEA in her garden with the Italian couple as her guests.

From the garden next door over a high wooden fence covered with purple clematis and espalier pears came both masculine and feminine laughter. It rolled in bursting waves which started separately, mingled, and retreated diminishingly as waves of the sea roll away into the sea only to gather and return in another huge breaker. As every wave of laughter crashed, Fräulein Hohler gave a slight shudder.

"That woman" (this was what Fräulein Hohler called Frau Herz, her next-door neighbor), "she allows anything to go on in her house! You observe, she herself makes as much noise as any of them." She clattered her cup and saucer onto the covered iron table before adding in an absentminded sort of way, "she belongs in the Rheinland of course."

The Italian couple shook their heads in simultaneous sympathy.

"You are from Berlin are you not, Fräulein Hohler?"

"Ja—ja, Berlin. It is so different in Berlin. Here they scarcely know there *is* a Third Reich, they are so foolish and easygoing." She leaned slightly but impressively toward the iron bench occupied by the Italian husband and wife. "They don't absorb even all the glorious things that for the Vaterland are being done by our wonderful Fuehrer."

"There are many people like that in our country," the husband said, "the ingrates!"

"Yes, so many like that in our country," said the echo, his wife, "they cannot understand what Il Duce is doing for them."

While they were talking the garden gate opened and a young American man hurried toward the front doorstep, but hearing voices, turned and waved gaily at the tea group. "Der Fuehrer and Il Duce meeting again over the teacups?" he called over laughingly while getting a latch-key out of his pocket.

Fräulein Hohler stiffened in her iron chair, teapot in hand. "Will you have a cup of tea, Herr Parker?" she asked with ice in her voice.

The American turned and slightly overdid a bow, declining the invitation. Then he opened the front door and went into the house.

"Ach!" Fräulein Hohler exclaimed with an access of guttural depth, "these impossible Americans!"

Conversation in Fräulein Hohler's garden lagged and tea and cakes were consumed in silence for a time, until the postman opened the gate and came in. As he approached the house he glanced over toward the tea table and with a perfunctory "Heil 'tler," scarcely raising his right arm at all, brought the mail to the table instead of going to the front door with it. He handed the mail across the teapot, which was covered with a huge embroidered cozy, to Fräulein Hohler with a smile and "Guten Tag." But instead of taking it from his hand Fräulein Hohler first sat even more erect than she already was and then with an exaggerated lift of her right arm she shot her hand stiffly forward and said "Heil Hitler!" in a loud and determined manner.

The Italians sipped their tea and looked vacant. The postman got rid of the mail, heiled again (this time more correctly), and walked briskly away.

After a few more attempts at conversation the teacups were put on the table and Fräulein Hohler was left sitting erect and angular and alone behind her red checked cloth, her antique teapot, and her assortment of bright colored peasant china. When the American man came out of the house again he merely bowed before opening the garden gate on his way out.

Meanwhile in Frau Herz's garden the Scotswoman had opened her tea basket and spread tea things on the rusty garden table, while Frau Herz and her other boarders, two young American girls and a middle-aged Englishman, were grouped about, some sitting in a sunny spot on the grass.

Frau Herz wiped her eyes. It always brought tears when she laughed so hard and it also made her high puffed bosom roll in spite of her tightly drawn dress. "Such funny mistakes in Deutsch you make, Fräulein Moore," she gasped at one of the American girls, "at the university what do they about you do?"

The other American girl spoke up: "They just think she's a freak."

Another burst of laughter from Frau Herz, an echo of the last, quite evidently covered up the fact that she did not know what a freak was.

When everything was quiet again the Scotswoman suddenly said "*Kaput*"—that's that—which again started the shrieks of mirth that Fräulein Hohler in her next door house objected to so much.

When the postman interrupted the gayety in Frau Herz's garden he was greeted in various ways. As he gave his usual careless heil Frau Herz said something to him in German that made him laugh, but at the same time he glanced over his shoulder nervously.

The tea party progressed. Jane Lofting, the older of the American girls, got a paper bag of pastries from her room which were greatly appreciated, as the table at Frau Herz's was scantily laid. Not that Frau Herz would have failed to provide real butter for breakfast, and better fare at other meals, but the cost was too high. She could not even afford the amount of butter allotted a house where there were boarders. It distressed Frau Herz that she could not show her guests the good living she had known before 1914 when her husband had been alive and her two boys had been very small.

As the party became engrossed in the bag of sweets, and as Frau Herz filled the gap in the conversation with "So . . . ," pronounced in a deeply satisfied Germanic way, the iron gate at the front yard of the house opened with a characteristic click that made Ann Moore look up expectantly. "Hello everybody!" the American from Fräulein Hohler's house called out, "What are you all doing?"

"Planting buttercups of course," answered the Scotswoman with a siren-like laugh. Which, having to be explained as a joke to Frau Herz, caused renewed merriment.

"Isn't he too *suss!*" mispronounced Miss Macpherson, the Scotswoman, with a coy giggle as Gus Parker rolled his eyes to heaven over his cup of tea and cakes.

"You sound so darned gay over here," he said gloomily, "I wonder if my month'll ever be up—wish I could move over now . . ."

"Do you think," Jane Lofting asked, "Frau Herz can sleep in the cellar so you can come over here, Mister?"

"Never mind, Herr Parker—for you I shall find the room when comes the time."

"I knew you would, Frau Herz—your heart's bigger even than your house . . ." He smiled at her gratefully as he put down his empty cup. Then he got up and shook himself out lazily. "How 'bout a walk before supper?" he said to Ann Moore.

But before Ann could answer there was another interruption which drew all eyes back to the front gate, and which drained the color from Frau Herz's face.

"Good afternoon," Frau Ranke called out, "may I join the tea party for a few minutes?"

The infinitesimal pause was covered by Miss Macpherson: "If you won't try to give me a German lesson!"

Frau Ranke stopped on her way to shake hands with Frau Herz and glared angrily at Miss Macpherson.

"It is so nice that you come, Frau Ranke," Frau Herz overdid her welcome a little, with great ceremony getting a seat for Frau Ranke. "Occasionally," she explained while bustling about, "Frau Ranke is kind enough to help Fräulein Macpherson with the Deutsch—Fräulein Macpherson is sometimes like a child, is it not so?"

An imp sprang into Miss Macpherson's voice: "Fancy, I am learning to write German so well that I'll be able soon to write a letter to Herr Hitler!"

For a second the air in Frau Herz's garden was suspended as if life had stopped for one beat.

"Do have some of these cakes," said Ann hurriedly handing a plate to Frau Ranke, "and tell us what opera is to be given next."

"Lohengrin," Frau Ranke answered as Ann dropped into the seat next her. But raising her voice she immediately added, "if war does not come first . . ."

"War?" "Oh, surely there will not be war!" "It all depends on Germany of course," Mr. Brooks, the Englishman, added to the other comments before lighting his freshly filled pipe.

"England!" snapped Frau Ranke. "England is doing her best to *make* trouble—encouraging the Czechs!" She snapped a cookie in two. "But we are ready—ach ja! We have Italy for our great ally, and if we need Japan she will help us also . . . That would bring you in, would it not?" She turned quickly to Ann with an evil gleam in her eyes.

"Why should that bring us in?" Ann took the plate and put it down casually on the iron table.

"Because Japan is your enemy."

Ann turned around swiftly. "We have no enemies, Frau Ranke." And before anything else could be said she spoke to Gus Parker: "I think I'll take you up on that walk, Gus."

They took a winding mountain road to a favorite spot which combined a view of wooded country with a downward vista of the red roofs and green trees of the town as it zigzagged about the brown stone spire of the münster.

"That darn Nazi!" Ann's voice shook a little. "She must be one of those Hitler Frauen—they seem to pick the fairly attractive looking ones. I bet she's getting something out of Miss Macpherson, to be giving her lessons—I'd better warn little Scottie, she's such an open book."

"Don't you worry—she's no open book. She's a very canny little Scot and a mighty nice one."

"I can't understand how you've stood that house you're in," Ann said as they moved on. "That Fräulein Hohler is a pain, and those awful Italians . . . What makes Fräulein Hohler look down on Frau Herz anyway—because dear funny old Herz is poor, you suppose?"

"That isn't the chief reason. It's because the old dragon is from some part of the North—up there they seem to look down on this neck of the woods. By the way, one of the Italians asked me once if Frau Herz is a Jew . . ."

"What did you say?"

"Definitely not! I said she is a very fine type of German."

"I think I know why she asked that—the Jews aren't allowed to keep servants, you know . . . One of those cute little things they are doing to them. Frau Herz can't afford a servant—but she certainly isn't a Jew."

"I didn't realize . . ."

"Perhaps you don't know how she suffered from the last war—she lost her husband and her elder son and then she nearly starved to death afterwards, during their depression."

"Maybe that's what makes her son Heinz such a queer customer."

"He's worse than queer—I think he's dangerous—I'm sure he's a party member and he's watching his mother as well as her guests. It's all so murky and unreal here, Gus—it's like a bad dream . . ."

Gus stopped short, gripped her by an arm and swung her around to face him, but before he could speak they both were conscious of a man in part-Bavarian costume looking at them intently as he pushed his bicycle up the hill. Gus let go her arm. "It's time for you to leave for home," he said. "If war is as close as some say—the newspapers are certainly trying to get the people's hair up over Czechoslovakia. Poor innocent Germans! And the wicked Czechs killing them every day along the border! I bet the Germans are marching in there right now, Chamberlain or no . . ."

"But my job at home depends on my finishing my course, Gus . . ."

"How 'bout a job in an internment camp?"

"I know."

"You're just the kind of girl I'd like to have around and make love to, you know—but I'm just that altruistic . . ."

They both laughed shakily. "Okay, I'm going—as soon as I can get things arranged."

On their way home again they stood once to watch a troop of young men, spades carried over their shoulders as if they were guns, marching down the center of a road in time to the song they were singing.

"What a lovely marching song!" Ann exclaimed, "I think I'd march anywhere to that song."

"But ominous, Ann. And spades! Drilling with spades . . ."

When they arrived at Frau Herz's house they found everybody gathered in the sitting room talking in loud excited tones.

"It is I that faulty am," Frau Herz was wailing musically. "I should of it have told—but Ich vergessen!"

"You're not to blame at all," the suntanned Englishman forsook his bad German. "The police should put notices about. Stupidity I call it, coming to the house in such an insulting manner—how was I to know I had to fill out their ridiculous papers in three days?"

"I can't think why I didn't remember to tell you myself," Miss Macpherson said vaguely.

Frau Herz went back to her native tongue: "They usually are not so strict—it must be that somebody has been talking . . ." Ann and Gus exchanged glances, but Jane Lofting broke out with: "Nice comfortable feeling, isn't it, to know someone is watching and listening all the time!"

Miss Macpherson laughed nervously: "I shan't buy another thing in their filthy little town."

Frau Herz started to speak, glanced around and closed her mouth, but her eyes looked appealingly at her guests.

Later, when Gus Parker joined Fräulein Hohler's boarders at the oblong supper table, he noticed how bleak one of the two Englishwomen appeared. As he struggled with his food he could not keep his eyes off Miss Heatherworth's nose, where all the blood from her cheeks seemed to have concentrated. The other Englishwoman occasionally glanced at her countrywoman anxiously.

"I hope your telegram good news was, Fräulein Heatherworth," remarked Fräulein Hohler.

Miss Heatherworth tried to clear her throat. "It was telling me to come home, Fräulein Hohler."

"I hope there is nothing serious . . ."

"Only war, Fräulein Hohler." Miss Heatherworth's voice was tight and dry. "It depends on how one reacts to it, of course . . . Everyone in England thinks war is about to break . . ."

The other Englishwoman sucked in her breath. The two Italians started an excited chatter, but Miss Heatherworth raised her voice and drowned them. "War," she repeated, "another horrible war not of our making . . . My only nephew will have to go . . . All fine English boys . . ."

Fräulein Hohler had been very carefully buttering a slice of bread with margarine. "Germany does not make war," she said calmly. "War is the last thing our wonderful Fuehrer wants. It's the Jews in England and America who are trying to make you believe Germany is going to make war!"

Gus looked up at a large picture of Hitler on the dining-room wall and checked an outburst, saying quietly: "Our papers are free to express whatever opinions they wish, and so are the British papers. They come pretty darn close to the truth too . . ."

Fräulein Hohler shifted her argument. "The Bolshevist press is the great menace of the world. The world one day will realize how the Vaterland has stood between it and Red Russia. How good it will be for all people when Germany her former glory has regained!"

Miss Heatherworth pushed back her chair murmuring something like an apology and left the room.

When the meal was over Gus stopped the other Englishwoman in the hall, as the Italian couple followed their landlady to her private sitting-room.

"Is Miss Heatherworth's family the jittery kind—I mean would they telegraph her just because they are a little anxious?"

"Not at all—they are very sober people. That telegram means there really is going to be war, they've seen signs that we here cannot see. Did you notice the groups of men standing around the town this afternoon, talking in undertones?"

"No—I wasn't in town this afternoon, Miss Brownson. And the way most of them have steadily denied the possibility of war! If we could only get an American paper, or the London *Times*—they haven't had the *Times* at any of the regular places for several days, or at least they've *said* they didn't have it . . ."

"Verboten," said Miss Brownson. "But in one of their local papers I read that the Czechs had announced they wanted to get all Europe into a war so Germany could be cut up and ended as a nation— and yet only a few thinking Germans seem to be worrying over such transparent suggestions as that."

"They don't think—they just feel. Are you and Miss Heatherworth going to leave immediately?"

"I shall ask her to wait a day or two—the job she's aiming at depends on her learning German thoroughly, you know."

The next morning the German newspapers had such headlines as: "Herr Chamberlain coming to Berlin to visit der Fuehrer on Thursday," "Our Fuehrer graciously will receive Herr Chamberlain," etc., and the reaction of the people of the town from the gloom of the day before was noticeable to everybody. When Gus Parker entered philosophy class at the University the Herr Professor beamed at him: "These silly people! Now they see for themselves the Vaterland would not dream of fighting England—we want only peace with the whole world. Der Fuehrer and Herr Chamberlain will put those wicked Czechs in their place—you will see."

Relief showed everywhere. Shopkeepers laughed and came to their doors with customers again. There even was a slight feeling of gayety in the air. The fruit and vegetable vendors on the market Platz chatted gutturally once more, and the little old woman who sold roses outside of a small café went in and had a mug of beer during the morning.

Gus joined the two American girls walking home to Frau Herz's for dinner.

"Isn't it grand that Chamberlain is coming over!" Jane exclaimed. "The whole place is so excited over it too."

"And most of them have been denying the possibility of any war!"

"Sure they have, Ann," Gus answered, "because they've been scared pink. I doubt if Chamberlain can really do anything now—the only possibility of stopping them short in their tracks, as I see it, is the letter I hear Roosevelt has sent both Hitler and Mussolini."

Miss Heatherworth postponed leaving until she should know the result of the conference between Mr. Chamberlain and Hitler, which later news said was scheduled to be at Godesberg. And at table at Fräulein Hohler's everybody made a desperate effort to hide the fact that they were marking time.

When the conference day came there was tension throughout Fräulein Hohler's house, and the usual laughter and banter at Frau Herz's was missing. At Frau Herz's breakfast table Mr. Brooks put his teacup down noisily during a silence.

"Isn't it a ripping thing for a man over seventy to do?" he asked the table generally. "Please God he can prevent war!"

"War," exploded Frau Herz, "always war! It took my husband and my eldest son—my little Heinz and I nearly starved to death afterwards all because of the way Germany was treated . . . If I believed . . ." She clapped her hand over her mouth to stop herself, turned almost purple in the face and leaned back shakily in her chair.

At midday of the same day, as Gus Parker and the two American girls came up the street from the University, they stopped short before Fräulein Hohler's house astonished by a new sight. Hanging by strings from a second-story window, flat against the house, was a huge red pennant with a black swastika in the center, so large it entirely covered a window on the first floor.

"Well I'll be damned!" said Gus.

"Wish you luck," the girls laughed as they went on to Frau Herz's for dinner.

"Have you seen the flag next door?" they asked their "House Mother," as they called Frau Herz, meeting her in the hall.

"Ja, ja . . ." she answered, immediately disappearing into the kitchen.

On entering Fräulein Hohler's dining-room, each of her guests was surprised. Fräulein Hohler, instead of being seated at her place, was standing behind her chair and, as each came in, she saluted with a very stiff and correct "Heil Hitler."

None but the Italians heiled, and they very limply; the others merely said good-day. During the meal only the clicking of silver against china was heard until Fräulein Hohler remarked that there seemed to be less noise at "that woman's" today. Nobody swallowed the bait.

After dinner the Italians, as usual, went to the sitting-room with Fräulein Hohler. Gus stopped the Englishwomen on the stairs and asked them to come to the sitting-room with him. Fräulein Hohler looked surprised when they knocked and came in.

Gus spoke immediately for the three of them. "Fräulein Hohler, why did you hang that flag out today—we are anxious to know?"

"To show the world the Vaterland and our glorious Fuehrer will not be dictated to by foreigners, Herr Parker."

Gus dropped onto the arm of a chair, although the two English-women merely stood rigidly together. "But don't you realize," he asked, "what a splendid thing the Prime Minister has done, coming over here at such a time of tension and crisis to try and avert war?"

"Deutschland does not need Herr Chamberlain or any other for-eigner to help her prevent war—the Vaterland stands alone and im-pregnable," Fräulein Hohler stood up in her excitement, her angular body with its thick neck and shoulders straightening as if on parade, "and she will purge the world of warmongers—the nations had better take care!" Her voice increased in volume with each word, her pale blue eyes turned almost black with excitement and fanaticism.

Miss Heatherworth's low musical voice was like a Station Announc-er's cutting in on a play just as murder hangs in the air: "Why do you take foreigners into your home, Fräulein Hohler?"

Fräulein Hohler came back to earth and gave up her dramatic stance, but there still was scorn in her tone. "Because I must, naturally."

Immediately there was a buzz of voices. Both Englishwomen started to break out angrily, but Gus Parker jumped up and his words filled the room: "Foreigners don't have to live with you, thank heaven! We'll pay what we owe and get out."

Fräulein Hohler's eyes focused on him quickly. "You took your room by the month, Herr Parker . . ."

"I don't think you'll hold me to it," he answered looking her coldly in the eyes.

Fräulein Hohler looked away.

"We'll pack now and pay as we are leaving," Miss Heatherworth said, going to the door with Miss Brownson.

Before Fräulein Hohler could say anything more the Italian man be-gan chattering and gesticulating to his wife, and turning on Fräulein Hohler he broke out in a mixture of Italian and German, telling her they were mortally insulted as allies, that they would require reparation, calling on Dio and Il Duce, and finally dragging his echoing wife out of the doorway with him.

When their packing was done, Gus and the Englishwomen went

back to Fräulein Hohler sitting stiffly at her desk. They paid silently, and as they filed out again Fräulein Hohler remained sternly erect and watched them go. Gus took the other two to Frau Herz's house to wait for a taxi. The door was opened as usual with a hearty welcome in such musical German that it soothed their ragged nerves, but they were not asked what had brought them. They went into the sitting-room where the American girls were talking at an open window, from which they turned with warm greetings.

Miss Heatherworth asked about trains and Frau Herz tried to be helpful without having a schedule in the house. Mr. Brooks walked into the room meditatively, took his pipe out of his pocket, filled it slowly while everybody watched him, and then remarked that the conference must be in progress.

"And if it isn't successful . . ." Ann walked over to Frau Herz's large radio and started fiddling with the dials while speaking in an exaggeratedly careless voice.

"Quite," Mr. Brooks said, finally putting the pipe in his mouth. "I'm going to try and get London on the air." Ann turned on a sudden blare of noise from the radio. But Frau Herz emitted a combination shriek and groan and rushed over to stop her.

"Oh, suss!" exclaimed Miss Macpherson, bursting into the room as Ann quickly and contritely switched off an English voice, "I want to hear what they say in bonnie England . . ."

"Please—oh, please, Fräulein Macpherson," Frau Herz's face was chalky as she put a hand on the Scotswoman's arm, drops of perspiration standing out on her upper lip, "you will not do that, Liebchen?"

"Now Frau Herz me dear, we mean no harm! That wee wireless could give us the news from our own countries, it's a good one—but we never have anything but the German stations on it. Now Frau Herz . . ." Miss Macpherson tried a wheedling tone.

Ann drew away from the instrument, but Frau Herz, with her hand on it as if defending it, spoke very solemnly.

"Fräulein Macpherson—all of you, my dear friends, I am sorry you to deny," she hesitated and looked over her shoulder at the door as the knob turned with an almost imperceptibly small noise, and then raising her voice slightly she went on, "there is Jewish propaganda on all the foreign stations, but from the stations in the Reich all the news that is good for us to get do we have . . ."

Heinz was fully in the room now and he stood in the center rubbing his chin thoughtfully. "Quite a speech, Muter," he said sarcastically, "considering one of your grandparents was a Jew."

Frau Herz seemed to grow tall and drawn and thin in the sight of the others as she looked at her son. "That would make you partly Jewish too, Heinz, Mein Sohn."

Heinz gave an icy laugh. "Not I, Muter. It is too far back of *me* to count."

The dumbfounded guests of Frau Herz were frozen into various positions, and it was not until Heinz had gone slowly and deliberately out of the room that they came back to life. Frau Herz herself looked as if she had suddenly shriveled into very old age, but she moved toward the door saying in a dead-sounding way: "A bed shall I make for you upstairs, Herr Parker."

The awkwardness finally was broken up by Miss Macpherson. "I hear," she said, "Mr. Chamberlain had a great ovation in the streets. The German papers do not know what to say about it, quite. Isn't it too wonderful him walking in and settling all their wee troubles for them?"

"I wonder," said Gus Parker.

Mr. Chamberlain went home from his first conference with Hitler. Immediately afterwards Czech atrocities again were played up in the German press.

"I couldn't get the *Times* again today," Mr. Brooks said after supper a few nights later," but I heard in town that Mr. Chamberlain had returned for another conference. It seemed to me that everybody on the Adolf Hitler Strasse was holding his breath except for groups of whispering men at several street corners—they looked at me with a blank look as I passed."

"I heard there is to be some kind of big compulsory meeting on the Münster square tonight," Miss Macpherson put in. "I think I will go and see what one of those things is like—it will be a jolly bit of fun ..."

"This no matter for fun will be, Fräulein Macpherson—it will mean war." Frau Herz's eyes fogged with tears and her voice dropped low. "War—I shall not face it again ..."

Ann put an arm around her: "Go to bed, Frau Herz, we'll bring you any news we hear—or would it be better for you to come to the meeting with us?"

"Danke, danke, kind friends," Frau Herz kept her face turned away from the others as she straightened some books on the center table, "I shall to the meeting not go—but I beg of you all, for your own sakes, very careful to be in what you do . . ."

"Of course, Frau Herz, do not worry about us," Gus Parker said as he crossed the room to hold the door open for her. "You get a good night's sleep."

In the thick crowd about the Münsterplatz Ann and Gus got separated from the others. Standing in the midst of motionless, silent people they listened to a ranting voice coming from a huge amplifier as they tried to study the faces nearest them. The voice, not Hitler's, was however trying to rouse the people from their lethargy.

"They're not showing a sign of anything at all," Ann whispered. "They look too depressed to be roused by anything, don't you think?"

Someone glanced at Ann, as anyone might at an interruption, but there was neither surprise nor annoyance in her face, and the docile waiting and listening continued until the speech was over and the heiling began. Then, as if they were part of some mechanism wound up ready for this moment, arms shot up and forward, hands with palms down, and a rhythmic sequence of "Heil, heil, sieg heil" rose into the night air. When this demonstration was over a small brass band burst out with the opening bars of *Deutschland, Deutschland Über Alles.* Suddenly the crowd came alive, and with still lifted arms put great feeling into their singing, some becoming very emotional and sad, others lifting inspired faces to the dark sky. The Americans stood unmolested and unnoticed, with arms down, through all the heiling and the singing.

The Horst Wessel song followed the other, and when it was over the crowd broke up while the local troops formed to march up the street to the music from their band. Ann and Gus had to wait for them all to pass—Brown Shirts, Black Shirts, and Hitler Youth down to boys of about eight years—before they could cross the street and so had the opportunity of seeing what a very military showing all these marchers made.

"What fools!" Gus exploded when they were safely out of the crowd. "Are they really so blind they can't see they're being worked up to some devilment?"

"But when they began to sing . . . Did you notice the fanatical expressions on some of the faces?"

"Very few it seemed to me, Ann—they all looked pretty automatic to me, except those that got emotional when they sang, but that wasn't fanaticism, that was just pure Germanism. They just seemed to me like a lot of trained animals in a circus."

"Gus," Ann took hold of his arm, timing her step to his, "do you think Chamberlain can prevent war?"

"No—I don't."

"Our consul told me several weeks ago the German army's full of communists, and so are the munitions plants in the North . . ."

"I don't think they're any different from the rest, Ann, they all think Germany should rule the world and they all obey orders—Deutschland über alles, you know."

"I don't believe Frau Herz can *stand* another war!"

"She won't have to stand it long, I fear, if they know she's Jewish—God, what a beast that son is!"

As they reached the turn which took them onto Frau Herz's hilly street Ann and Gus simultaneously raised their faces to the blue-black mountains barely showing against the night and drew in deep breaths of the exhilarating air.

"With a country like this . . . Oh, how can these people be so warlike in such a land . . ."

"Maybe it was Siegfried and Brünnhilda that started them—or Alberich the dwarf making swords underground for them . . . No, no, it was the gold—ah, yes, it was the Rhein Maidens' gold that started everything . . . Doesn't gold always start people into evil ways?"

"Look," Ann interrupted, "she's got the whole house lighted up! Oh, my goodness, do you suppose she's been afraid of something or someone?"

"Heinz!" Gus exclaimed under his breath as they crossed the front yard to the house. Opening the front door with a latch-key he said, "Hurry and tell her we're back."

Ann ran up the stairs to the second floor. Almost immediately her voice came back down in a shriek: "Gus! Come quick!"

She was standing just inside Frau Herz's bedroom door when Gus reached her, a hand covering her eyes. He stopped beside her, a little breathless from his race up the stairs, and in a flash he saw the reason for her call. For a second he also was too stunned to move, but in that second his mind recorded the most prominent details of the room: the sun-faded walls, bare except for two large portraits—one of an older and one of a very young German officer—the denuded bureau and the stript and swept look that filled the atmosphere. Unconsciously he put an arm around Ann as his eyes returned at last to what they first had seen: Frau Herz's bed.

Ann's hand dropped from before her eyes as she watched Gus start slowly across the room. With fascinated horror she saw him gaze at the body stretched limply across the big down comfort that almost covered the bed, and then stoop over an old army pistol which lay on the floor beneath a stiffly overhanging hand. She watched him, herself still detached from the scene, look the pistol over carefully as if to memorize its design but without touching it.

"Must have taken only one shot," he said tonelessly, "right through the heart."

Ann suddenly became conscious of her own presence there and made a small movement away from the door jamb—but she did not speak.

Gus stood up slowly and slowly glanced around the room in search of something. His eyes quickened and he went to the bureau and picked up a scrap of folded paper, but he held it unopened in his hand as he looked over to Ann.

Ann came to him immediately, and in spite of a shakiness in his hands he unfolded the paper and they were both able to read the words it held in German: "For me there can be no more war," signed Edita Herz.

Gus's hand dropped with the paper in it, and he repeated "No more war" as they continued standing motionless by the old bureau. And as they stood in a horrified vacuum, as if they waited for a word that must make all things sane again, they heard footsteps on the stairs. They were heavy military footsteps and their deliberate tread on the stairs took away any initiative of movement the two Americans might have had.

Finally the ascent was finished and the footsteps came toward Frau Herz's room. They stopped in the open doorway a second, and then Frau Herz's son, Heinz, walked in dressed in full SS uniform.

He looked the situation over slowly and minutely, ending with a coldly amused gaze at Ann and Gus. "So . . ." he said mockingly, "our guests witness a tragedy."

Quickly then he put out his hand for the paper Gus still was holding, and while he read the few words, Gus straightened and, taking Ann by the arm, moved toward the door murmuring some words of condolence.

Heinz went over to the bed and looked down at what once had been his mother, his light blue eyes expressionless and his straight-line mouth closed tightly. Then he stooped and picked up the pistol, and as he stood up again he said, partly to himself and partly to the Americans who were going out the door: "So . . . Ach ja, this way it is better."

Within the Day
Edd Winfield Parks

THE COVER ON THE BED MOVED GENTLY, as Jack Maitland drew his head back to escape the warm light beating upon one corner of the pillow. A languid eye watched the minute hand move toward eight o'clock, a languid arm went out to shut off an alarm which had not been set.

He was twenty-one. Somehow, this morning, that was not of major importance; not as important, at least, as he had thought it yesterday afternoon when he struggled with wording a telegram properly. I HAVE NEITHER SMOKED NOR DRANK . . . drunk . . . drank. Words troubled him, and both these words seemed bad, in that connotation.

Then his vexation definitely started; his mind flinched with embarrassment even at the recollection. NOR TOUCHED A WOMAN . . . he had first written, then recoiled from the musty indirect phraseology. Literally, it wasn't so. Remembrance of touches, halted once at least because five hundred dollars bulked too heavy as a price to pay, shamed him again. Why could a man not think of something pleasant, on a day when pleasure was in order? For that telegram was distinctly something to forget, with its lame NOR YOU KNOW. LOVE.

"Two telegrams, Jack."

"Thanks, Bob." Jack allowed his suite-mate to depart, after he had brought them to the bed, with a casualness which suggested that telegrams were a normal part of the day's routine.

He ripped open the first.

DEPOSITING FIVE HUNDRED YOUR CREDIT TO-
MORROW CONGRATULATIONS MAN OUR LOVE
                                    DAD

315

His skin glowed warmly. Objects spattered through his half-conscious mind—Europe, Ford, wife, whiskey, cigarettes, dancing women, Hawaii—as he opened the second telegram.

FORGOT IT WAS YOUR BIRTHDAY AM
TRULY SORRY CONGRATULATIONS LOVE
EDITH

The words had no meaning. His eyes focused for a second on a colored stamp that said a telegram next Sunday would delight a mother's heart. Sorry? The word could mean anything, or nothing. Sorry that he was a man, now, or that she had forgotten to send a present, or. . . . It was not like Edith to forget. Slowly he cursed the inexorable thought-machine which ground steadily on its circular track, arriving nowhere.

Warm light played upon the bed. With a sudden mental effort he forced his legs to throw back the covers, forced his body upright. Abruptly, over-night, spring had come to New England. By the shaded steps of Holworthy Hall he could see a small blackish lump of snow, on the glinting trees the first opening buds. The Yard was painfully bright, and almost barren of life. He looked at the clock: ten after eight.

On his way to the shower, Jack noticed the shot glasses, and the pitcher of musty water on the table. Under one glass was a quarter, to placate the biddy for the extra task and the unusual disorder of the room.

No longer need he excuse himself redfaced from these small parties to read in the Farnsworth Library, or retire into a glum solitude in one corner of the room, more alone than if the jesting, chattering boys had been so many clothes-horses. They did not care if he neither drank nor smoked, they told him with too much emphasis, as long as he did not care what they did.

It was a goodly philosophy, but somehow, for him, it worked only for the first minutes. His sensations must have a startling kinship with the turtle's when ringed small boys poke with sticks at the head bewilderedly retreating within the shell, for in those moments that glasses were held aloft and merry toasts to the loss of feminine virtue or the gain of masculine renown were repeated, his neck seemed tangibly to shorten, his head to grow blocky with a sodden weight. All that was over and done with.

The squat black bottle with an absurdly elongated neck was on Bob's desk. He drew the cork, inhaled the peaty fragrance. Sorry I forgot . . . It seemed to shout within his head. But it was sorrow which, properly, was forgotten and care which mattered not. He raised the bottle suddenly, and allowed the mellow yet tingly liquid to flow into his throat. He choked, burned, belched; with careful rapidity he replaced the bottle and gulped from the stale contents of the pitcher.

His first drink gnawed angrily at his stomach, but he was conscious also that a heavy hand had been removed from the back of his neck. Fresh water cleared the thick spittle from his throat, eased the burning within. Fresh water on his face and breast and legs, water unexpectedly icy with the sting of needles, shot him into wakefulness.

As he vigorously rubbed the towel over his flesh, he reflected that *medium* was the precise word which fitted him: medium length, medium weight, mediumly attractive irregular features, barely medium mentality and physique generally. Only a few days of trifling were necessary for him to fall dangerously behind in his classes; a few days of laziness brought countless days of steady, irksome driving. Only by constant, relentless effort through four years of playing had he made the basket-ball team in the middle of his senior year, and the dubious glory of a minor letter which he was too self-conscious to wear.

Medium. That meant that he must buy things at a high price which better men took in their stride. Five hundred dollars . . . He finished knotting the blue and white striped tie, tossed the vest on the bed with a slight feeling of relief, and put on his coat. On the way out, he jammed the *Crimson* into his pocket. Last night was not his turn; there would be nothing from the editorial columns to mock him in the cold hour of breakfast.

"Bacon and eggs, toast, black coffee. Leave off the potatoes."

The counter was thick with students. Ten till nine. And the counter-boy asking blandly, "How'll yer have yer pertaters?"

"No potatoes, and no cream."

Breakfast became a battle, with pushing elbows crowding from right and left, with a hurried counter-boy who shoved at him a plate decorated with eggs, bacon, and a small dipper of mashed potatoes. He could empty those on some dirty plate, he reflected, while he raised his voice to refuse the third cup of milky coffee which had been thrust at him.

A small notice in the *Crimson* stated that John Raker, the young

English Communist, would lecture in Economics 51 at eleven that morning. He had planned, nebulously, to cut his one class that day, but Raker promised some excitement. His visit was earlier than planned, but deportation proceedings were threatened, and the young Englishman desired to sail before the date of trial.

Jack Maitland walked to the desk. "Pack of Camels, and a *Times.*"

The cigarette felt large yet flimsy. He drew the smoke into his mouth, then expelled it immediately. For a beginner, smoking was a full-time job. The smoke curled into his eyes and nostrils. If he strangled over liquor and cigarettes, what could he hope to do with women? He dropped the cigarette into the coffee-cup, rolled the paper in his hand, and started out.

"Check, please."

"Oh, er . . . here."

His room was clean and orderly, now, with glasses and bottles stored in the closet. On his desk were a large package and a small letter addressed in small, precise handwriting. Home-made candy and chocolate cake—he stuffed a piece of fudge in his mouth before he picked up the letter. He turned it over slowly, realizing that he did not want to read it.

Dear Jack—

I knew Easter that it was no use, that we couldn't go on. I'm in love, truly in love, and I know now for the first time how you felt last Christmas. I hope with all my heart that we can always be good friends.

You may never know how much I hate to write these lines.

Affectionately,

Edith.

He had no sense of emotion. Only a certain numbness, as of a heavy hand clapped once more on the back of his neck. Automatically his feet carried him to the fireplace, where he tossed the envelope into the ashes. Only a few words on paper: sorry I forgot. The letter followed the envelope; then, deliberately, he struck a match on the hearth and lit the letter and the envelope. He walked back to his desk, collected the telegrams and threw them on the tiny fire.

He remembered again the objects which had spasmodically raced through his mind for ages—Europe, Ford, wife. That could be crossed off now. There was no need of thought. Cigarettes—he reached into his pocket, and carefully extracted a cigarette, carefully lit it with shielding hands that could feel no breeze.

A picture of a boy in knee-breeches doggedly drawing on a huge cigar came back to him, of a boy who sobbed in agony while a grave, tight-lipped father watched him vomit. A proposition, a promise, and five hundred dollars in the bank. Yes, and a letter which said that now, with another man, she understood. The back of his neck felt tightly knotted.

The clock struck eleven. When he rose from the chair he realized that his right foot tingled painfully, and that his cigarette had gone dead after that first puff. It took time and effort, apparently, to break good as well as bad habits.

He collected a water glass, which he filled from the basin, a shot glass, and the ungainly bottle. He lighted the cigarette again, poured a drink, and drained it. With the gestures which he had seen Bob employ a hundred times, Jack reached for water, drank, and drew immediately on his cigarette. He coughed. It was no use. He threw the cigarette viciously at the grate.

When he arrived, ten minutes late, the lecture room was crowded. Jack edged into a corner seat on the front row. The blond young Englishman was just beginning to speak, evidently, for he was announcing that to his regret he could not remain to answer questions, as he was sailing that night and must catch a one o'clock plane for New York.

Without ado he began to talk of the downfall of the capitalistic system, spicing his satirical thrusts with casual, effective wit. But Jack found it increasingly impossible to follow that agile mind which presented informally such devastating certainties. His own mind was amazingly light, and strangely not amenable to reason. Phrases better forgotten plagued him endlessly. When Raker said that love must be achieved through blood and revolution, he could think only that love by force was meaningless, if applied to individuals. Unselfish hatred . . . you will never know how much I hate . . . planned economy . . . only a few words could change all plans. . . .

His mind functioned smoothly. This man in the beautifully tailored tweed suit who leaned so negligently against the desk was delineating a delightful dream, of a world in which there would be no waste and no want. Waste must be eliminated by force. The dream took into account everything, except the individual; therefore it took into account nothing.

"I'm thinking of the floods in my section, and the sun. Can't you do something about the sun? It's the most wasteful thing I know, freezing the world in winter and burning it in summer. Can you have the scientists build an asbestos jacket for the sun, to conserve the heat?"

The elderly professor who had written many authoritative treatises on economics suddenly guffawed. Jack flushed. It was his own voice, grave and pondering, which had filled the silence. He had not intended to speak, had no conscious memory of opening his mouth. But the words echoed back at him.

The clock struck twelve. The students waited a moment for a final word from the lecturer. When none came, they surged for the door. Jack Maitland rose slowly. He was not confident that he could walk steadily.

The room was empty, crowded with loneliness. Jack opened a trunk drawer, and pulled forth his black lettered sweater. A few times he had worn it in the privacy of his own room, and looked in the mirror at the crimson H. Sweaters were not worn on the campus; no one seemed to know why, but they were not. He folded it under his arm, and started for the Varsity Club.

At lunch he felt uncomfortably warm. Even in displaying his trophy among his companions he had waited too late. His head buzzed with the effort of eating soberly and with not remembering.

"Round of pool, Jack? We've got three. Dime a corner."

"Suits. With you in a minute."

He got up and walked into the billiard-room. Harold Bates was smoking with obvious enjoyment; spring football practice had ended last Saturday. The other two were track men. He lighted a cigarette, dusted a cue with powder, and leaned against the table.

"Match for break?" asked Harold. "Odd man out."

Jack broke. The click of ball against ball was nice. In general, he was accustomed to paying for the sport, for he played rarely. Today, however, he aimed more rapidly along the stick, and shot harder. A close slice was usually less difficult for him than a straight-in shot, but mainly, now, the ball rolled unerringly into the pocket.

At the end, his partner applauded lustily, his opponents offered bright satirical comments which were as integral a part of the game as the shots.

"You can't beat nigger luck."

"Unlucky at love, lucky at pool."

That remark brought back all that he had tried to forget. As he collected the eighty cents which he had won, and made innocuous parting remarks, he was conscious of wheels which turned with monotonous regularity: sorry I forgot . . . depositing five hundred . . . a man now . . . you'll never know . . . He hung the sweater in his locker, and put on his coat.

Three o'clock. He could study, or read a magazine in the Union, or go to his room, or—none of those seemed festive. The ground was too wet for tennis; squash was tiresome now, for it was played indoors. Twenty-one. This was an occasion which would never be repeated, and he felt desperately a desire to be gay, to break from the routine. Ford, Europe, liquor . . . he wanted no more of that, for the present. Women. He thought of debutantes and shopgirls, but he could think neither of names nor of faces.

Alice. He remembered the joke, long since threadbare, that Alice had picked a name which would follow the University's in the telephone book, so that weak-minded students would remember it.

He walked to the booth and leafed through the pages of the directory. Seven blocks away. He would walk. When he came to the shabby brownstone house he did not want to go in, but now he was ashamed to turn back. The bell sounded through the door.

The woman who opened it was boldly pretty, in a florid, rather stout way. She had a lavender hat on, and was drawing on her gloves.

"Well, come in. Tight again? This is a hell of a time to come, when all the girls are out except Mamie and me, and I'm all ready."

Jack could not speak. He was conscious, vaguely, of purplish decorations, but he saw nothing distinctly except the thick red lips and generous breasts of the woman.

"Oh, Mamie! Come here. It's five for me and three for Mamie, big boy, but I'm in a hurry."

The woman who was coming down the steps looked old and fat, and not overly clean. He reached for his bill-fold.

"Five it is."

"O.K. If my boy friend honks, Mamie, holler to him that I'll be out in a minute."

He had walked so hurriedly back to his room that even now, in the shower, he felt pressed for breath. The warmth soothed his flesh. Out in a minute. She had kept her word. He shoved the hair from his eyes. It was nothing, a matter of a minute or so. Time enough to read a letter . . . or a telegram. Sorry. Why should he be sorry? Congratulations man. The words seemed barbarous in their irony.

On the bed, naked, he watched the first fly buzz against the ceiling. They would be plowing dark land for cotton and corn, at home now, and his mother would be superintending dark men who broke the garden and transplanted shrubs and varnished the screen doors and windows before hanging them in place for the summer. It was good work which left the body warm and tired, and the mind in a half-drugged peace.

"I have read a book." He had read, and tried to comprehend, but the total result, for some reason which escaped him, was not peace.

Only the land bred peace. He was rich enough in a boy's way to do all that a boy could want to do, but he could only think. There were objects and images on which to build a life, but there were also illusions to be moulted. Other lines from that poem of Tennessee ran through his head:

> A child keeps asking,
> Where was I before I was born? And shall I say
> O questioning son of man, I do not know
> Where you are now after you are born?

He did not know. He knew only that the click of ivory ball against ball was associated with a handsome woman who promised to be back in a minute, and who came, with a boy—a very small and shamed boy —behind her, that words and years were somehow jumbled with all the things which he had been. Liquor, cigarettes, women . . . eighty cents and five hundred dollars . . . only a few lines, only a minute . . . a man now. . . .

"Hey, Jack, what's the package?"

"Birthday, Bob. Cut yourself a piece of cake."

"Why keep it a secret? Well, I'll blow you to dinner."

"No, you have dinner with me. There's a place I want to go. And we'll see a show afterward. I reserved seats for Leatrice Hope's revue."

"We'll go where you please, but it's my dinner if it's your show. Where are we going?"

"The *Stella d'Italia.*"

"Why, man, no one goes there any more. Joe is still working off the gin he served us in prohibition days."

"Maybe so, but that's where I want to go. When I was a soph, I went there with you and Dave Beckett, and I watched you drink cocktails and dago wine, and all I had was coffee in my cup."

The close noises of the subway held conversation to a minimum. Jack began to compose a letter in his mind, which would treat with dignity the loss of all romantic hopes. "I am sorry—truly sorry—that . . ." I hate to go above you; that was not right, it was tagged with brown eyes, while Edith's were a deep blue. Love must come by hate, but not to him. "We have, I fear, grown too far apart to understand each other; what I feel had better be left unsaid . . ."

That damned florist: after all, he had ordered cut flowers for Easter. He had not intended to send a potted plant. His mind turned backward on himself. He was too petty. This was not the cause. One loved where one would; and the letter he thought to write was not worth the writing. Only a few words more . . . the final words of a gentleman. Huge white thighs floated before him. Out in a minute.

They were walking toward a dimly red star, then climbing the dirty steps to the restaurant.

"Two dry Martinis, Joe. How's the world?"

"Not good. It was much better so when we served the Martini in the coffee-cup."

The drink tasted oily, somewhat bitter. But it eased the tight constriction above his eyes. He could hear the taut muscles of his neck pop as they relaxed slightly in their pressure.

"Two Italian dinners, Joe, and two bottles of dago red."

He gorged the food into his stomach. The wine tasted vinegarish, but he could swallow it without effort. They lighted cigarettes.

"Your lungs aren't bellows, Jack. Let the smoke trickle out easily."

He was conscious of Bob's amused tolerance, but somehow that did not seem to matter. The dim, smoky room looked infinitely pleasant in an indistinct way; the cigarette for the first time was not a conscious source of effort. There would be other days.

The musical comedy was under way when they arrived. At first, the stage would not focus before his eyes. It did not matter, greatly; only another show, but enough to hold thought in check for an hour. The orchestra moaned rhythmically, as girls in patterned brocade performed quick and intricate movements, and a blond tenor sang indistinguishable words about a flower garden.

Jack closed his eyes. When he opened them, the same girls were performing the same involved patterns, but he could see only white flesh and, on each girl, three large red roses.

Through the rows of dancing legs came a tall girl with close-cropped brown hair. Her long dress was white, dotted with red roses. He gasped. Here was loveliness. He listened tensely as she sang of flowers that would die, but of love that would live forever. The words were silly, he knew, and thought transiently of a love which was already dead, but the words mattered not.

A stuporous haze bereft him of thought. When Leatrice was on the stage, he saw and felt clearly, with no need for thinking; when she left, he subsided into an automaton who waited to be called to life. The plot meant nothing, until the blond tenor deserted her for another girl. Then Leatrice began plaintively to sing: "You'll never know how much . . ."

The tall, clean-limbed girl seemed to shrink in size, as her brown hair merged into blond, her brown eyes into blue. Another girl roamed the stage restlessly, a girl of no certain height or coloring. Waves of words and phrases beat upon him: how I hate to write these lines . . . I'm sorry that I forgot . . . only a minute ago I was happy, only a word. He could not distinguish the lines of the song from the words which ran tumultuously through his head to the rhythm of the music.

The curtain dropped. The lights blinded him. Automatically he followed Bob to the foyer.

"Smoke?"

"Thanks, Jack. She's a marvelous actress. Must be thirty if she's a day."

Jack did not want to talk of her. Thirty, or fifty—years were not important. He did not want to talk about anything, but talk was a necessity which could not be avoided. When the warning bell rang, he could not remember a topic they had chatted about so easily; apparently, however, he had been casual enough and sensible, for Bob had made no comment.

The orchestra was playing *You'll Never Know*. Presciently he seemed to hear the tune at a hundred dances, to hear gay, painted young girls lisp and twitter in his ear how much they loved that song.

As the lights went out, he slumped in his chair, waiting. Out in a minute. . . . The tinsel miniature world before him seemed lifeless until Leatrice came on the stage. He waited, expectant, for that breathtaking mirage when a beautiful tall brunette merged partially into a beautiful small blonde. The actress who talked and sang was superlatively competent, but she no longer stirred him.

He saw instead a slender girl in a black bathing suit who patiently attempted to dive time and again, and who laughed nervously when she hit the water resoundingly flat. His heart caught again as it caught when her head struck the bottom of the shallow concrete pool. She had spluttered, strangled, half-cried; then "sorry I'm so clumsy," she had said. Black words typed in capitals on yellow paper—SORRY I FORGOT.

The girl on the stage was singing, as she gazed soulfully into the eyes of the tenor, "You'll never know . . ." Suddenly, once more, she seemed a symbol, a distant promise of what he might have known. The muscles of his neck grew taut and hard.

The lights flashed on. He applauded frantically; he must see her again. The curtain went up. Leatrice smiled and bowed and kissed her hands to the audience. She was a beautiful woman, and nothing more.

As they were undressing, Jack caught Bob's half-humorous, half-sardonic glance.

"You're one hell of a glum companion at your birthday feast, Jack."

"Sorry, Bob. Guess the growing pains have been too much for me. See you tomorrow."

The coolness of linen felt grateful to the skin. His head throbbed painfully, in time to music; snatches of the song rolled in ceaseless repetition in the circular grooves of his brain. An indeterminate girl, two girls in one, came and went in tight images before his eyes. He opened them with a distinct effort, then closed them again.

Love and hate, one must conquer love with force, thin it out until it stretched to nothingness. The graceful lecturer paused. An asbestos jacket around the sun. How thoughtful his voice had sounded.

Tomorrow he must write a letter, the last letter. There would be no more specials on Sunday morning, no need to remember to send one each Friday morning. "I am sorry—truly sorry—that we can be nothing more than friends, but I shall value always the days"—that rhymed, it wouldn't do—"the hours we have spent together. The experience . . ."

The pillow was uncomfortably hot against his cheek. He turned over quickly. The bed whirled over and over, the pit of his stomach thumped against his throat. He reached a steadying hand out to find the wall, and pressed his palm firmly against it. His heart pumped heavily, the noise sounding loud in his ears. Gradually the bed became steady, the tumult in his stomach quiet.

His birthday was past. Tomorrow, today, there were classes to attend, and divisionals to study for, and a routine of living which had some months to go.

Yes, and a letter to write. Where was he? Experience . . . "Experience keeps a dear school, but a fool will learn in no other." Self-expression and experience were valuable; at least, he had heard that many times. He had been repressed for always, until today. That was over. He had learned not to turn quickly in bed, when one had drunk too much, and that a handsome woman with quivering breasts . . . out in a minute.

It was all experience, but it contained no meaning; nothing save disgust. His mind seemed to bite with cold thought: old Franklin had selected his words with precision. A fool would learn in no other, but a fool might not—probably would not—learn even by experience. If he learned nothing he was a fool. Q.E.D. The proposition, whether of logic or of geometry, was complete.

His letter, however, was not written. His mind ached with the endeavor to hold that high pitch of concentration. It was no use. There were objects to be bought, wines and liquors and cars and trips to strange cities, and pipes . . . there were things to be forgotten. Little charred words which jumped back from the ashes to which he had consigned them. Love and hate . . . dollars in the bank . . . a man who was but a boy—out in a minute . . . you'll never know. . . . He felt infinitely old, with an age to which wisdom is denied. Sorry I forgot. . . .

BIOGRAPHICAL NOTES

JOHN PEALE BISHOP was born in Charles Town, West Virginia, May 21, 1892. He attended Mercersburg Academy and graduated from Princeton in 1917. After the first World War he became managing editor of Vanity Fair. In 1922 he went abroad to France and among his friends in the expatriate group were Ernest Hemingway, Scott Fitzgerald and Archibald MacLeish. In 1943 he was Consultant in Comparative Literature at the Library of Congress. Bishop died on April 4, 1944. Author of: *Many Thousands Gone* (stories), 1932; *Now with His Love* (poems), 1932; *Act of Darkness* (novel), 1935; *Minute Particulars* (poems), 1936; *Selected Poems,* 1941.

MALCOLM COWLEY was for many years the literary editor of *The New Republic*. He is the author of *Exile's Return* (1935); *Blue Juniata* (1928); *The Dry Season* (1941), and the editor of several other books, including *After the Genteel Tradition* and *The Portable Hemingway*. The essay published here, *William Faulkner's Legend of the South,* won the essay prize in the John Peale Bishop Memorial Literary Prize Contest.

ROBERT DANIEL was born in 1915 in Memphis, Tennessee. He was educated at the University of the South and at Yale University. He is now teaching at the University of Oklahoma.

CHARLES EDWARD EATON was born in 1916 at Winston-Salem, North Carolina. He studied at the University of North Carolina and at the Graduate School at Princeton. His first book of poems was entitled *The Bright Plain.*

BREWSTER GHISELIN was born in Missouri in 1903. He attended the Universities of California and Oxford, and has been teaching English, mostly at the University of Utah, since 1929. He has published stories, poems and articles and recently a book of poetry entitled *Against the Circle.*

EUNICE GLENN has had criticism published in *The Sewanee Review* and poems in the *New Mexico Quarterly Review* and other magazines. Her first published short story appeared recently in the *Prairie*

Schooner. A native of Georgia, she studied at Louisiana State and Vanderbilt Universities and the University of Chicago. She has done editorial work in New York City.

ROBERT B. HEILMAN is Professor of English at Louisiana State University where, after completing graduate work at Harvard, he has taught since 1935. He is co-author, with Cleanth Brooks, of *Understanding Drama,* and has published articles and reviews in *The Sewanee Review, The Southern Review, The Kenyon Review, Quarterly Review of Literature, Accent,* and other periodicals.

BERNARD HERINGMAN was graduated from the Park School, Baltimore, in 1940; attended Princeton University, 1940-42; Bread Loaf School of English, 1942; Johns Hopkins University, A.B. 1943; Johns Hopkins Graduate English Department until 1944. His verse has appeared in the *Nassau Lit, The Chimera, The Sewanee Review* and *Princeton Verse Between Two Wars.* He has also written for radio.

KATHERINE HOSKINS was born in 1909 at Indian Head, Maryland. She attended Smith College and has spent considerable time abroad. A volume of her poems, *A Penetential Primer,* was published in 1945.

RANDALL JARRELL was born in Nashville, Tennessee in 1915. He was graduated from Vanderbilt University and taught at Kenyon College and the University of Texas. He has contributed essays and poems to *The Southern Review, The Kenyon Review, The Partisan Review* and *The Sewanee Review.* His poem, *The Märchen,* included in this anthology, won the poetry prize in the John Peale Bishop Memorial Literary Contest in 1945. He is the author of two books of verse, *Blood for a Stranger,* 1942, and *Little Friend, Little Friend,* 1945. Mr. Jarrell was acting literary editor of *The Nation* during 1946.

LEROY LEATHERMAN was born in Louisiana in 1922. He attended Vanderbilt University and Kenyon College. His work has appeared in *The Sewanee Review.*

ANDREW LYTLE was born in Murfreesboro, Tennessee in 1903. After a year of study in France, he attended Vanderbilt University and the Yale School of Drama, then spent one year on the stage. He received a Guggenheim Fellowship, 1940-41, and has been managing editor of *The Sewanee Review* and a teacher of history at the University of the South, 1942-3. He has written a biography and two novels and contributed to the agrarian symposia *I'll Take My Stand* and *Who Owns America?* Mr. Lytle's story, *The Guide,* printed here, won the story prize in the John Peale Bishop Memorial Literary Contest in

1945. He is the author of two novels: *The Long Night,* 1936, and *At the Moon's Inn,* 1941.

HERBERT MARSHALL MCLUHAN is a Canadian who studied at Cambridge University after graduation from Manitoba University. Subsequently he taught at Wisconsin and St. Louis Universities and is now at Assumption College in Windsor, Ontario.

MARY OWINGS MILLER was born in Columbia, South Carolina, and studied at Winthrop College and the University of South Carolina. She carried out additional graduate study at the Harvard Summer School, Radcliffe and the University of Pennsylvania. She is the editor of *Contemporary Poetry,* the *Distinguished Poets Series* and the *Contemporary Poetry Library Series;* and has contributed to *Poetry, Voices, Poetry—Scotland* and *Meanjin Papers* (Australia).

WILLIAM VAN O'CONNOR was born in 1915, attended Syracuse and Columbia and taught at Ohio State University, Louisiana State University and Stephens College. He wrote, with his wife Mary Allen O'Connor, *Climates of Tragedy.* He has contributed to *Poetry, The American Scholar, The Sewanee Review, The Kenyon Review,* etc. Mr. O'Connor was recently awarded a Rockefeller Foundation Fellowship in Humanities to do work in literary criticism.

GEORGE MARION O'DONNELL was born in Mississippi in 1914, attended Vanderbilt University, returned there in 1939-40 as the Fellow in Creative Writing, and since 1941 has taught English at Alabama Polytechnic Institute. This year (1946-1947) he is on leave, teaching at Harvard. He has contributed verse and prose to many magazines, and a collection of his poems appeared in *Five Young American Poets: 1940.*

EDD WINFIELD PARKS was born in Tennessee and studied at Harvard and Vanderbilt Universities. He has taught English at Vanderbilt, Duke and the University of Georgia. He is the author or editor of several books, notably *Segments of Southern Thought* and *Long Hunter.*

ELEANOR ROSS was born in Norwood, North Carolina, in 1920. She graduated from the Women's College of the University of North Carolina in 1940 and has since taught English in the North Carolina Public Schools for several years. She held the Creative Writing Fellowship at Vanderbilt University in 1942.

JAMES ROSS was born in Norwood, North Carolina, in 1911. He attended Louisburg and Elon Colleges. His novel, *They Don't Dance Much,* was published in 1940. His stories have appeared in *The Partisan*

Review and *The Sewanee Review*. He was with the U. S. Army in Belgium.

NATHAN ROTHMAN was born in New York City in 1904. He was educated at the College of the City of New York, Columbia University and New York University. Mr. Rothman is a teacher in the New York City high schools and reviews for *The Saturday Review of Literature*. The essay printed here is a portion of a book on James Joyce's influence in American writing, still in manuscript.

ROBERT WOOSTER STALLMAN was born in Milwaukee, Wisconsin, 1911. He took his Ph.D. at the University of Wisconsin in 1942. He has been an instructor in English at the University of Wisconsin and at Yale and an assistant professor at the University of Kansas. He has published essays on Dryden, Keats, Hardy, Housman and John Peale Bishop, and has in preparation a *Bibliography of Modern Criticism* and a *Critique of Modern Criticism*.

PETER TAYLOR was born in Trenton, Tennessee in 1917. He attended Vanderbilt University and Kenyon College, graduating from Kenyon in 1940. His stories have been published in *The Southern Review, The Partisan Review* and *The Sewanee Review*.

PERIENT TROTT was born in McKeesport, Pennsylvania and now lives in Colonial Beach, Virginia.

PARKER TYLER was born in New Orleans, Louisiana and lives in New York City. He is the author of the following published volumes of poetry: *The Metaphor in the Jungle and Other Poems* (1941); *Yesterday's Children,* a poem for drawings by Pavel Tchelitchew (1944); *The Granite Butterfly,* a Poem in Nine Cantos (1945); and two books on the movies: *Hollywood Hallucination* and *Magic and Myth of the Movies.*

MARY N. S. WHITELEY is a frequent contributor to *Poetry: A Magazine of Verse, Smoke, Harper's Magazine,* etc. She has published articles on music and other subjects, but this is her first story to appear. Her first book of poems will shortly be published.

LOUIS B. WRIGHT was born in Greenwood county, South Carolina in 1899. He took his B.A. at Wofford College and his Ph.D. at the University of North Carolina in 1926. He was Johnston Research Scholar, Johns Hopkins University, 1927-8; Guggenheim Fellow in England and Italy, 1928-9 and the summer of 1930; Visiting Scholar at the Huntington Library, 1931-2. Since 1932 he has been a member of the permanent research staff of Huntington Library. Author of *Middle-*